THOSE RADIO TIMES

DEAR SIR,—

     I certainly agree
With those who praise the B.B.C.;
A pair of phones, a crystal set,
Ten bob a year—for this I get
A store of knowledge, wealth of fun,
To cheer me when the day's work's done;
Whatever other folk may say
I thoroughly enjoy a play,
While comedy and bright revues
Are just the things to banish 'blues';
Lowbrow I'd be considered as
Because I'm rather fond of jazz—
But highbrow too!—I love each note
Of music which great masters wrote;
By foreign talks I strive to learn,
I'm there when opera takes its turn,
For weather forecasts, news reports,
For talks on travel and on sports;
When Mr. Baldwin 'takes the air'
Or when the Prince is in the chair
I listen in; by Greenwich time
I set my watch, and Big Ben's chime.
I listen to the church bells' ring,
I hear the congregation sing.
And from the broadcast pulpit glean
Comfort from him who speaks unseen.
O give to me the happy mind,
O give me the contented kind,
That pleasure, knowledge, wealth will find
Whatever be the programme!

A LISTENER'S LETTER, 10 AUGUST 1928

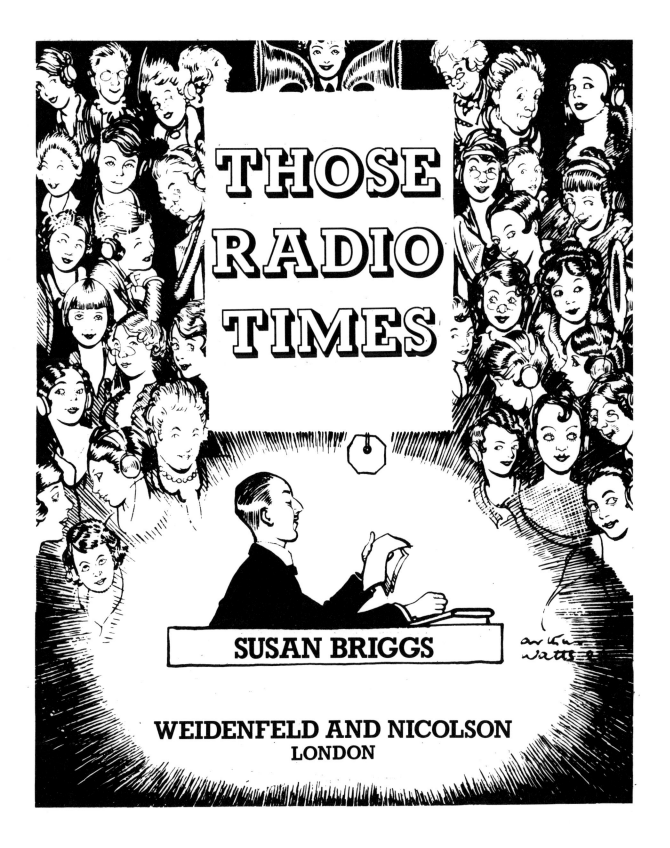

THOSE RADIO TIMES

SUSAN BRIGGS

WEIDENFELD AND NICOLSON
LONDON

Designed by Margaret Fraser for
George Weidenfeld and Nicolson Limited
91 Clapham High Street
London SW4

ISBN 0 297 77929 X

Colour separations by Newsele Litho Ltd

Set, printed and bound in Great Britain by
Fakenham Press Limited
Fakenham, Norfolk

CONTENTS

Author's Acknowledgments

I should like most of all to thank my husband, who has helped and encouraged (but never overwhelmed) me throughout the writing of this book. My grateful thanks are also due to the following kind and knowledgeable friends: Leonard Miall and Pat Spencer of the BBC History Unit, never at a loss for the answer to any question on broadcasting; Geoffrey Cannon (formerly Editor) and David Driver of *The Radio Times* and their colleagues; Mrs Jacqueline Kavanagh and her helpful staff at the BBC Written Archives, Caversham; Raymond Mander and Joe Mitchenson, founders of the unique Theatre Collection, whose knowledge and enthusiasm extends to radio; Cecil Madden, connoisseur of radio pictures; Ronnie Hill, who wrote and provided me with the words of 'Here's Looking at You'; and the ever-resourceful and patient Margaret Fraser and Anne Dobell, the designer and editor of the book.

I should also like to thank the staffs of the Bodleian Library, the Victoria and Albert Museum, the BBC Reference and Periodicals Libraries, the BBC Photographs Library and the BBC Popular Music Library.

Publishers' Acknowledgments

The publishers would like to express their thanks to John Hore of the BBC for permission to use *Radio Times* pictures, to David Stoker and Ron Shipley of the Periodicals Library for allowing them to photograph their bound copies of *The Radio Times*, and to Geoff Goode Photographics for taking the photographs.

Picture Sources

Numbers refer to pages
t: top   b: bottom   r: right   l: left   c: centre

The Radio Times: 1, 3, 5, 10b, 11 (1932), 15 (1937), 17tr (1932), 18–19t (1931), 18b (1932), 20tr (1934), 21tl (1926), 22l (1937), 22tr (1937), 23tl (1937), 37b (1927), 38tr (1936), 39tr (1935), 39b (1937), 40tr (1930), 40c (1930), 41tl (1936), 41tr (1938), 43tl (1938), 43tr (1937), 43b, 44tl (1930), 44bl (1930), 44r (1930), 45b (1936), 47tr (1937), 47bl (1938), 48b (1924), 49tr (1934), 54l, 55r, 58l, 58br, 59tl (1930), 59tr (1930), 60tr (1924), 61b (1934), 63tr (1933), 63bl (1932), 63br (1929), 64tl (1936), 66b (1930), 69bl (1931), 70bl (1927), 70br (1924), 71t (1936), 71br (1937), 72tr (1924), 72bl (1936), 72br (1938), 73tl (1935), 74tl, 74tr, 75 (1923), 76, 77l (1924), 77r, 81t, 81b, 83t, 84 (1938), 85tl, 85tr, 85bl, 85br, 87b, 88t (1929), 89tl (1939), 89tr (1934), 92, 93, 94b (1939), 94t, 95 (1937), 96br (1938), 97b (1936), 98bl (1934), 100b (1926), 109 (1936), 110 (1928), 114br, 116tl, 116tr (1938), 116b (1939), 117tr, 117b, 119t (1935), 120tl, 120tr (1938), 120bl, 120br (1928), 121b, 124tl, 124bl (1931), 124br (1939), 126b (1937), 127br (1932), 128 (1928), 129 (1935), 136t (1936), 137tr (1938), 138bl (1928), 140–1t (1936), 141cl (1937), 141cr (1938), 142br (1928), 155, 158 (1936), 159 (1939), 160 (1926), 161tl (1931), 161r (1933), 163, 165 (1934), 170b (1927), 172t (1926), 175 (1931), 177b (1935), 180 (1928), 184t (1925), 184bl (1929), 186t (1935), 186b (1928), 188tr (1933), 188b (1934), 189bl (1932), 189br (1934), 191, 202b (1937), 203b (1936), 206br (1937), 207 (1939), 208b (1924), 209tr (1931), 209b (1928), 215 (1937), 222l, 222r, 225cr, 227t (1936), 227bl (1924), 227br (1933), 228 (1935), 230tl (1928), 230b (1930), 232 (1938). *BBC Year Books*: 21bl (1936), 27 (1929), 89b (1936), 111 (1930), 127tr (1931), 135 (1936), 140cr (1940), 141b (1939), 169 (1939), 184br, 188tl (1930), 189t (1938), 199 (1940), 204tl (1938), 204cr (1938), 205t (1939). BBC Photographs Library: 10t, 16tr, 16br, 17tl, 17b, 19b, 31, 66t, 91, 92, 96t, 97t, 107, 117tl, 121t, 127tl, 138tl, 138br 139t, 139b, 140b, 142tl, 142bl, 143tl, 143tr, 143b, 145, 154t, 170tr, 171, 173tl, 174b, 176tr, 177t, 200tl, 200tr, 200b, 204b. Radio Times Hulton Picture Library: 38b, 39tl, 41br, 60br 61t, 67b, 68b, 69t, 114t, 173t, 192l, 192r, 209tl, 211t, 211br. Bodleian Library, Oxford: 43c, 44ct, 45tl, 48t, 49bl, 72tl, 99tr, 102tl, 134, 142cl, 225t, 229t, 229bl, 229br. *The Broadcaster*: 38tl (1922), 53, 64tr, 86, 218, 221, 224b (1922). *The Bystander*: 46 (1923), 50t (Bodleian), 50bl (Bodleian), 50br (Bodleian), 99tl (Bodleian). *Children's Hour Annual*: 101tl (1935), 101tr (1936). *Daily Express TV Annual 1950*: 60l. *Daily Mirror Reflections*, vol 128, 1934, by W. H. Haselden: 122b, 153. Victor Gollancz Ltd: 144tr. *The Illustrated London News*: 16tl, 29, 45tr, 62tl, 62tr, 62bl, 62br, 65, 67tl, 70t, 100tr, 104, 115tl, 118 (Mander and Mitchenson Theatre Collection), 133, 174t, 185tl, 212–3. Cecil Madden: 203t. Mander and Mitchenson Theatre Collection: 51t, 102tr, 103t, 103b, 118 (*Illustrated London News*, 1929), 142tr. *Men Only*: 211bl (1939). Oresko Books: 106, 185b. *Popular Wireless*: 80, 214 (1922), 216 (1922). *Punch*: 20br, 22br, 23tr, 23bl, 35tr, 35br, 36, 47cl, 56, 63tl, 64br, 67tr, 68tl, 68tr, 72cr, 73tr, 73bl, 73br, 74b, 82b, 83b, 88b, 98t, 99b, 114bl, 119b, 124br, 126tl, 126tr, 126b, 127bl, 136b, 137tl, 137bl, 149, 170tl, 173b, 176tl, 176b, 182, 183, 187bl, 187br, 190, 197, 201, 208t, 223t, 223b, 225bl. *Radio Magazine*: 99r (1934), 138tr, 224t. *Radio Pictorial*: 9, 47br, 49tl, 49r, 71bl, 87tl, 90cl, 96bl, 97c, 115tr, 122tl, 122tr, 123l, 123r, 125, 140cl, 151, 178t, 178b. *Television Magazine*: 194 (1928), 210t (1928), 210b (1928). Victoria and Albert Museum: 19r, 41bl, 51b (Louis Wain). *Wireless Magazine*: 40tl (1925), 57 (1925), 100tl (1925), 217.

INTRODUCTION

DO YOU WANT A BIT OF WIRE
FOR YOUR WIRELESS?

SCRAPBOOK AND HISTORY LESSON

'What's all that wire for?' somebody asked the comedian Harry Tate in an early 1920's sketch. 'Wireless, you fool!' he replied.

Similar paradoxes abound when you produce a picture book about wireless. Curiously enough, there are at least as many pictures relating to the early history of sound broadcasting – and every kind of picture at that – as there were wires.

In this survey I have looked for and discovered them in the most unlikely places. I have found many photographs, of course, some in the archives of the BBC, more outside, including photographs of people the BBC would have preferred to keep anonymous. I have also found sketches and blueprints, cartoons and caricatures, advertisements and illustrations of every kind, from cigarette cards to the wireless sets themselves. They come to life best when you add the words actually used at the time, so that this book is an anthology of contemporary comment also.

The phrase 'The Radio Times' is more than the title of a journal, just as *Those Radio Times* is more than the title of my book: it conjures up a whole society and culture. I found particularly evocative the words of a popular Henry Hall song of 1934, *Radio Times*:

> A wireless-set near, to bring us good cheer,
> In Winter-time or Summer-time
> For leisure time and pleasure time
> The daily times that Big Ben chimes
> Are Radio Times

And I discovered that throughout the whole period covered in my book the contents of *The Radio Times*, the first number of which appeared on 28 September 1923, are satisfyingly comprehensive.

I may be unusual in acknowledging this. In Val Gielgud and Holt Marvell's detective story, *Death at Broadcasting House* (1934), one of the characters is described as 'wandering restlessly up and down, looking at the uninspiring backs of the Controller's collection of bound volumes of *The Radio Times*'. To me, however, these volumes have been far from uninspiring. Like the *BBC Year Books*, they combine facts and features, and like them, also, they are profusely illustrated.

The lack of pictures in the radio programmes themselves was felt by some early commentators to be an advantage, not a handicap. As a contributor to *The Radio Times* put it in 1929: 'Listening in the dark prevents attention being distracted by eye-catching objects, and the result is that scenes – particularly in radio drama – can be built up, and characters pictured, with an amazing vividness.' This view persisted. In 1932 a listener's letter printed in *The Radio Times* said: 'When there is no light the faculty of hearing alone is employed. . . . When a play with effects is being broadcast, one can picture oneself at the scene of the play, especially if in the firelight, as the fire has a way of creating visions.' As the apocryphal imaginative child was to say a few years later: 'I like wireless more than television – the pictures are so much better.'

By 1939, the end of the period covered in this book, ideas on such subjects had become more sophisticated. In June of that year, for example, Janet Adam Smith asked, in a *Radio Times* article called 'Seeing Pictures', 'What do you see when you listen?'. It depended, she said, on the type of programme and the type of listener. 'Everyone's answer is different. Listening to the News, some people see the fretwork pattern on the loudspeaker, the fire flickering, Mother knitting, and make no mental pictures. Others see the dinner-jacketed figure of the Chief Announcer . . . I should hazard,' she went on, 'that the ideal listener should be capable both of working his picture-making faculty as hard as a movie-camera, and of shutting it off altogether.'

In choosing my own pictures, I have had every kind of reader in mind. Indeed, I have tried in this book to combine two elements which are not easily reconciled, each of which has had a place in the history of broadcasting – the scrapbook and the history lesson. The word 'scrapbook', with earlier and very different Victorian associations, was first used in relation to radio in December 1933, when Leslie Baily presented the first of his *Scrapbook* programmes. Whole tapestries of sound were woven, despite the primitive recording methods which meant that celebrities could not be recorded outside and played back later. They had to be brought physically to the studio.

As always, a paradoxical advantage was seen in such a limitation of the available technology. Even when recordings did exist, they were used only if the protagonists were dead or otherwise inaccessible. A virtue was made of the necessity for live performances.

The object of the *Scrapbook* programme was to recapture the immediacy of history, and this is my object also. As Leslie Baily put it proudly in 1937: 'We appoint history to live itself again.' His *Scrapbook for 1901* included a contribution from Marconi, and we can now listen as often as we like to the last recorded words of the best-known pioneer of 'our radio times'. The *Scrapbook* programmes caught impressions as well as recorded words, and they brought in music too, the kind of music that carries with it whole chains of associations.

The *Manchester Guardian* claimed in 1937 that the *Scrapbooks* so treated 'social history' that it became 'a form of entertainment'. The charge was too heavy. The best history lessons involve re-creating atmosphere as well as presenting facts, and the BBC excelled in these as it developed its educational programmes. Its best history teacher, Rhoda Power, sister of Eileen Power,

the brilliant medieval historian, was as enterprising in her own way as Leslie Baily. Going back deep into the past, she and her colleagues restored the Middle Ages to life for the children of Britain. The photograph of 'The History Lesson', reproduced overleaf, is my second inspiration.

The BBC itself was so engrossed in its own history – and self-conscious about the way in which to write it – that it, too, fused the concepts of the scrapbook and the history lesson. 'Reminiscence has a particular charm', wrote the editor of *The Radio Times* complacently in 1933, after the tenth anniversary number had brought in many letters from readers who still possessed their copy of the first issue ever produced. 'It is clear that so short a period as ten years', he went on, 'can suffice to give retrospect its charm.'

One of the most interesting of all the *Scrapbook* programmes concerned the year 1922 itself, the year of the founding of the BBC, in which the producer even went to the lengths (in 1937) of creating an aural mock-up of the pre-Savoy Hill 2LO studio at Marconi House, complete with 'chatter, telephone-bells, engineers testing on a piano, clatter of typewriters'. By

A schools talk at Elstow, 1926.

MEETING THE NEW TEACHER.

then the very name of the call sign 2LO was rich with nostalgia. Indeed, it was not only 2LO which had faded into history, but the whole of the Savoy Hill years of the BBC itself. The years before 1922 were thought of as pre-history. They included some landmarks, however, like Dame Nellie Melba's broadcast, by courtesy of the *Daily Mail*, in 1920. The BBC's first chief engineer, and inventor of its regional scheme, Peter Eckersley, represented such continuities until his forced resignation from the BBC in 1929 because of his involvement in a divorce case. He had been the first broadcasting star in the pre-BBC days of 'W-r-r-rittle Calling!'

The Radio Times itself made the most not only of every anniversary but of every backward glance and every forecast of the future. A feature, *The Dear Old Days*, appeared in 1930; *Do You Remember?* in 1937; *Here's Radio for Remembrance* in the same year; and, also in 1937, a complete 'Memories' number of *The Radio Times*. An article on the tenth anniversary of the Corporation asked the retrospectively poignant question 'How many more changes will broadcasting have undergone by 1946?'

TEN YEARS OF LISTENING

IN 1922 I GOT INTERESTED IN WIRELESS

IN 1923 MY CRYSTAL SET BEGAN TO FUNCTION

& IN 1924 IT PASSED THE EXPERIMENTAL STAGE INTO THE DRAWING ROOM.

WITH 1925 CAME THE GLIMMER OF VALVES,

& IN 1926 I GOT MY FIRST LOUD-SPEAKER.

IN 1927 I GOT A LOUDER-SPEAKER

& IN 1928 A REALLY-LOUD-SPEAKER.

IN 1929 I ADDED A (NOT VERY) PORTABLE.

IN 1930 I SWITCHED OVER TO AN ALL-MAINS SET

& IN 1931 A RADIO-GRAM.

NOW IN 1932 I HAVE GOT EVERYTHING — SO I'VE TAKEN OUT A LICENCE!

In my book I have tried throughout to catch the elusive present as well as the sense of the past and the future. Insofar as it is a scrapbook, it is never afraid of nostalgia. As the authors of the *Scrapbook* programmes put it: 'We pick and choose, laying a cherished oddment beside the quaint choice of a moment ago. Voices from the past. Songs of yesteryear. Events relived. This oddness, this variety, these strange juxtapositions are the fascination of a scrapbook.' Insofar as it is a 'history lesson' it aims not at completeness but at representativeness.

My chapters include some not very strange juxtapositions. I continue this introduction with 'Cavalcade', a glimpse of the whole broadcasting sequence from 1922 to 1939, a necessary element in the history lesson. I try to pick out the landmarks here – some landmarks in broadcasting, some landmarks in national history to which broadcasting lent a new dimension. This is the only chronological section of the book.

I go on in the first chapter, 'The Miraculous Toy', to recall the time in the early 1920s when people referred generally to 'the wonders of wireless'. The wonder began with the simple crystal set, but before long there was as much talk about the wonderful design of receivers as there was about the design of cars.

'Everybody's Listening In', the title of my next chapter, was the name of one of the first (1922) of many radio songs. In Britain – unlike in the United States – a listening public was built up rather than a listening market, and in this chapter I describe who listened in and in what circumstances.

'The Bradshaw of Broadcasting', the title of my third chapter, was the nickname given to *The Radio Times* in its very first editorial in 1923. The analogy between *The Radio Times* and the Bradshaw railway timetable was a sign that broadcasting, like railways, changed not only modes of communication but the sense of time. ('May you never be late for your favourite wave train.') In this chapter I describe the history of *The Radio Times* itself, a highly controversial journal at first because of the jealous rivalry of the conventional press. *The Listener*, also described in this chapter, was controversial too, for far longer; nobody would have dreamed of calling it a Bradshaw.

'Hullo Children!' speaks for itself. These were the children of the country's first radio times and within the great broadcasting audience they were always given a special place by the BBC. Indeed, long before the Corporation was called 'Auntie' (at a date later than that covered by this book) it had dozens of 'aunts' and 'uncles' on its staff. The most famous 'uncle' of all, Derek McCulloch ('Uncle Mac'), used the phrase 'Hullo Children, Everywhere'. While it lasted it was as

well-known a greeting as J. C. Stobart's 'Grand Goodnight' was a benediction. J. C. W. Reith, of course, the first Director General of Broadcasting House, was the father-figure behind the scenes.

'What are the wild waves saying?' is the first line of a poem by Joseph Edwards Carpenter (1813–85). It was used during the 1920s as an advertising slogan for Igranic (radio) Coils, but I have used it to cover most of the studio programmes presented by the BBC, recognizing that the waves under Reith's command were not very wild, and that there were commercial waves outside his command altogether. There was, however, the danger of perpetual interference. The miraculous toy was not immune from oscillation, howling and the like.

'Personality Parade', chapter six, introduces the broadcasters, some of them stars to start with, some stars made by radio. These are my cigarette-card characters; some of them are still alive. Very few, if any, would have won a hundred per cent rating in a popularity poll. Personalities, like programmes, divided the great audience, and chapter eight, 'What the Other Listener Thinks' (the title of the correspondence column of *The Radio Times* before the Second World War), sets out details of what came to be called 'listener response'. It was not until 1936 that the BBC introduced audience research, but long before that unsolicited correspondence would arrive in sacks to be sifted by an officeful of BBC officials.

Chapter seven, 'Quaecunque', the BBC motto from the mid-thirties, provides the title for my chapter on religious broadcasting broadly interpreted, and I place it before 'What the Other Listener Thinks' because, while most listeners did not think that this was their favourite listening, Reith did. Religious programmes were 'that branch of work which rests . . . upon an instinctive sense of fitness', as he put it in 1928. Yet for most listeners there was an element of mystery to be approached, with awe, in the ether itself, and as far as the broadcasters themselves were concerned, it was not only those making religious programmes who were expected to elevate as well as entertain. Education, as we have seen from the example of 'The History Lesson', was expected to do both. *The Listener*, indeed, was first conceived of as an educational journal, an adjunct to the learning process.

As my title for chapter nine I have chosen 'The Microphone at Large', the heading of a regular column in *The Radio Times* in the late 1920s and 1930s. For me it means outside broadcasting as it evolved from the song of the nightingale in the Surrey woods to the voice of Neville Chamberlain on his return from Munich.

Chapter ten, 'Nation shall speak Peace unto Nation', the BBC's first motto – pre-Chamberlain and pre-

Appeasement – traces the development of Empire broadcasting and the first beginnings of broadcasting in foreign languages. Reith pioneered the first: the second was a by-product not of peaceful but of stormy international history, the beginning of the war of words. 'Nation shall speak peace unto nation' meant 'telling the truth' as well as speaking peace – in Arabic and Portuguese, before German and Italian entered the repertoire.

Most of this book is about sound broadcasting, with the pictures attached. The BBC's first regular television service started in 1936, however, and there were now pictures on the screen as well as pictures on the page. The service was launched with a specially commissioned song, *Here's Looking at You* by Ronnie Hill, and in my chapter eleven (with this title) I look at television from its earliest experimental days until the moment on 1 September 1939 when the service closed down 'for the duration' with a Mickey Mouse cartoon.

This well-known break in time is not quite my own shutdown: *The Mystery of the Beam* illustrates with chapter and verse, as well as with pictures, the influence of broadcasting on the imagination. We thus return by a circuitous route to the 'Miraculous Toy' and the fascination wireless continued to exercise, even when the technical miracle was commonplace. Wireless encouraged people to dream as well as to listen, and some of my own most 'cherished oddments' in this book have more to do with fantasy than what was actually heard on the air. The fantasy still lingers when the facts are forgotten.

CAVALCADE

Scrapbook, as conceived in radio terms, suggests a patchwork of impressions pieced together on empty pages. In fact broadcasting, as it developed, carried with it also the sense of a cavalcade, a procession through the years, a journey through time.

The word 'cavalcade' was not much used before 1932, when Noël Coward gave it what he later described as 'artificial respiration'. It was in that year that C. B. Cochrane produced Coward's *Cavalcade*, which immediately aroused immense enthusiasm and was serialised in the *Daily Mail*. Domesticity, drama and patriotism were blended. In his speech on the opening night Coward himself exclaimed, 'In spite of the troublous times we are living in it is still a pretty exciting thing to be English!' and it was this sense of a particularly English cavalcade which was to linger, not least during the darkest years of the Second World War.

There were no references in the 1932 show to BBC broadcasting, which by then was indubitably British, if not English. The Voice of the Announcer, however, was to be heard in the wartime film of *Cavalcade*, and in 1936 the BBC broadcast a radio version of the original show, which proved as much of a success as it had been on the stage. Indeed, it was singled out as one of the best productions of that year.

Sir Philip Gibbs was to link the ideas of scrapbook and cavalcade in the following year when trying to account for the popularity with both old and young listeners of Leslie Baily's *Scrapbooks*. They were enthusiastic about them, he claimed, 'for the same reason that they liked *Cavalcade* by Noël Coward. To them it is a revelation of history'. Soon, as Coward himself wrote in 1941, there were 'Cavalcades of fashion, Hollywood Cavalcades, . . . Cavalcades of practically anything that can be cavalcaded'.

The BBC cavalcade began for different listeners at different times, as broadcasting reached them and swayed them. It reached them, too, at different moments in their lives: the oldest listeners were born 'B BBC', while for young listeners, of whom Princess Elizabeth was representative, the radio cavalcade had been in progress for the whole of their lives. They might have said when listening to *Scrapbook*, according to Sir Philip Gibbs, 'How very extraordinary! How very amusing. Their fathers and mothers spoke like that, thought like that, lived like that, behaved like that. . . .'

Leslie Baily described how, during one of the first television rehearsals at Alexandra Palace in autumn 1936, some of those taking part 'fell to comparing the birth of television in 1936 with the birth of broadcasting in 1922. . . . Suddenly,' Baily reported, 'our reminiscent conversation was pulled up with a shock when a tall and lovely young actress remarked that of course *she* couldn't remember a time when there was no broadcasting, no wireless set in the house, no radio news and entertainment. "You see," she said, "when the BBC started I was – let me see – just two years of age".' She would now be – perhaps is – over sixty and the two-year-olds of 1936 over forty-five. The procession continues.

The BBC recognized on its tenth birthday in 1932 that there were a number of landmark events in its own past. The day when the stationery changed – though not the initials – 1 January 1927 – was one. The starting of the regional scheme, with the opening of the Brookman's Park service, was another. The biggest of all the changes, however, the move from Savoy Hill to Broadcasting House, came in 1932 itself, a few months before the BBC's tenth birthday, although there was to be one other equally big change in 1936 (in retrospect at least) with the opening of the regular television service – the first in the world – at Alexandra Palace.

These were institutional landmarks; there were landmarks in programmes too. As early as 1930, the *BBC Year Book* produced a list of selected events in the history of the old company. It already had a touch of nostalgia. Many programme 'firsts' were included, proudly and comprehensively chosen to illustrate the range of broadcasting and the pioneering spirit of the BBC: the first General News Bulletin, the First Talk and the first Children's Hour (all on 23 December 1922); the first Religious Address (Christmas Eve, 1922); the first Outside Broadcast, *The Magic Flute* from Covent Garden (8 January 1923). The list passed on, in 1923, to the first Dance Music programme and the first Weather Forecast – as distinct from report – (both on 26 March) to the first broadcast of Election

Results (6 December). In 1924 came the first French talk by M. Stéphan (12 February) and the first broadcast of the Song of the Nightingale (19 May). 1925 brought the first broadcasting experiment in telepathy (12 November), while in 1926 came the first broadcast of the Changing of the Guard at Buckingham Palace (5 April), and, on the same day, incongruously, the first broadcast dancing lesson.

The personal 'cavalcade' of many early listeners – and broadcasters too – had included comic and inconsequential private memories as well. The laughter echoed not only through its broadcast jokes. 'The Broadcasters', who wrote *The Radio Times*' light-hearted gossip column 'Both Sides of the Microphone', looked back fondly in November 1930 on the 'Dear Old Days'. To them funny little happenings in early studio life at Marconi House and Savoy Hill meant as much as the building of 'the glittering white palace of Broadcasting House'. 'We were lately discussing the old days with Percy Merriman of the "Roosters" (who were among the first artists to broadcast)', they reported in November 1930.

'There were no tests then,' he said, 'no palaver, no contracts, no rehearsals to speak of – the announcer simply said "There's the microphone – and good luck".' The Roosters' first broadcast of Army Reminiscences lasted for two hours. The shirt-sleeved conductor said 'Tipperary in F, boys', and off they went. Mr Merriman recalls junior members of the BBC staff pouring water from jugs into basins to suggest a rippling stream. Even more curious is the reminiscence (quite unauthenticated) of a popular novelist who tells how, while he was actually broadcasting his first talk, twenty schoolchildren, in charge of a clergyman, were shown round the studio (the only one then in use).

In the eyes of 'the Broadcasters', the Roosters, the novelist, the clergyman and the twenty schoolchildren were as much part of the cavalcade as Reith and his colleagues.

The memories written in words could be broadcast in words and music too, and there were landmark programmes for many of the BBC's big birthdays and on great days like the day of the move from Savoy Hill, when 'A Great Panorama of 1922–1932', written and constructed by Lance Sieveking, compressed 'ten years' broadcasting in one hundred and sixty one-and-a-half minutes!' (see page 17).

By the fiftieth birthday in 1972 the 'select list' of pre-1927 dates in the 1930 *BBC Year Book* had become even more select. 226 events were singled out in 1932: there were only 30 in the *BBC Hand Book* for 1972. By then a date had to be very special indeed to be included; among the post-1927 'firsts' were the publication of the first issue of *The Listener* (16 January 1929); the first

Round-the-Empire Christmas Day programme and broadcast message by King George V (Christmas Day 1932) and the first television outside broadcast (the Coronation of King George VI on 12 May 1937).

There were a few new dates for the pre-1927 period in the later list, however. In long-term perspective the introduction of the ten-shilling broadcast receiving licence on 1 November 1922 took pride of place, even over the first daily broadcasts, and there was one addition to the entry for 26 May 1926, fascinating in the light of later history. The item in the 1930 list read simply 'first Broadcast from the House of Lords. Speeches at the International Parliamentary Commercial Conference'. The 1972 *Hand Book* entry added after 'speeches', 'by the Prince of Wales and the Rt. Hon. Winston Churchill'. There were few Churchill landmarks in the history of broadcasting before the Second World War: the BBC was very nervous of allowing rebels within the political parties the chance of airing their views. One remarkable omission from both lists is the General Strike of 1926, when Churchill, then Chancellor of the Exchequer, wanted the BBC commandeered.

There was one curious correction in the 1972 *Hand Book* list of dates. For some reason the 1930 *Year Book* had given 15 November 1922 as the date of the first programmes broadcast from the London station of the BBC, 2LO. In fact the first programmes from London were broadcast on 14 November, one day before the Birmingham and Manchester programmes began.

There were other significant differences too, all demonstrating that the 'revelations of history' are always incomplete. The 1972 list, unlike the 1930 list, singles out the first broadcast of the chimes of Big Ben to usher in the New Year on 31 December 1923. It is the sound of these chimes that, more than any other sound, registers the national cavalcade.

The 1930 list does not mention, either, the first issue of *The Radio Times* on 28 September 1923, probably because it concentrates on programme 'firsts'. *The Radio Times*, as the title of my book suggests, provides the source for my own selective chronology. Yet its first number, costing 2d – a price which was maintained, like the licence fee, through the period covered by my book – included in addition to details of programmes not only chatty 'gossip about Artistes' and the 'Uncles' Corner', but, surprisingly, 'a Song of Ancient China'.

My own select list of BBC dates provides the content of this chapter. But two interesting questions arise in relation to the choice of episodes in the broadcasting cavalcade.

First, every listener would make up his own list. The individual listener's list might begin with his very first experience of listening to broadcasting, and Alasdair Clayre has collected a remarkable anthology of vernacular impressions. A Yorkshire woman, for example, recalled

'playing in the street, and I went round to my next-door neighbour's house and I saw this round cone, you know, on the wall. And I went in to my mother and I said, "Mother, Mrs. Buckle's wall is singing." "Don't talk so silly," she says. So I says, "There is, there's some music coming out of the wall." So she went to have a look and she said, "Oh, it's amazing," she says.'

A Scottish woman remembered listening to the broadcast of George V's death with her family 'because,' she said, 'families tended to sort of sit round and listen to events like this, and I remember we even drew the curtains, you know, as a sort of token of mourning. . . .'

In the second place, there were already before 1939 some events in national life which today would be called 'media events'. As the media became dominant in national life, it was the sense of a mass audience listening together which carried with it the feeling of participation in history.

In the beginning, however, what fascinated listeners was the novelty of the association of the media with events which most of them would only have read about

(continued on page 24)

There's always good reading in **The Listener** 3ᵈ *Every Wednesday - a BBC Publication*.

Savoy Hill

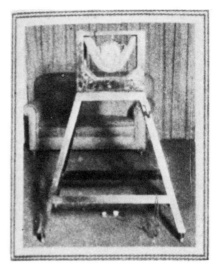

'We went to inspect sundry possible sites for the launching of our enterprise,' wrote Reith after the BBC's arrival in Savoy Hill in 1923. '. . . Finally, as dusk was falling, we came to Savoy Hill. It seemed the worst of all. . . . What a depressing place it was. It had been used for some mysterious L.C.C. medical activities . . . , and much dirt and depression had accumulated.'

In its heyday Savoy Hill (*right*) was 'the hub of British Broadcasting, a pioneering centre of radio wizardry'. 'Thousands of our readers who have acquired the radio listening habit and possess receiving sets in their homes will be interested in these photographs of the centre of British Broadcasting,' wrote *The Illustrated London News* in March 1924, one year after the opening of Savoy Hill (*above*, one of the photographs, 'the microphone at 2LO, where speakers and entertainers stand'). 'Those who hear the familiar words "London calling" will be able to picture in their mind's eye the scene where those words, and the sounds that followed, have their origin. The veil of mystery has been lifted from that cave of wizardry . . . but the inner secrets must remain a mystery still.'

The great Marconi himself (*bottom right*) greeted a new decade of broadcasting from Savoy Hill in 1930.

'2LO calling'

The words 'Savoy Hill' were already
nostalgic when, in 1931, *The Radio
Times* referred to the Savoy Hill days as
'the stone age of broadcasting'.

Yet there was plenty of nostalgia in
the BBC even then ... with a
'panoramic' programme (*above*); the
photograph of Reith (*left*) locking the
Savoy Hill door for the last time, and
the words in the 1932 *BBC Year Book*
introducing 'The Old Order Changeth':

The setting sun, and music at the close,
As the last taste of sweets, is sweetest last.

The engineers who 'pulled out the
plugs' and 'dissed the mics.' on the final
night at Savoy Hill, 14 May 1932,
themselves felt the passing of an era.
One by one the numbered studios 'off
the Strand' were closed as Leslie
Woodgate's Theatre Orchestra 'played it
out' (*top left*, Studio No. 9, Savoy Hill).

'A worthy edifice'

B.B.C. Military Band   Queen of the Typists leading office cats   Sound-effects experts imitating nightingales   Announcers announcing   Mr. A. J. Alan

'Names and descriptions of Broadcasting House,' Val Gielgud and Holt Marvell began their detective novel, *Death at Broadcasting House* (1934), 'have varied from the complimentary to the scurrilous.... It has been called "Majestic", "A Worthy Edifice, well fitted to house the marvels it contains", "A Damned Awful Erection" ... "Sing-Sing" (by certain frivolous members of the BBC staff who had heard this term applied to the new building of the Deutsches Rundfunk in the Masurenallee).'

Calling it no names, art-critic R. H. Wilenski praised the 'contemporary' style of 'B. H.' (as broadcasters themselves soon began to call it). 'The Radio is a product of our epoch. It rightly refused to do its work and conduct its business in any type of romantic fancy dress.... It has no flavour of the past ...', rather a 'radio-aeroplane-steel-and-concrete tang'. Raymond McGrath was one of the distinguished modern artists commissioned to design the new B. H. studios (*opposite right*, McGrath's design for the Vaudeville studio).

The inscription (p. 145) was not so modern. Yet the architect who advised the BBC on its interior decorations favoured new styles, and Eric Gill, who carved Prospero and Ariel *in situ* (*opposite below*), was modern enough to be controversial – more so with Ariel than with Prospero. The Unionist MP for St Pancras found time to move in the House of Commons that the whole group should be removed on grounds of impropriety. By contrast, a shopkeeper in Upper Regent Street was heard remarking to a customer, 'Have you seen our statue?' with 'not a hint of scandalised laughter; just pride'.

THE RADIO TIMES

Broadcasting House Number. Price 2d.

ADRIAN HILL

'A damned awful erection'

Triumphal Car: The Spirit of Broadcasting addressing Britannia · Rude Boy · Eminent Broadcasters · Office Boys (disguised as Cupids) pulling— · Allegorical Car: 'The stimulating effect of broadcasting on married life' · Interferers · Spirit of Detection

London - Broadcasting House, Portland Place.

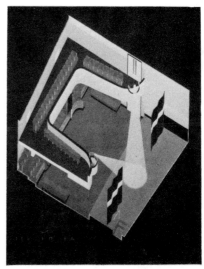

The frieze (*top*) by Arthur Watts depicted the 'cavalcade from Savoy Hill to Broadcasting House on 14 May 1932'. Adrian Hill designed the front cover of a special Broadcasting House number of *The Radio Times* (*opposite below*, 18 May 1932), which featured a mock inaugural luncheon. It began with 'the Hungry'un Rhapsody' and ended with the 'Dough-Mess-Stick Symphony' by Richard Strauss. The best item was the Trout Quintet by Chewbert.
Centre left, a publicity photograph for the opening of Broadcasting House.

'Tree of memory'

Daventry calling . . . wind and rain
Against my voices fight in vain . . .

You shall hear their lightest tone
Stealing through your walls of stone;

Till your loneliest valleys hear
The far cathedral's whispered prayer,

And the mind of half the world
Is in each little house unfurled.

The giant high-power transmitter
(*above*) of the British Broadcasting
Company, 5XX, opened on 27 July
1925, captured the imagination of the
listening public as much as 2LO or
Savoy Hill. It was built on the ancient
site of the Dane Tree, and, as Alfred
Noyes put it in his poem 'Daventry
Calling',

Dark and still
The tree of memory stands like a sentry . . .
Over the graves on the silent hill.

No poems were written for the
Droitwich transmitter which opened on
7 October 1934 (though its 700-foot
mast was six times greater), but the
BBC commissioned paintings by
Rowland Hilder (*top right*). There was
poetry in prose, too, in Reith's
description of his symbolic drive
successively to Droitwich and Daventry
'to put the transmitters to bed' on his
last night in the BBC, 30 June 1938,
when he signed the visitors' book
'J. C. W. Reith, late BBC'.

"LISTEN, DEAR. ISN'T THAT FROM 'LOHENGRIN'?"
"NO, SILLY! IT'S FROM DROITWICH."

Crisis

How Londoners heard the news during the Great Strike, according to Low, the famous cartoonist of the London *Star*.

The challenge of the General Strike of 1926 was faced by the pre-Corporation BBC. Opinions differed as to whether this was Daventry's finest hour. Ellen Wilkinson felt 'pain and indignation', Gilbert Murray confidence, and Reith relief when it was all over and he could personally announce its ending (*above*, producer's note of Reith's announcement on 12 May).

This was only one kind of crisis in a divided society which was seeking unity. Economic crisis created more divisions during the 1930s than the General Strike had done. The day after J. M. Keynes advocated more public spending before the microphone in April 1931, sales of national savings certificates fell 250,000 to 170,000 and Joshua Stamp had to be called in to restore order. Later in the decade John Hilton (*bottom left*, 'the poor man's lawyer, doctor, psychologist all in one') tried hard to establish real communication with ordinary listeners on topics that mattered most to them.

Political crisis was reflected most in controversial, pre-election political broadcasts, but these were planned by the parties, not by the BBC, and the international crisis soon overshadowed all else. Objectivity counted then.

There was one peculiarly British crisis (with Commonwealth implications and world-wide interest), Edward VIII's Abdication, with broadcasting stage-managed personally by Reith. During Edward's farewell speech not one telephone call was received at New York's largest telephone exchange. (*Centre left*, a pre-Abdication broadcast of Edward VIII, 1936.)

Ceremony

As Sherriffs sees them—the

CORONATION
COMMENTATORS

A. W. DOBBIN
Inside Buckingham Palace, overlooking the courtyard

JOHN SNAGGE
Opposite the Palace

HAROLD ABRAHAMS
In Whitehall

GEORGE BLAKE
At Middlesex Guildhall

MICHAEL STANDING
In the Abbey Annexe

HOWARD MARSHALL
In the Triforium

THOMAS WOODROOFFE
On Constitution Hill

S. J. de LOTBINIERE
In the Abbey Control Room

FREDERICK GRISEWOOD,
television commentator at Hyde Park Corner

"ALBERT, I'M SURE THE DEAR KING AND QUEEN WOULDN'T WISH US TO STAND TO ATTENTION *ALL* THE TIME."

'Audible pageants'

(phrase used by the *Daily Mail* of an earlier royal broadcast)

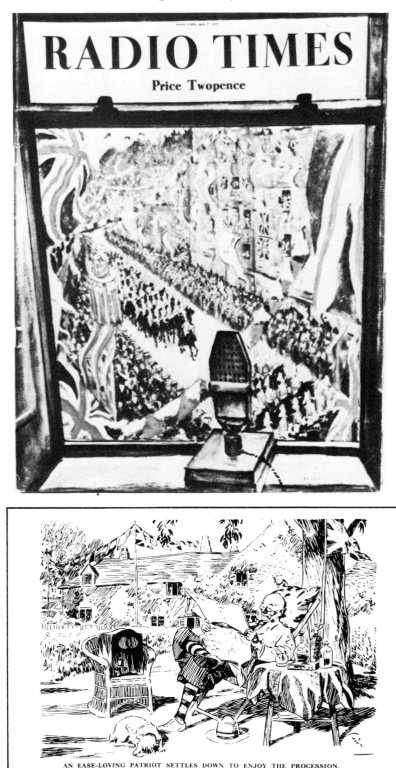

Voice of Announcer: 'The Procession is now leaving the Palace'.

AN EASE-LOVING PATRIOT SETTLES DOWN TO ENJOY THE PROCESSION.

The BBC responded more naturally to national ceremony than to economic and social unrest. Reith, indeed, believed that the aim of broadcasting was to unify sentiment and opinion, not to divide it.

The Coronation of George VI in 1937 was a broadcasting landmark (*top left*, Nevinson's famous front cover for *The Radio Times*, 7 May 1937). *Punch* joined in the popular 'cavalcade' with these three cartoons. 'To review broadcasting in 1937', the *BBC Year Book* stated, 'is at once to recall the historic part it played at the Coronation, on 12 May, of King George VI. For then, by the wonder of radio, every one of the King's subjects at home and in the remotest outposts of the Empire was able to see, with the inner eye of the mind, the pomp, the pageantry, the solemn ritual of the ceremony at which the Sovereign dedicated his life to them. They could follow, too, the outward and return journeys of the triumphal cavalcade, and at night hear the King himself speak to them. That day's broadcast was the most elaborate and complicated of the kind ever undertaken by the BBC.'

Letters of appreciation flowed into the BBC from all over the world. 'The Canadian people feel they are really part of the Crown now, and not just on the outside edge,' reported a Toronto listener, while the Coronation made one Pennsylvanian feel 'that your King was my King'.

in newspapers. In 1934 'G.S.', the writer of a letter to *The Radio Times*, looked back on the first Royal Broadcast ten years before. George V's opening speech at the British Empire Exhibition at Wembley on 23 April 1924 had been perhaps the first event to make the general public aware of broadcasting. 'G.S.' described his reactions and experiences on that day.

In Leeds, where the writer was then staying, a local electrician-turned-radio-dealer was permitted to rig up eighteen loudspeakers (the old horn-shaped pattern) around the pedestals of the statues in the Town Hall Square. He and his set were perched at the feet of Queen Victoria herself. He smoked a nonchalant cigarette. All eyes in a vast crowd were upon him. He was the miracle man. Occasionally he touched a knob, and for a moment or two the air was full of strange wailings and whistlings.

The eighteen little loudspeakers did their best, but it was impossible, what with the grunt of passing trams and all the sneezing and coughing (for it was a cold morning), to catch every word the King said; but we heard his resonant voice, and that of the Prince, and heads were bared whilst the Bishop of London led us in prayer. The loudspeakers, the statue, the Town Hall itself, faded from our consciousness.

Reith himself, writing in *The Radio Times* beforehand, looked forward to the 'Great Event', as he called it, not without a trace of nervousness:

'. . . Providence will surely have smiled on us on April 23rd. It is perhaps the biggest thing that has yet been planned. It will be history, wonderful and magnificent, if it succeeds, and abysmal disappointment if it be marred. . . .

One can visualize the crowds in the great cities where demonstrations have been arranged participating in what is, I suppose, one of the greatest ceremonials in Empire history. And one can hear little children in far distant villages saying 'I have heard the King.'

In those early days of broadcasting Reith naturally appreciated the novelty, 'first', element of the occasion – 'the biggest thing [in broadcasting] that has yet been planned' – but when he went on to 'visualize the crowds . . . participating in . . . one of the greatest ceremonials of Empire' he was unconsciously looking ahead to an era of 'media events'.

During the 1930s, after the opening of the Empire service in 1932 made such link-ups technically possible, the broadcasting of great national occasions bound together scattered imperial audiences just as Reith had foreseen and hoped. There were, of course, sad as well as festive imperial occasions, and radio covered and contributed to them all. 'In the darkest hour the whole nation turned instinctively to the BBC for its lead,' wrote John Trent in *Radio Pictorial* on 31 January 1936. The death of the King was a broadcasting as well as an imperial event. 'The Voice of the Nation became an awed whisper,' Trent went on, 'expressing and reflecting the grief of the Empire.' Less than a year later Reith's own grave words before the Abdication Broadcast, '. . . This is Windsor Castle. His Royal Highness the Prince Edward', not only introduced to millions of listeners the news of the event and Prince Edward's own commentary on it, but came later to constitute a vivid and integral part of their memory of it. In the same way Stuart Hibberd's solemn reading of the radio bulletin, 'The King's life is drawing peacefully towards its close', became for millions an inextricable part of the memory of the King's death.

The funeral of one king, the abdication of a second, and the coronation of a third, three new and testing experiences for the BBC, all occurred in the space of sixteen months. The Coronation was the first large-scale modern 'media event' in that it was the first outside broadcast by television – not only in England but anywhere in the world. 'We are happy to think that some of its [television's] earliest opportunities will have as their setting the historic pageantry of next summer,' said R. C. Norman, Chairman of the BBC, in November 1936 in his speech inaugurating the regular television service from Alexandra Palace. Norman was referring to the Coronation of Edward VIII, one 'media event' destined never to happen.

In May 1937 television, nevertheless, used the opportunities of 'the historic pageantry' of the Coronation, as the BBC Chairman had predicted. The identity of the King had changed, but the Coronation took place on the day originally planned, May 12th. It did more to boost television than any other single happening. As the *BBC Hand Book* for 1938 put it:

When the King and Queen neared Hyde Park Corner in their Coronation Coach on May 12, they were seen not only by the throng of sightseers lining the route, but by an army of people scattered over the Home Counties, from Cambridge in the north to Brighton in the south.

The television phenomenon would have been hailed in any other age either as a miracle or as a piece of witchcraft. But these were 'those radio times'. It had been long awaited and long expected. Yet it made a remarkable impression on everybody, 'from owners of broadcasting receivers to owners of racecourses'.

As the *Hand Book* went on:

Trains were an improvement upon stage coaches; mechanized flight, on ballooning; but television is an improvement on nothing. It is something new under the sun.

Television as a medium was 'something new', yet in an obvious sense the message it offered on May 12th was an old one. What the cameras showed was a genuine cavalcade in the oldest sense of all – 'a festive and solemn procession with horses'.

THE MIRACULOUS TOY

IT IS MORE BLESSED TO BUILD THAN TO RECEIVE

C is for Crystal

I have a little magic box
    Cased in with windows clear;
It has a Fairy who unlocks
    Sweet secrets to my ear.

My Fairy in a Crystal lies
    Imprisoned out of sight,
For though I stare with all my eyes
    I never see her quite.

Sometimes she sleeps and nothing says
    Until her dreams are stirred –
But you must learn to know her ways
    Before she'll say a word.

You mustn't bang upon her door
    With sticks and things like that
But you must use, nor less nor more,
    The Whisker of a Cat.

Then when you've tapped the Crystal well
    Where it most brightly gleams,
The Fairy to your ear will tell
    A dozen different dreams.

From 'A Broadcasting Alphabet' by ELEANOR FARJEON,
The Radio Times, 7 October 1927

'WHEN some people can no longer deny the existence of a newly-discovered force, they save their faces by waving it aside with a superior gesture. They call it a toy.' So wrote Reith with feeling in *The Radio Times* in March 1924 at a time when vested interests hostile to broadcasting were at their height. He went on to compare those who hoped to make wireless fail by ridicule with the 'flat-earthers' of the time of Copernicus. 'Some people called wireless telegraphy a toy,' he wrote. 'Some few still persist in calling broadcasting a toy. Now what is a toy? The dictionary says it is "a plaything for children", "a trifle". Well, if wireless served no other purpose than to be a first-class plaything for children, I for one would hold that it had still a very great part to perform in moulding the life of the nation.'

Reith's editorial was called 'The Miraculous Toy'. For him the miracle lay as much in the infinite scope of broadcasting, 'its untold possibilities for good or evil', as in the mystery of the workings of 'the newly-discovered force' inside the 'little magic box'. 'Miracle' and 'magic', 'mystery' and 'romance', were all words which featured often in early writings about broadcasting. The excitement felt by early wireless enthusiasts was communicated by Peter Eckersley, Chief Engineer of the BBC, who called his article in *The Radio Times* in November 1923, 'The Romance of it All'.

'Think of the chain of events between your ears and the spoken word in the studio,' he wrote, going on to anticipate the rhetoric of micro-technicians: 'In London a little coil wound of wire as fine as small thread moves 1/1000 of an inch only, and its motions are faithfully interpreted as feeble electric impulses. These are passed to valves which amplify the feeble sounds produced until so great are the energies released that the transmitter itself can be heard quivering in sympathy – and would to Heaven we could find exactly where! The movements of that fine wire coil of not more than 1/1000 of an inch finally controls horse-power. If one ever really sits down and thinks of the connections involved, of the myriad particles of electricity obedient to one's will, of the many contacts that might (and sometimes do) go wrong, one wonders that anything ever goes through.

And you, with your aerial tied up with string . . . there, indeed, you have a miracle! . . .

There are forty-eight millions of people in the British Isles, and nightly flowing past their houses, ready to be tapped, is this "concourse of sweet sounds".'

Among the forty-eight million potential listeners was one huge group of actual wireless enthusiasts, the children. 'To the child mind,' wrote the Editor of *The Broadcaster* in October 1922, a month before the BBC was born, 'radio will appear as a wonderful toy that has superseded the fairy books of our own youth. The loud-speaker in the nursery will be a familiar spectacle in the near future, and one that will represent to the parent an invaluable means of introducing quietude into the precincts of the playroom.'

Children, indeed, were the first listeners to have their own programmes regularly provided for them, not by fairies but by 'uncles' and 'aunts'. The first Children's Hour was broadcast in December 1922. There were *BBC Children's Hour Annuals* before there were *BBC Hand Books* for the grown-ups. A story in one of the earliest of them, *Hullo Boys!* (1925), illustrated the

At last the box was connected and placed on a table by the bed

'magic' theme. Paul, the little invalid boy, receives a surprise present from a mysterious lady visitor:

> ... The very next day a parcel arrived, by his father, and while he was unwrapping it with eager, feverish fingers, two men entered the room and quietly set about fixing wire.
>
> 'Dear Paul,' said the little note that came with the parcel, 'Here in this box are some fairies, and they have nothing to do, you may be quite sure, but to amuse little boys like you. Here is the music, the song, here are the Uncles and Aunties you miss so much, and they are all yours, and yours alone.'
>
> 'Paul,' said his father, 'this is a wireless set. And it is just for you; so you can work it yourself, and listen to all the music you want.'
>
> 'Father,' replied Paul, 'it is a box full of magic!'

This sentimental story was written for his 'nephews' by one of the radio 'uncles', but by the mid-twenties the children themselves often exhibited a hard-headed and matter-of-fact approach to wireless. Filson Young commented sadly on the blasé attitude of a typical knowing child. 'All the apparent overthrow of natural laws and forces,' he wrote, 'all the defiance of seeming impossibilities, all the genius and striving, experiment and research that made it possible for him to share at his own fireside an entertainment with a million other children, were no more miraculous to him than the running of the water from the bathroom taps when they were turned on for his evening ablutions. . . .' For such a child there was no miracle in the wireless.

One way of dealing with miracles has always been to seek a physical explanation. In the early days of broadcasting, 'wireless hobbyists' of all ages attempted to understand the 'miraculous toy'. The science fascinated them more than the magic. Soon wireless seemed neither miraculous nor a toy: the mystery, too, began to diminish before the onslaught of thousands of serious amateur and professional 'constructionalists'.

Journals like *Popular Wireless* were full of articles with titles like 'How to make a crystal set in half-an-hour (so simple a Child can make and fix it)', and 'Oscillation' (with comic illustrations of wicked 'oscillators' being ostracized by their neighbours). The editor of *The Broadcaster* invited readers to 'Write to me about your Wireless Worries', while the editor of *Wireless* boasted that if *he* were wrecked on a desert island 'with nothing more than a keg of nails and a few empty biscuit boxes, he would establish wireless communication within a day'. *Desert Island Discs* was still almost twenty years away.

Schoolboys were encouraged to take up the wireless hobby and thousands did so. In *Hullo Boys!* in 1925 'Uncle Clarence' wrote:

> The facts teach us that boys generally love radio, and I regard it as being psychologically true that this hobby is not

DETECTIVES LOCATING AN OSCILLATOR

only the latest, but the best! It is far deeper in its interest than the simpler things boys did when I was young and, by the fact that it requires more thought, it is a mind-trainer and a thought-builder. It is amazing how a boy's grasp of knowledge increases in proportion to his study of this latest game, which is a fascinating hobby and a piece of remunerative work rolled into one.

To my mind, there never was a greater example of profitable interest in a hobby for young and old alike. Every hour – every minute – spent in getting down to the depths of radio, this never-ending science, bears fruit; and who knows but what the schoolboy dabbler of to-day will not be the Marconi of tomorrow. Ask a schoolmaster if it isn't true that those of his boys who are wrapped up in radio are quicker in the grasping of knowledge and the application of other things; their minds, it seems, are more susceptible to learning; they are, shall I say, more intelligent. Radio is the tonic of a boy's brain; a thrilling, yet mysterious, something which, though regarded as a hobby, is that, and a heap more. Which are the most progressive countries? Those whose people are mostly easy-going peasants and traffickers, like Russia and some of the Eastern countries, or those whose populations are mostly quick-witted business men and artisans, like Britain, America, and Germany, and in which of these two groups of countries is radio manifest? There are upwards of fifteen millions of radio listeners in Britain and the United States alone. Therefore, boys, those of you who make your radio sets with 'nose on the grindstone', carrying yourselves into the night with your experiments, be doubly encouraged that you are on the great highway to success in some calling in life. . . . Even if you do not actually build your set yourself, you cannot listen to broadcasting even for an hour without learning something, while you are enjoying yourselves. Does not radio bring to you the acknowledged experts on their different subjects as private tutors into your own home?

Not all grown-ups adopted such an enlightened attitude to the educational value of the new hobby. In February 1925 'Halyard', the columnist of *Wireless Magazine*, criticised the headmaster of a large grammar school in Yorkshire who had issued a circular to the parents of his boys in which he pointed out that wireless was interfering with the work of 'an alarming number of the boys in his school'. He suggested that wireless had been found responsible in many cases for skimped homework, and quoted a case in which a boy had to do his homework in a room where a loudspeaker was in operation, and another case in which a boy made a pretence of doing his homework while wearing a pair of headphones.

'Halyard' wrote:

I have had a most interesting chat with the headmaster of a similar school in a neighbouring county on the subject of wireless and the schoolboy, and I must say that there is most decidedly another side to the question. The views expressed by the Yorkshire headmaster are somewhat extreme.

The headmaster who was so kind as to give me his experience and views pointed out to me that wireless is not the only thing which causes a boy to neglect his homework. There has always been something which the lazy boy has been able to spend his time over in preference to homework. Such things as the scout movement, choir practices, music lessons and the cinema have all, in their day of popularity, made sad havoc of the schoolboys' homework and progress. The majority of schoolmasters view the question of wireless and the schoolboy with equanimity and the most progressive of them are determined to use wireless as an educative force.

It always seems a great pity to me when schoolmasters refuse to take advantage of some new progressive force such as wireless undoubtedly is in these days. Is it not all to the benefit of the schoolboy of to-day that he can hear, in his own classroom, the best of the world's music and the greatest of the world's living scientists? Is it not far better for a boy to read ravenously the pages of a wireless paper in preference to the pages of a juvenile magazine which attracts its readers by impossible stories of adventure and school life?

Alec Waugh, the novelist, writing in *The Radio Times* on 'Wireless and the Modern Boy' on 1 May 1925, divided wireless enthusiasts into two classes:

There is, on the one hand, the boy who is concerned with wireless as an ingenious mechanical contrivance, and on the other, the boy who regards it solely as a medium of entertainment. To the first class of boy the nature of the thing heard is of casual matter. He has in his own room or workshop erected a machine with which it is possible for him to hear words spoken in London, Bournemouth, Cardiff, Paris, and he is immensely proud of his achievement . . . . His radio conversation is not an affair of 'How good *Midsummer Madness* was last week', but of crystals and loud speakers. He is like the artist who works at his art for his art's sake only. He does not think of it as a directly utilitarian activity.

Waugh was writing about boys everywhere. For boys in boarding schools wireless was, 'of course, such an entirely new thing' that it was 'impossible to dogmatize on its regulation'. He went on:

At Harrow, for example, while any boy may set up a wireless set in the workshop, to listen in houses is a monitorial privilege. Only those, that is to say, are allowed to have wireless sets in their studies who can be trusted not to use them in work hours, and so it would seem that radio activity in boarding-schools at any rate, will be confined to that type of boy who is interested in wireless as a mechanical contrivance simply, who will fix up his own set in the school workshop and experiment with wave-lengths at such hours as he may be free to leave his house – the hours, as a matter of fact, when the least interesting portion of the programme is being broadcast.

And such a boy is, I believe, in the minority. The average boy regards wireless as a means of entertainment simply. He does not care twopence whether he is listening to Cardiff, or Paris, or Berlin, as long as what he hears amuses him. He is no more interested in the technique of the business than are 99 out of every 100 film-goers in the process by which moving pictures are projected on the screen in front of them.

The boy 'concerned with mechanical contrivance' may have been in the minority, but in 1926 there were enough of him – and of his father and his older brothers – to cause *The Radio Times* to exclaim: 'If Charles Dickens, the great Broadcaster of Human Nature, returned to earth and visited a modern house, he would think that he had strayed by mistake, not into a human home, but into some kind of scientific exhibition or workshop.'

The high point of the wireless constructionist had already been reached by 1926. As the valve set playing through loudspeakers replaced the simple crystal set and earphones, the necessary new techniques went beyond the skill of most amateur 'hobbyists'. The novelty of wireless had, in any case, worn off. As Reith had hoped, interest in the programmes broadcast began to replace interest in the 'miracle' of broadcasting. As early as May 1924, Reith had pointed out in *The Radio Times* the dangers of concentrating too much on 'the technicalities, the means by which, and so on'.

We say 'Come and listen to my wireless set', and we lead our friends into a room where there obtrude on the attention wires and valves and boxes and switches, and, to crown all, a horn. The attention is distracted by all this paraphernalia and by the tuning preliminaries which ensue. And then we all sit with our eyes glued to the loud speaker and come to the conclusion that the sound is metallic and unsatisfying, and that we do not like our music tinned. Whereas, our minds are obsessed and distracted by the agency, and the music has not a fair chance.

Tell your friends to 'Come and listen to the Unfinished Symphony', and let the music come on them mysteriously and spontaneously from some invisible source. Camouflage the loudspeaker, hide it behind a screen, in a cabinet, on the top of a bookcase – anywhere where people will not sit and stare at it. Why plant the whole apparatus down in the most conspicuous part of the room? If one wants to dance, do let it be done to music and not to a horn. I am convinced that the effect of music and many other things is marred by the obtrusive visibility of the source from which they come.

There was one group of listeners who keenly endorsed Reith's objections to over-concentration on 'the means by which': women had never shared the wireless construction craze, though they early became the most devoted and regular listeners. 'That women will not be interested in the mechanical side of broadcasting is a fact, for the natural indifference of the fair sex to any knowledge of what "makes the wheels go round" is inevitable,' wrote Sinclair Russell in *The Broadcaster* in October 1922. 'Enterprising photographers may picture pretty women standing before transmitting sets and operating switches with dainty fingers. Such studies, however, are a picturesque rather than a practical reflection of the interest of the opposite sex in the mechanism that lies behind the magic of Marconi.'

Most women seem happily to have accepted this low evaluation of their capabilities, and even to have encouraged it. The lady columnist of the *Wireless Magazine* in 1924 and 1925 wrote coyly under the by-line 'Wireless Femininities', which was illustrated with a picture of a head-phoned lady of leisure sipping a cup of tea in an armchair.

In February 1925 she wrote:

Every woman must have noticed how different her point of view about wireless is from that of her husband or son or any other male belonging to her.

To women wireless is a joy, a distraction, a companion, or an excitement; but it is never what it is to men – a toy.

It seems to women that the last thing men want to do with their wireless set is to listen-in. They want to play with it and fiddle with it incessantly, just as they do with their cars. Putting it up is a huge joy, and what a ruthless one! The friend who installed mine heartlessly hacked a corner out of each door from the sitting-room to kitchen, so that he could earth to the sink water-pipe. . . .

One visitor always pulls out the set every time he comes and plays with the catwhisker, 'to see how it's working today'. But I've never known him listen-in for five consecutive minutes – with the grand exception of the last election night.

My sympathies go out to a friend of mine who says she never hears any broadcasting because her husband is such an efficient wireless hobbyist. 'Which means that whenever there's grand opera, which I adore,' she sighs, 'he's taking down the old set, or putting up a new one, or sitting in front of it twiddling buttons and things to make it work better for listening-in. Listening-in!'

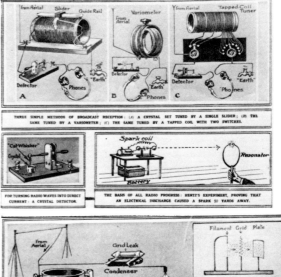

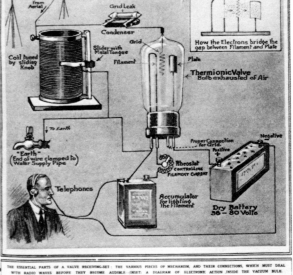

'How the Miracle of Broadcasting is Performed.'

The Radio Times itself printed an article in the same year called 'Fashions set by the wireless: innovations for women listeners', which helped to confirm the feminine stereotype:

Gold and silver net caps, designed specially to prevent the hair being disarranged when listening with ear-pieces, are being sold in large numbers to women wireless enthusiasts.

'These nets were originally intended for evening wear on the way to dances and other functions,' a saleswoman told a representative of *The Radio Times*. 'Now they are being bought almost exclusively for use at wireless listening parties. After using the ear-pieces, the hair is liable to be slightly pulled out of place, and these nets prove just the thing to prevent this.'

LISTENING IN

Fashion, being notoriously fickle, is always difficult to forecast, but experts say that the first item of feminine apparel to suffer eclipse by wireless will be the bandeau, which has had such a great vogue since Mlle Lenglen introduced it, or rather popularised its use, three or four years ago. Women listeners prefer the net cap, and as the ear-pieces themselves partly surround the head, the bandeau will have to be consigned to the limbo of fashions that have had their day.

Wireless, in fact, will tend to simplify rather than to complicate women's dress of the future. The woman enthusiast, who will soon be numbered in her hundreds of thousands, will not want to be hampered by superfluities of dress when busying herself about the task of tuning-in. Tassels and ribbons and lace are liable to become entangled with the leads, as she bends over her set, and for this reason they will be discarded.

The feminine role was established in childhood: schoolgirls were not expected to share the wireless constructionist hobby with their brothers. *Hullo Girls!* the *BBC Children's Hour Annual* of 1925, contained stories of fairy circles but no circuitry. Only one story in *The Broadcaster* showed a more liberated woman: in *Angela Gets It Done*, the heroine crawls gallantly among the chimney pots erecting an aerial. Angela, however, was a shining exception which proved the rule; most women in wireless stories and articles conformed to the 'helpless' norm.

There were helpless males also. 'Why should people want to know how this magic vaguely known as "wireless" does its tricks?' asked Ivor Brown in *The Radio Times* in November 1933. He objected to the high proportion of incomprehensible technical articles with titles like 'Sidebands and Heterodynes' in the new *BBC Year Book*.

Filson Young, also, preferred to concentrate safely on listening. 'I know nothing of anodes, grid-leaks, reactions, condensers, oscillations, induction, variometers, or super heterodynes,' he had written complacently in the *Saturday Review* in 1924, two years

before he became the BBC's own radio critic. 'All these words (except the last) mean something to me, but they mean something quite different from what they mean to the instructed wireless amateur, whose aerials thread the skies above suburban back gardens. They are excellent mysteries.'

Young and other non-mechanically-minded listeners actually enjoyed the sense of *mysterious* power they experienced when they turned on the wireless. They did not want to know too much about the 'miraculous toy', and while, for Young, a paid radio critic, wireless was no plaything, it nevertheless remained a miracle. He wrote of 'his little magic cabinet by means of which, on the manipulation of certain knobs and plugs, I am nightly in communication with the wonders or inanities of the ether'. He even confessed to 'revelling in the easy flattery of the wireless cabinet, which makes me believe that I am engaged in scientific research when I turn the knobs'.

By the beginning of the thirties, 'turning the knobs' was electronically a far more sophisticated process which left less to the skill of the listener. Filson Young looked back with nostalgia to the days when 'it used to be a matter of some skill to tune in a wireless receiver to different stations and wavelengths, and weird howlings and cracklings accompanied this geographical exploration of the ether'. A visit to see the wonders of Radiolympia in August 1933 made him feel almost useless:

Now the most elaborate sets seem to be made fool-proof. Turning a single dial to a given wavelength, in the certainty that the station required will be immediately heard, is as easy as setting the hands of a clock. All the elaborate and skilful work of construction, the almost miraculous affair of transmission, these are hidden away from the listener, who can therefore feel no particular pride in the achievement of the miracle.

The radio advertising of the day reflected changes in attitudes: 'The "Wonderful-it-Works" Years are Over' ran the caption to a Pye advertisement of 1933, going on to claim:

Pye lead on to the era of 'Beautiful-it-Recreates' . . . The technique of aggressive knobs and dials, the survival of the experimental era in the outward appearance of radio, belong to a chapter that is closed by the introduction of Pye Cambridge Radio. Realistic entertainment and artistic beauty of design have long since overshadowed the miracle of radio in the minds of listeners. There is no longer any excuse for the test-bench technique, as perhaps there was in the earlier days when the marvel of music from the air alone excused anything. That phase has survived too long.

Pye, in the business of selling radio sets, naturally stressed the importance of the quality of receivers in

A short wave receiver in use for the broadcast of the Boat Race in March 1927

their advertising copy; the BBC, in the business of transmitting programmes, naturally emphasised the quality of what was transmitted. By the early thirties, however, they shared a common situation: for neither was it now enough to point to the 'miracle of radio'. The fact of broadcasting was taken for granted and only improved quality in sets and programmes could impress the no-longer-astonished listener.

Yet there was still romance in broadcasting for those who cared to look for it. With the opening of Broadcasting House in 1932, attention shifted from the 'miraculous toy' to the miraculous toyshop. 'London's Terrifying Tower of Silence' was the title of an article by Harold Nicolson in the *Evening Standard* in March 1931. Nicolson, who was allowed a preview of the building, found a kind of romance in the functional modernism of the architecture. 'Stark it may be, but oh! how strong! how true!' he wrote, intrigued by his visit to the sound-proofed studios in 'the palace of sound required to be a citadel of silence'. At different times Broadcasting House was compared with a ship, with a fortress, with a towering cliff, and was even nominated one of the 'Seven New Wonders of the World'.

There was romance and magic in the 'toy factory' too. In 1933 E. P. Leigh-Bennett wrote an astonishing publicity booklet, 'A City of Sound', about Hayes, the headquarters of the Marconi Company. For Leigh-Bennett, Hayes was the most magical place in the world:

You are left with a blurred vision of a huge white-coated company of men and women, boys and girls in an almost endless vista of wide, sunlit rooms. And of the batteries of machines they control. And you are troubled with protracted indecision as to which are the cleverer, the humans or the machines?

. . . Even the Coil-Winding Shop at Hayes seemed a romantic spot to Leigh-Bennett:

Days could be spent with unflagging interest in this part of the factory. . . . Machines are winding miles and miles of copper strands on reels; the strands being in some cases as thin as the hair on your head; and even so these have already been coated with enamel. Forty-eight thousand turns of the reel, adjusted to the nicety of half a turn! A coil, and then a layer of paper, and then another. A metal strand so fine that you must hold it up to the light to see it. A girl watching a needle on a gauge for nth degree accuracy. The extreme delicacy of touch needed in this department – a woman's job. No man could handle such work successfully.

At last women had been given credit for superior wireless skills!

Eventually Leigh-Bennett reached the inner sanctum, the Hayes Power House. He approached it in a spirit approaching reverence:

. . . You do not talk much in this big Power House; mundane speech seems out of place – futile. But you realize, as you stand on this faintly quivering floor, that all those thousands of fingers in the high buildings round and about, moving so dexterously at this moment, and all those hundreds of machines coughing, jerking systematically, flashing in organized revolutions, are drawing their energies and excellencies from this soporific centre. And in that one thought lies the lure of the place. Of the eight thousand people working here to-day how many have felt these pulse beats; know even where the great heart lies? Very few; and it does not matter. But if you are from outside this community and have come to look within it, seeking knowledge – here will be found an inspiration.

The BBC itself found sober satisfaction – if not inspiration – in the healthy increase in wireless licences sold in the early thirties, despite the Depression. An editorial in *The Radio Times* in January 1931 described the figures as 'unanswerable proof of the rapidity with which Broadcasting has sloughed the skin of Novelty and Luxury and taken its place in contemporary life as a fully-fledged Necessity. The wireless set,' the editor went on,

. . . no longer displayed as a mark of great prosperity or scientific acumen, has gained an accustomed place in the home. The novelty of 1922 has become the day-to-day routine of 1931 and now, had Broadcasting been no more than a clever toy, would be the moment for it to be put away in the cupboard with other forgotten playthings. That it is something more than a toy, that it has won its place as a necessity, the possibilities of which are as yet unreckoned, is proved we venture to think, by the evidence of those 409,000 additional licences.

The following year *Punch* himself, speaking in the character of 'The World' (after visiting the Radio Exhibition at Olympia) commented, 'Whatever else has happened to me, at least I've become a place fit for hearers to live in.' And by 1933 Hilda Matheson could write, as of a period of ancient history:

At first, the possession of a receiving set was entertainment in itself; it was a game, a hobby, a magic box, from which one extracted unexpected and exciting sounds. The radio industry in general did not in those days look much beyond this stage, since people were ready enough to buy sets for the sake of a new experience. Programmes seemed then less important than mechanism.

By then, when television, the subject of a later chapter, was still being treated as a miraculous toy – although never, perhaps, to the same extent as wireless – there were children, the most matter-of-fact listeners of all, who remembered nothing before radio. In 1937 Derek McCulloch, 'Uncle Mac', wrote to them in the Children's Hour Annual:

If you were born in 1927, probably without realising it you grew up at the time when all the wonderful and elaborate devices I have just mentioned were ready for your pleasure, and, naturally enough, you accepted these things as part of your everyday life. Among the greatest of all inventions at that time was one called a crystal set. As you probably know, it consisted of a small crystal and a 'cat's whisker', coupled with an aerial and earphones, and with this equipment it was possible for people to listen to all sorts of programmes sent out by the British Broadcasting Company, first from Marconi House, and later from Savoy Hill.

In about 1927 – the year we have in mind – the crystal sets were beginning to be put on one side, and their place was being taken by better sets fitted with loudspeakers. That was just progress, and we all thought it was wonderful not to have to use earphones, although even to this day there are many listeners who still prefer to stick to their old-fashioned crystal sets.

The crystal set was, by the end of the thirties, itself an object of nostalgia. A *Punch* cartoon of June 1939 shows a used-car salesman showing a customer an antiquated 'bargain'. '£5, and it's got a built-in crystal set,' is his selling point.

The summer of 1939 was no time for nostalgia, however. Only fifteen years after Eckersley had written eloquently of 'the Romance of it all', the message which *The Radio Times* gave its listeners in June 1939 was more prosaic: 'Is your set doing its job? Is it as good as it was?' And the final pre-war Radiolympia, which ended the day before war broke out, was described unromantically as 'dignified, orderly, instructive and practical'. It would have been easy to claim that a nation going to war had no need of miraculous toys, had it not been for the fact that the most miraculous toy of all, known in 1939 to only a handful of people, was radar.

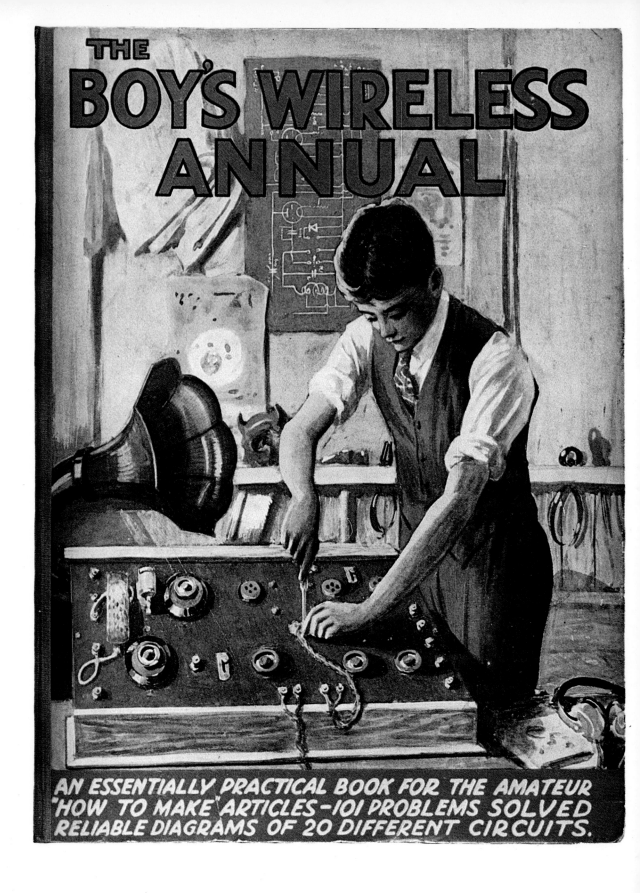

THE BOY'S WIRELESS ANNUAL

AN ESSENTIALLY PRACTICAL BOOK FOR THE AMATEUR
"HOW TO MAKE" ARTICLES — 101 PROBLEMS SOLVED
RELIABLE DIAGRAMS OF 20 DIFFERENT CIRCUITS.

'A kind of wizardry'

(Dame Nellie Melba on the subject of wireless)

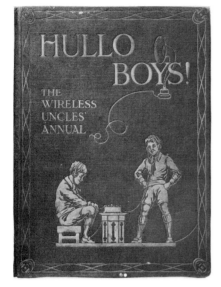

Wireless was a hobby long before the BBC became a Company, let alone an institution. It was a hobby both for men and boys. According to the editor of *Wireless Constructor*, men fell into two categories – 'handy-men' and 'ready-maders' – and wireless, he felt, not surprisingly, was 'a godsend' to the former, 'A heaven-sent hobby which seems to satisfy every longing.' It could be frustrating, of course, particularly after cats' whiskers gave way to more complicated 'super-hets':

I made myself a wireless set
The beast was styled a "super het" . . .
It whooped just like a whooper,
A chronic Babel-swooper.' (1933)

Husbands naturally knew more than their wives (*top right*, *Punch*, March 1925). Boys often knew more than their fathers, not to speak of their mothers. Caption of the *Punch* cartoon (*bottom*):

MOTHER: 'What makes the radio squeal so, Johnny?'
JOHNNY: 'Well, mother, if you must know, what you call squeals are really the self-oscillations of the thermionic valves, brought about by altering the potentials of the high and low tension batteries and varying the relations of the capacitative and inducive quantities in the receiver.'

The constructor's effort was not always rewarding, as a prize-winning limerick of 1928 showed:

After three or four hours hard fight,
I get my 'set' working all right;
I put on the 'phones,
Then hear, in sweet tones,
'Good-night, everybody — good-night.'

Newly-married Man (busy with wireless construction). "SWEETHEART, HAVE WE ANY TWEEZERS IN THE HOUSE?"
Wife. "I'LL RUN AND LOOK, DEAREST—ER, WHAT IS IT THAT DARLING WANTS TO TWEEZE?"

A CHILD OF THE RADIO AGE.

YOUR FIRST WIRELESS SET.

WHEN YOU HAVE YOUR FIRST WIRELESS SET INSTALLED FOR YOU—

DO NOT DELAY—

TO TAKE FULL ADVANTAGE—

OF ITS ENTERTAINMENT—

FOR ONCE—

YOU GET—

BITTEN—

WITH THE SUBJECT—

YOU WILL—

NEVER AGAIN—

HAVE—

MUCH—

LEISURE FOR LISTENING.

Wireless words

"WIRELESS TERMS ILLUSTRATED"

"THE WAVE LENGTH" AT BOGNOR

"WIRELESS TERMS ILLUSTRATED"

"BROADCASTING"

Dear Old Lady (writing to the B.B.C.): '. . . And will you please send me the pamphlet telling me how to osculate.'

'Should broadcasting invent a vocabulary of its own?' asked *The Radio Times* in October 1932. The question came too late. There already was such a vocabulary: 'From Microom to Etherphile', to quote one title.

Nonetheless, there were old words in the vocabulary, like broadcasting itself, as well as new ones, like radio; and the only argument was how they should be declined or conjugated. Reith himself used his authority to say that 'broadcasted' was wrong. He could not quite drive out 'listeners-in', though he felt 'in-listeners' would be better. *The Listener*, by leaving out the 'in' set the new style in 1929. From the beginning the title of *The Radio Times* had incorporated the new American word 'radio', not the old negative word 'wireless' (c.f. horseless carriage).

Much of the fun of the developing vocabulary lay in the associations surrounding technical words, particularly 'oscillation' (Wireless Enthusiast: 'I could not hear anything last night. The people next door were osculating all the time'). The 'Wireless Enthusiast' himself could be called, *inter alia*, 'radiomer', 'radiard' (or 'radienne'), 'etherphile', or 'radiofan'. Competitions were often organised to invent and choose between such exotic designations.

Television introduced more new terms and further new problems. The word itself was a hybrid, half Latin and half Greek, as many people, including C. P. Scott of the *Manchester Guardian*, noted. He went on to ask, 'What good, then, can come of it?' 'Let us build our language for posterity and with dignity and not make it a laughing-stock,' wrote a critic of the words 'television', 'super-heterodyne' and 'picturedrome' in 1937.

'Looker-in' was as controversial as 'listener-in'. 'Looker' was the term used in the official Selsdon Report on Television in 1935 although the simple word 'viewer' was winning when television was shut down in 1939.

It would have been unwise, given what happened to television, to have called 'television followers' 'Bairdists', as one inventive viewer suggested in 1932, following the trail of 'ohm', 'ampère', 'watt', and 'decibel'. (How many people knew that the last of these commemorated Alexander Graham Bell?)

Foreign words could be fun, too, not least *franglais*, not yet described as such. A French 'commentator' (and the word was deemed ugly in any language) could be heard saying 'le centre forward a fait un bon kick vers le goal'.

'Purely modern...'

Curious effect of a piece of ultra-modern
music on a very receptive listener

George V's wireless set, a gift from the BBC in 1924, was 'purely modern', and the first valve sets of the early 1920s looked 'scientific' with their dials and control panels. But designers soon tired of the scientific look and sought 'disguises' in the form of furniture of all periods, real and imaginary, from 'Stuart' (sic) to 'Chippendale' (above, advertisement for Western Electric's 1922 version, 'a twentieth-century invention encased in an eighteenth-century style') and beyond. The *BBC Hand Book* of 1928 objected to disguised wirelesses and urged listeners to treat their sets like valuable clocks which 'will do much more than tell you the time'.

The 'ultra-modern' followed after 1930, and 'Pseudo-cubistic' (*top right*, *Punch*'s comment, 1936) took the place – for a few listeners at least – of pseudo-Jacobean and pseudo-Japanese (*bottom right*). Edison sets boasted 'long, low lines, fitted for this long low age' (Pye advertisement).

The general depression in the radio industry did not prevent British designers from producing 'models... better in design than any to be found abroad'.

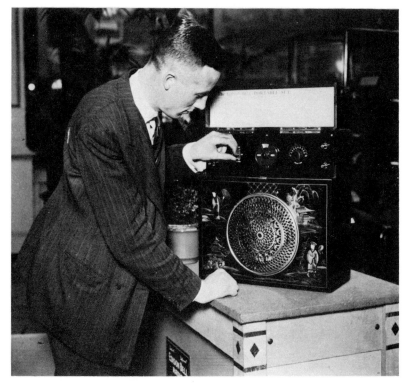

'Sensations in suburbia'

SENSATION IN SUBURBIA

In 1930 *The Cabinet Maker* made a stand against crudely decorated 'jazz age' sets and appealed to furniture makers to regard the radio set as a piece of furniture, simple and functional, yet 'conveying an idea of the mystery of the medium'. Soon there were beautifully veneered wooden cabinets, often fairly plain except for loudspeaker apertures, incorporating popular 'art deco' motifs in fretwork. Pye's 'sunrise' virtually became a trade mark. A few radio manufacturers took up *The Cabinet Maker*'s challenge more seriously: Ekco invited top designers Serge Chermayeff and Wells Coates to work on radio sets. The latter's best-selling circular set of moulded bakelite (*top left*) was shown at Radiolympia in 1934, described as 'a practical proposition', the black version cost 10s 6d more than the brown 'walnut' and sold less.

Meanwhile Murphy commissioned Gordon Russell, the distinguished furniture maker, to make wooden cabinets 'of a quiet dignified style in harmony with any good furniture whether modern or old'.

There was no real equivalent to the German 'People's Set' (*cf* the Volkswagen): British listeners in peacetime demanded as much variety in their sets as in their programmes.

"THIS IS OUR LATEST NOVELTY—A WRITING-DESK THAT TURNS OUT TO BE A WIRELESS-SET."
"THERE'S NOTHING MUCH NEW IN THAT."
"AH, BUT THIS IS A WRITING-DESK THAT TURNS OUT TO BE A WIRELESS-SET THAT TURNS OUT TO BE A COCKTAIL CABINET THAT TURNS OUT TO BE A WRITING-DESK AFTER ALL."

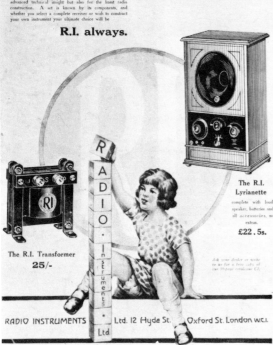

WELL BUILT

Good Building is the outcome of good knowledge correctly applied. In Radio the monogram R.I. stands not only for advanced technical insight but also for the finest radio construction. A set is known by its components, and whether you select a complete receiver or wish to construct your own instrument your ultimate choice will be

R.I. always.

The R.I. Transformer
25/-

RADIO·Instruments·Ltd

The R.I.
Lyrianette
complete with loud speaker, batteries and all accessories, no extras.
£22.5s.

RADIO INSTRUMENTS · Ltd. 12 Hyde St. · Oxford St. London W.C.I.

Sir Edward Elgar

HEARS MUSIC AS IT SHOULD BE HEARD!

SIR EDWARD ELGAR, the great British composer, says, "There are people who are music-starved—who cannot go to concerts, to recitals, to the opera. Such people *need* a Marconiphone. To be able to hear, in your own home, all the important musical events of the day is the great advantage of wireless — and I find that with a Marconiphone you hear them as they *should* be heard."

"People need a Marconiphone"

'Are you getting square-wheel reception?' asked Captain Mullard in 1924. For those 'ready-maders' who preferred to go to the dealer rather than construct their own sets, the very question provided a justification for their inactivity. If you needed an even stronger justification, by the mid-1930s you could respond to Frank Murphy's personally signed advertisement: 'I shouldn't be appealing to you on moral grounds if I hadn't complete faith in Murphy sets' (*opposite*, *top left*, typical Depression-style advertisement, 14 February 1936).

There was an immense diversity of radio advertising lines. In 1924 Polarphone had offered 'faultless reproduction: Science's last word – Society's first choice'. Ekco showed their 'very latest car set' with a pretty girl (*opposite*, *bottom right*), while R. G. D. offered numbered sets (*opposite*, *top right*).'R. G. D. instruments are built for those for whom the mass-produced, the "commercial grade" is not good enough,' potential customers were told. 'Such people take it for granted that

their kind of instrument will cost more than ordinary.' Advertisers offering cheap sets were in the minority, though hire purchase deals were common – '27/9d now!'

There were some distinguished intermediary salesmen. If you could not always have Elgar (*top right*, 1930 Marconiphone advertisement) you could very often – if you wanted a Bush set – have Christopher Stone and his radio puns: 'the importance of a strong cabinet' or 'a switch of power'. 'I'm sure most of us have heard about "the power of the press" at some time or another,' he exclaims in one advertisement. '. . . On this BUSH model the "Power of the Press" enables you to receive any of your five favourite radio stations at a touch.'

There was a new power switch in the late 1930s: 'If what we carefully refer to as a natural emergency arises,' wrote Murphy of their All-Purpose Portable, 'and you had to spend hours in an air-raid shelter, a set that keeps working under its own power anywhere would be worth its weight in gold.'

SOLD FOR A SONG!

TYPE 'K'
f6·15·0

Mullard
MASTER·RADIO

Manufacturer's message

'Where tomorrow is made'

Pye advertised its wireless sets and components from Cambridge, 'the town where tomorrow is made', but where 'the traditions of the University persisted'. One advertisement showed two men entering a College cloister: 'Come on, Cambridge is not all colleges,' says one to the other. 'Of course,' the advertisement goes on, 'he may have been thinking of the University Arms, but we like to feel that he was referring to our factory' (*top right*, extract from Pye advertising leaflet, *c*. 1934).

Oxford was not left out of the reckoning either. R. G. D., the self-styled 'Aristocrat of Radio', advertised its products from 'the creamy heart of Oxfordshire', but threw in 'an old College tutor' for good measure: 'There in the corner [of his rooms] where a bookcase used to be, stood an R. G. D. radio-gramophone. His host switched it on. They played it all the evening. Perhaps you can guess the upshot. He wrote to us that day and our dealer took him a similar model.'

Lissen, maker of 'the constructor's luxury set', stressed the modern rather than the mellow approach in its advertising (*bottom right*). Other manufacturers, like Ever Ready, Philips and Mullard (*opposite*, *top right*) simply stressed the wonderful difference between new sets and old (*opposite*).

IN THIS NEW YEAR OF 1934, RADIO LED BY PYE RECOGNISES A NEW RESPONSIBILITY BOTH ARTISTIC AND MUSICAL TOWARDS THE HOMES OF GT. BRITAIN

W Stanley

PYE CAMBRIDGE RADIO

The LISSEN SKYSCRAPER 7

SEVEN-VALVE, SUPERHET

COMPLETE WITH SEVEN VALVES £8·17·6

THE CONSTRUCTOR'S LUXURY SET

'Is your set doing its job?'

LOOK AT THE DIFFERENCE IN TONE—

BETWEEN AN OLD SET AND A NEW EVER READY

In August 1931 'J. C. S.' summed up the problems of old sets and their owners in *The Listener*:

Tu Quoque

'Listeners, look to your sets!'
But how often the fellow forgets
    When his grid doesn't leak
    Or his speaker will squeak
That he mostly deserves what he gets.

When he growls to The Radio Times
For example, in scurrilous rhymes,
    Has he really forgotten
    His aerial's rotten,
His earth's one of Life's Buried Crimes?

If he fancies the BBC like
Pianos that buzz when you strike,
    Sopranos who quaver
    Or tenors who waver
They don't for the love of their 'mike'.

The stuff that's provided at source
Is perfectly faultless of course,
    While the horrors you get
    Are the fault of your set
Plus occasional static or Morse.

LITTLE WILLIE WIRELESS

Little Willie Wireless
    Was feeling rather weak.
I asked him what had happened,
    He could barely raise a squeak.

I sent him to the doctor
    Who murmured with a frown:
'The trouble must be valvular,
    The little chap's run down.'

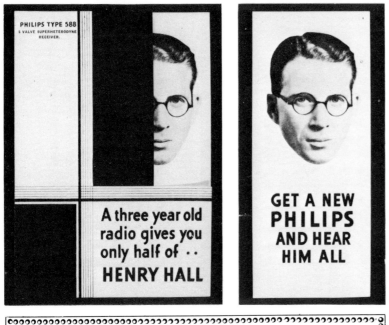

PHILIPS TYPE 588
5 VALVE SUPERHETERODYNE RECEIVER.

A three year old radio gives you only half of ·· HENRY HALL

GET A NEW PHILIPS AND HEAR HIM ALL

'No more lost chords'

IN THE WILD NIGHT
THE URGENT CALL FOR HELP COMES
TO THE COASTGUARD BY
THE AID OF THE EXIDE BATTERY

AND THE TWIN OF THIS BATTERY
MAY BE IN YOUR OWN WIRELESS SET
GIVING, PURE AND POWERFUL,
THE FLOW OF REASON AND OF SOUL

Exide

THE LONG LIFE BATTERY

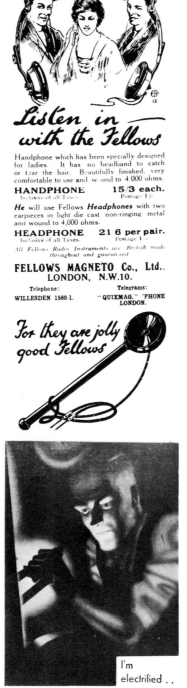

Listen in with the Fellows

Handphone which has been specially designed
for ladies. It has no headband to catch
or tear the hair. Beautifully finished. very
comfortable to use and wound to 4,000 ohms.

HANDPHONE   15/3 each.
Inclusive of all Taxes.   Postage 1/-

He will use Fellows *Headphones* with two
earpieces in light die cast non-ringing metal
and wound to 4,000 ohms.

HEADPHONE   21 6 per pair.
Inclusive of all Taxes.   Postage 1 -

*All Fellows Radio Instruments are British made
throughout and guaranteed*

FELLOWS MAGNETO Co., Ltd.,
LONDON, N.W.10.

Telephone: Telegrams:
WILLESDEN 1560-1.   "QUIXMAG." 'PHONE
            LONDON.

For they are jolly good Fellows

I'm
electrified . .

Make me myself again through—

Mullard
THE · MASTER · VALVE

LINER ABLAZE
IN
MID-OCEAN !

HALF-WAY across Atlantic. Fire
breaks out ! Deadly peril. Urgent
S.O.S. Passengers and crew rescued
... by ships summoned *through
Marconi Valves.* Most British pas-
senger-carrying ships use Marconi
Valves. So do ninety per cent of
British whalers...whole Norwegian
whaling fleet . . . all Imperial Airways machines ... Empiradio Beam
Wireless . . . Metropolitan Police.
For their reliability. For their wide
range. For their long life.

● *In cases like
these, when unfailing efficiency is essential, men insist
on Marconi Valves*

FIT

MARCONI VALVES

TO YOUR RADIO SET

There were as many styles of advertising radio accessories as there were accessories themselves. 'No more lost chords!', Cossor promised users of their valves. Triotron showed a lady covering her ears – 'Are you a victim of Dialitis?', adding, 'Dialitis is a modern complaint, best defined as a tendency to fiddle with the radio'. The simple cure was to use Triotron Valves.

Users of Mullard valves *c.* 1928 were promised Many Happy Radio Nights (*opposite*). In 1930 a more up-to-date Mullard advertisement suggested the release of a new force rather than a new cure for a new complaint. A personified electrical current (*right*) exclaims 'The microphone has changed me. I was SOUND. Now I am ELECTRICITY . . . I flew to the transmitter. . . . A million pounds of machinery flash us into space . . . down your aerial . . . into your set . . . into your valves. Make me myself again through Mullard, the Master Valve.'

'What connection is there between Love and Pure Power?', asked Lissen. 'Imagine a lover pressing his suit with blurred words and mumbled articulation. Yet many people put up with the same kind of inferiority in their radio reproduction. The Lissen New Process Battery will change all that.'

'Radio enchantment'

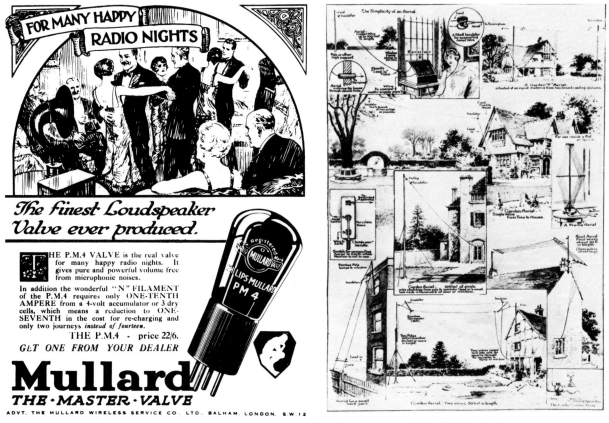

'The British wireless advertiser has the pull over the American wireless advertiser as regards the artistry of wireless advertisements,' *The Wireless Magazine* wrote confidently in 1925. But it nevertheless 'gave the palm' to the following 'just lovely' American advertisement:

'Christmas – and the whole world is young again. The air is a-quiver, the ether crowded with Yule-tide music. The carols, the simple songs that carry us back to a rose-tinted childhood are beating – beating – beating their soundless tattoos at our hearth stones. Radio is the magic key which translates it all into glorious sounds. Only a Scrooge, untouched by the Christmas spirit, will leave the key unturned. Of course for the utmost in radio enchantment, you will equip your set with [x's] tubes.'

'Radio enchantment' might mean the right aerial (*above, The Illustrated London News*, 1922) or, perhaps, music 'piped' to a bedside extension speaker (*left*, Stentorian advertisement, 1936).

Drawings by wireless

THE WINNING ENTRY

MR. HEATH ROBINSON'S ORIGINAL

THE WINNER OF THE SECOND PRIZE

Wisecracks and gimcracks

"IT CERTAINLY DOES GO MUCH FASTER THAN THE LAST ONE."

MR THIKKED: 'When I read about these developments in wireless, it makes me think a bit.'
MISS SMARTE: 'Isn't it wonderful what science can do?'
(Caption of *Punch* cartoon, May 1921)

'Wireless set for sale, or would exchange for intelligent parrot.'
(Newspaper advertisement, 1924)

ALWAYS A FLY IN THE OINTMENT
SANDY: 'Yon wireless is wunnerful. Think o'hearin' the sairmon frae the kirk in yer ain' hame an' nae collection tae worry aboot!'
JANE: 'Aye, but ye ken ye ha'e to pay a licence tae the Government afore ye can listen in.'
SANDY: 'Och! aye – thocht there wis a catch in it somewhere.'
(caption to cartoon in the Sydney Bulletin, September 1925)

Spectatress (seeing players wearing ear-guards). "DEAR ME! HOW CAN THEY LISTEN-IN WHILE THEY ARE PLAYING?"

'It's just occurred to me—perhaps there was nothing on'

'Wonderful, wonderful! And to think it takes five hours by train!'

'Tune in – keep listening'

(theme song of Radiolympia, 1933)

An early mobile radio exhibition: (*right*) a car full of radio-receiving apparatus with a frame aerial on the roof at the Lord Mayor's Show, 1922.

Though the first 'All-British Radio Exhibition' of 1923 seemed 'a very small thing' in retrospect, at the time it was proudly described as 'a magnificent demonstration of the extraordinary progress which wireless has made, a triumphant vindication of the belief that British goods hold their own against the world'.

For Filson Young it had seemed almost impossible then that 'there could be enough variety of apparatus to furnish material for a show that would attract the public'. To most people, however, it seemed extraordinary that the exhibition should fill two 'immense rooms'.

By 1939, 'Radiolympia', by then identified with one place, was a glamorous attraction in itself. Even the name, coined in 1932, had glamour ('If it's Radio, it's Olympia'). Throughout the 1930s the Exhibition focused on specific annual themes: in the summer of 1939, Radiolympia Theatre was transformed into the Hollywood Bowl.

The organisers of Radiolympia made the best of any kind of business. So, too, did BBC stars, some of whom seemed more at home there than in Broadcasting House. Yet even intellectuals in the BBC gave Radiolympia their blessing. 'The listening public would be dull indeed,' wrote *The Listener* in 1935, 'if it regarded switching on and off as its sole function and never evinced a legitimate curiosity about how broadcasting is developing.'

There was a serious side to Radiolympia too, with lectures by scientists like Sir William Bragg on 'The Means of Communication'. One keen visitor in 1934 described it as 'a College, a place where a man or woman can graduate as a listener'. But above all it was a great show, at which to delight in the techniques and arts – and fun – of broadcasting.

The style had been set in a year of depression, 1929. 'Music there will be: a hum of harmony that subtly fills the entire building, creeping its melodic way around the walls and climbing to the overhanging dome. And yet, it will be music segregated, organized.' Music was played, also, for the workers before the crowds assembled, real 'music as you work', deemed 'conducive to good working'.

(*Opposite bottom*, inside Radiolympia.)

Hello Everybody !

Here I am at the exhibition waiting to welcome you all. We've got here the finest and most representative wireless show you have yet seen.

'Optimism, London'

(suggested telegraphic address for Radiolympia, 1933)

The first nighters who wouldn't miss Radiolympia!

EAST END FEATURE

THE **RADIO TIMES** 2ᴰ

RADIOLYMPIA NUMBER

OLYMPIA

FIRST BROADCASTS FROM THE RADIO EXHIBITION

RADIOLYMPIA'S SPECIAL THEME SONG

Tolchard Evans, composer of "Listen-in on Your Radio."

"LISTEN-IN ON YOUR RADIO"

(*Words by Stanley Damerell*)
(*Music by Tolchard Evans*)

"Listen-in on your Radio,
We just want to say 'How-do';
Listen-in on your Radio,
We've a programme here for you.
Songs old and new,
Dance-music, too,
Sung by request;
Listen-in on your Radio,
Listen North, South, East and West.''

'Watts in the aerial'

(punning title of *Radio Times* article, February 1924)

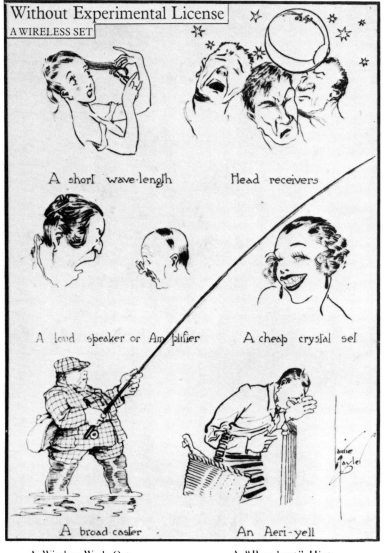

Without Experimental License

A WIRELESS SET

A short wave-length   Head receivers

A loud speaker or Amplifier   A cheap crystal set

A broad caster .   An Aeri-yell

A Wireless Wash-Out—

—And a Little Local Disturbance

A "Broadcast" Hint

THE CRYSTAL RECEIVER

The language of radio gave birth to a spate of new jokes about (female) 'loudspeakers' and 'crystal receivers' and (seaside) 'wavelengths' some of which are shown on this page (from *The Bystander*, 1923).

Radio even provided embattled married couples with a 'Superlative Insult':

HUSBAND: 'Perfidious! Coquette! Shameless One!'
WIFE: 'Idiot! Wretch! Listener-In!'
(from *Buen Humor*, Madrid, reprinted in *The Radio Supplement*, December 1923).

Radio gave archetypal stories a new lease of life and *The Radio Times* enjoyed telling them:

ALL MODERN IMPROVEMENTS

It was the familiar farmhouse scene, interior setting. The night was of the bitter sort, a wailing wind and the slash of savage rain.

The girl, with terror in her eyes, sensed her parent's purpose even before he spoke.

'Father,' she gasped, 'would you send me out into the world on a night like this?'

His lips grimly set, the old man pointed to the door. One monosyllable. 'Go!'

Choking back a sob, the girl took one all-seeing look at the old home, then vanished into the storm.

Silence, save for the wind and rain.

*   *   *

The old man tottered across the creaking kitchen floor and dropped trembling on his knees beside a table. In an instant his bony fingers were fumbling with a long black box.

'It used to be the style in melodrama,' he groaned, 'to keep burnin' a lamp in the window for ye, a light to guide ye home. But times have changed now, so I'll sit here night and day, with these here contraptions on my ears, just waitin' and prayin' for your dear, dear voice to come to me over the radio.' (20 June 1924)

There were pockets of resistance to radio too. In November 1929 *The Radio Times* told the story of the BBC Official who visited his old college.

'After dinner, in the common room, a don, anxious to appear friendly and in touch with life as it is lived outside our great universities, asked, "And what are you doing now?" The broadcaster explained modestly that he was connected with "broadcasting – you know – wireless". This explanation was greeted with a cackle of laughter. "Wireless! Really, my dear fellow, you'll be telling us next that you've taken up *roller skating*!"

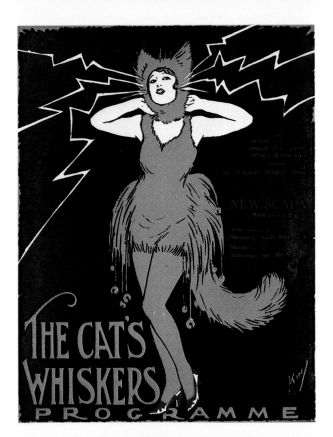

LISTENING IN.

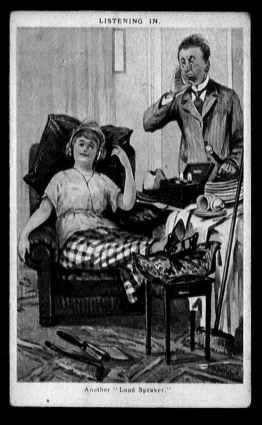

Another "Loud Speaker."

LISTENING IN.

There goes that point again.

LISTENING IN.
And they call this Wireless.

LISTENING IN.

EVERYBODY'S LISTENING IN

The Broadcaster

September 1923

1/- NET

POWER by WIRELESS by Prof. A.M. Low

Everybody's listening
Sitting at home and listening
Everybody's listening in.
　　Pick 'em up as they go
　　To and fro, to and fro . . .
Mother and Father think it's grand
Quarrelling who shall first begin.
For a seaside trip nobody saves up,
All they do is pick the wireless waves up
　　Everybody's listening,
　　See how their eyes are glistening,
Everybody's crazy on the game of listening in.

Lyric of popular song, 1922

WHEN this 1922 song lyric was written the word 'everybody' was a wild poetic exaggeration. There were, in fact, only 35,000 licensed listeners in December 1922. The BBC did not know, indeed, just how many people were regularly listening in to particular programmes until, after long hesitation, it started a listener research service in 1936. It did know the licence figures, however, and there was a great leap in the first year: there were just over half-a-million licensed listeners by the end of 1923, and probably just as many illicit unlicensed ones. 'Readers who are not experiencing the pleasure of listening to broadcasts are missing one of the greatest wonders of our time,' wrote the newly-appointed radio correspondent of the *Illustrated London News* in August 1923.

Although the early BBC had no more details of listening habits than it had of listening figures, it had its own gallery of particular kinds of listener. At one end was the 'Ideal Listener', willing to listen to all kinds of programmes (and often poor and culturally deprived, until wireless transformed his life). At the other end was the 'Ordinary Listener', whom Filson Young, the BBC's own radio critic, described as 'that shy and elusive bird'; 'the 'Compleat Listener', who 'hears, marks and inwardly digests, and who gives to broadcasting its permanent values'.

Other types included the 'Family-Ridden Listener', who 'lives with seven other members of the family, the wireless continually switched on', and his friend the

'Model Listener', to whose house the 'Family-Ridden Listener' escaped for planned and peaceful listening. Then there was the 'Habitual Listener', saturated with too much listening, whose sin was 'mental gluttony, the desire to do two things at once', and, even worse, the 'Bad Listener' 'who prefers to do the talking himself' and the 'Wicked Listener' who indulged in the vice of background listening, 'turning on the set when he wants to be livened up by noise'.

A sad figure, dear to the heart of the BBC, was the 'Lonely Listener'. The poet Wilfrid Gibson imagined her life – he was sure that it was a she – happily transformed by wireless, in this poem printed in *The Radio Times* in November 1926.

*Into her lonely cottage every night
Comes music, played a hundred miles away;
And now each dumb and solitary day
Melts into music with the dying light:*

*And as she hearkens, unto her it seems
That she is one with the vast listening throng
Held rapt together by the strains of song,
Made one in music, dreaming the same dreams:*

*And her old heart, not lonely any more,
Sweeps on ethereal melodies afar
Through aerial regions, and, a singing star,
Among the singing stars she seems to soar.*

In November 1932 – exactly ten years after the birth of broadcasting – the 'Five Millionth Listener' joined the family of listeners. *The Radio Times* featured him: Mr Cecil Fox, 'a cellulose sprayer of Wood Green . . . an amateur of ten years' standing who has built his own radio-gramophone and who likes, in this order, Vaudeville, Dance Music, Sir Oliver Lodge, and talks by archaeologists'. Mr Fox sounds remarkably like the original 'Ideal Listener'.

Before a 'Ten Millionth Listener' could appear on the scene and be featured in *The Radio Times*, the

Second World War had broken the sequence. In September 1939 the total number of current wireless licences was just over nine million. As the BBC frequently pointed out, however, for each licensed 'Listener' in the statistics, there were perhaps four listeners, on average, sharing the wireless set in each home. Thus, even in 1923, when the *Illustrated London News* began to cover radio topics, there were probably already two million people who lived in homes possessing a radio set. Many of them, in those early days, would have been taking turns with a single pair of headphones within the family.

Early critics of broadcasting treated the listening habit as if it were a disease. Thus, the *Bystander* complained in 1923: 'This wireless-in-the-home business is not a healthy outdoor game. It is not even a gentle indoor exercise. But it is becoming the national pastime. It is one of those epidemics that you sicken for, catch, and spend an inordinate amount of money getting rid of.'

That was one angle. Wireless was often to be found in hospitals in the early days, but as a cure, however, rather than as a disease. University College Hospital was the first London hospital to install radio sets for the patients in 1923. *The Broadcaster* was as enthusiastic as the *Bystander* was critical: 'It [wireless] helped the staff in their efforts to brighten the lives of those who are not able to participate in the ordinary enjoyments of life.'

The 'good of humanity' was a theme often stressed throughout the first decade of broadcasting, and in *The Radio Times* articles appeared with titles like 'The Blessing of Radio', 'With Healing in its Wings', 'Wireless and Health', 'The Perfect Spiritual Healer' and 'A Second Doctor'. In January 1927 an 'invalid lying on his sick bed' wrote: 'You may be depressed and weary after a long illness; you may be anxiously awaiting an operation on the morrow; you may be a chronic invalid confined to your continual couch, but when you put on the earphones or switch on the loudspeaker, your burden, for the time being at least, well-nigh disappears.'

Whether cure or disease, the wireless epidemic was certainly sweeping the country in 1923, but the condescending *Bystander* was wrong in choosing the medical analogy: unlike influenza or measles, this epidemic was destined never to recede. Nor was disease, it was believed, the only burden that could be lightened by broadcasting; poverty, too, could be alleviated. 'A Good Fairy in Mean Streets' was the title of a typical article in *The Radio Times* in September 1924. Begbie, described as 'one of the best informed writers of the day on questions affecting the welfare of the poor', wrote eloquently: 'Broadcasting is the good fairy of the slums; it is the genius of Romance. The younger people of East

London must surely be moved by these things in those deeps of character which are partly conscious, partly unconscious, and help to determine human destiny.'

Begbie did not stop there:

Never before in all the black history of slumland has such a light shone upon the darkness of human ignorance and domestic wretchedness. . . . Imagine what it must mean to East London when the Queen's Hall Orchestra floods its foul courts and dark alleys with the majestic strains of the Fifth Symphony, or when the pain and longing of Chopin come beating against the souls of men and women whose only knowledge of music hitherto has been got from the rattle of a street-piano outside a public-house. Imagine, too, what it must mean to the minds of those men and women whose only serious mental effort hitherto has been to grasp the right and wrongs of their economic condition, when a man of science speaks to them of the stars . . . I am quite sure that for many thousands of those who are the base and foundation of our national life broadcasting is almost a passion, and that they go to it as the poor students of the Renaissance went, first, to anyone who could teach them to spell, and, afterwards, to the monk's school and the colleges of Oxford and Cambridge. It is the beginning of a new life for them, the life of the imagination, the life of the eternal spirit.

Begbie was patronising towards the poor: others doubted how poor they really were if they could afford a wireless. 'The prevalence of broadcasting continually surprises me,' wrote the novelist, E. V. Lucas, acidly, in the same month as Begbie. 'Every Sunday I am more and more impressed by the good clothes of those whom we are accustomed to call "the poor", and particularly of the splendour of their younger children, but even more I am impressed, coming into London by any line that intersects mean streets, by the number of "the poor" who can afford wireless sets. It goes to show what a lot of rubbish is talked about these very fortunate people.'

'These very fortunate people' were also the target for the class-ridden wit of the condescending *Bystander*. 'Our charlady on Monday spent one-third of her half-day expatiating upon her daughter's installation in the Fulham Road,' he wrote in April 1923. '"Our Grace," she said, raising the edge of her apron to its time-honoured use, "she 'eard it lovely on Saturday. So did we all, come to that. 'Er 'usbing, wot works at Lot Road, 'e's fitted one up proper, 'im bein' an elick-trishun on the Toob, out of a cigar-box of 'is father's 'an some wotsisnames – *you* know. It was a fair treat an' no mistake. We might all 'ave bin sittin' in the theatre . . ." I mean, one must retain some vestige of dignity, if *these* people are listening-in.'

Punch joined the *Bystander* in these disagreeably diverting class-ridden games. This cartoon caption dates from December 1923:

COOK: 'What are we having tonight, M'm?'
MISTRESS: 'Why, I've just told you: clear soup; fillet of sole; cutlets; cabinet pudding.'
COOK: 'I meant on the wireless, M'm.'

With this exchange the idea of 'Music While You Work' was born, almost twenty years before the programme of that name boosted the morale of factory workers in the Second World War. Even *The Radio Times* made its own contribution to this vein of humour in April 1925 with a cartoon in whose caption the new cook is saying to the Mistress, 'I'm afraid I won't be able to stay after all. I see you only have a crystal set in the kitchen!'

Such tired jokes in various forms lingered on into the thirties, adapted to take account of new developments like the portable radio set. Thus, in January 1937, *Punch* commented again:

Plumber: *'Might we 'ave the portable, Lady? Me and me mate works better to music.'*

Reith himself had his own strong sense of class-consciousness, but he thought that it was a mistake to over-emphasise the value of wireless as a therapy either in illness or in poverty. He wanted broadcasting, above all, to be part of normal everyday life. 'It must and does appeal to every kind of home,' he wrote in 1924 in *Broadcast Over Britain* (in the same month as Begbie's article). 'Perhaps,' he went on, 'in the early days it was felt that it would be of interest only to those who, for reasons of distance, infirmity or poverty, were unable to participate in activities of others more favoured than they. . . . This conception . . . is an entirely mistaken one, and must be attributed to lack of imagination. . . . I believe there is no home, however favoured, to which some quota of additional interests, new and live, may not be borne through this amazing medium.'

Reith put the spotlight on the favoured, not the deprived, home. He liked to win converts for wireless among the rich and the powerful, the great and the good. Many years after the event, he described in his autobiography, *Into the Wind*, how, in 1923, he 'suggested that the Archbishop of Canterbury and Mrs Davidson might dine with my wife and me one evening; they could then be introduced to it [Broadcasting] . . .' They graciously accepted the invitation and 'in the course of conversation before dinner I pressed, unseen, the switch of the wireless set; in a few seconds the room was filled with music. . . . The guests, who were "entirely amazed", enquired if it were not necessary to leave a window open'. (Reith's approach was completely successful, for the next day the Archbishop summoned a meeting of ecclesiastical leaders to the House of Lords – the beginning of the BBC's Religious Advisory Committee.) Fourteen years later Reith was to derive equal pleasure from a distinguished listener. In 1937 Queen Elizabeth told him 'We listen as a family'.

Despite Reith's reservations about the idea of broadcasting 'shining a light into humble homes', it continued to attract writers. The blind 'set free' by wireless became another favourite poetic and artistic theme. 'At the familiar sound of "London calling",' wrote 'Bartimeus' of Somerset in a letter to *The Radio Times* in August 1928, 'there is a comforting feeling that I am on the same terms as sighted people who, for the time being, are equally dependent on hearing and imagination only.' 'Thus,' he went on, 'I possess a key of a kingdom where blindness is unknown and I can wander at will.'

In 1927 a lady reader, Morwenna Lyne, contributed some verses on the same theme. The poet first describes herself and a group of friends enjoying together the visual delights of nature and home: '. . . green buds, purple crocus, the last new book and Baby still asleep.' Belatedly they remember their blind friend sitting silently in a corner:

And then (our thoughts had not quite gone)
Somebody switched the wireless on,
And made us, one and all, embark
Upon your ocean of the Dark.

At 'London calling', you were free
Of the wide realms of minstrelsy;
The whole world's music-makers gave
Themselves to light your living grave;
And friendly voices from the night
To you, without the need of sight,
Brought news and greeting, laughter, song ...

And these to all of us belong —
We, blind in this republic too,
Made equal citizens with you.

MR. HEATH ROBINSON'S "USES" FOR WIRELESS!

The Radio Times itself occasionally adopted this sentimental-poetic language – if not actual verse – about blind listeners. It asked in October 1927:

Do you remember Millais' picture of *The Blind Girl*? A girl with Titian-red hair sitting on a stone by the roadside, her lips curled in a smile of enchantment as she listens to her sister's description of the rainbow? One day there is another wonderful picture to be painted. It will show a blind boy with earphones, intently listening – and, perhaps, that same slow smile of sheer delight will hover round his lips. How much broadcasting means to the blind, the blind alone can tell.'

There was a practical purpose behind these sentimental words, however, which was to advertise a concert to be given in aid of the Wireless for the Blind Fund. The fund was to provide every blind person in the United Kingdom with a wireless set. Naturally it was the favourite charity of the BBC, who issued free licences to the blind and gave prime broadcasting time to the Fund's appeals. *The Radio Times* co-operated by giving generous coverage to the Fund's concert advertisements, often illustrated in the spirit of Millais (*below*):

'I'm afraid you'll have to speak a little louder – you see we keep the telephone on the same table as the wireless.'

While it was boasted that wireless freed the blind, it was also feared that, like television later, it would enslave the multitude. Critics warned that broadcasting would produce a nation of passive non-participants. A whole series of 'liquid' metaphors expressed such fears. In one illustration to an article music was shown literally coming out of a tap (*right*); Reith himself compared the ease of listening to broadcasts with 'the milk left on the doorstep', and Filson Young wrote of the danger of listeners becoming 'empty buckets to be

pumped into by other people'. The playwright L. du Garde Peach described the unintelligent listener as 'a sponge'; the novelist Richard Church wrote of 'spoonfeeding' listeners; while both Leonard Woolf and E. V. Lucas compared listening to the wireless with 'dram-drinking'.

Dignitaries sometimes attacked broadcasting from a public platform. The Bishop of Hereford, Dr Linton Smith, in a speech opening a music festival in May 1930, deplored the serious devitalising effect of broadcasting on the life of the nation. 'It will be a bad day for England if people become content to look on at football and not play, or listen to wireless and not sing or play,' he warned. The same theme was developed by the writer of a prize-winning letter to *The Radio Times*: 'It is so easy to watch and listen,' he wrote. 'One day, possibly, the earth will have been transformed into one huge feather bed with man's body slumbering sweetly on top of it and his mind, like Desdemona, smothered underneath.'

Sport on tap

SHOOT MAN SHOOT

Tense with excitement . . . . thrilled. Almost seeing the game, so clearly does he hear it. Can you wonder that he shouts? Such radio is new to him. It comes as a revelation that broadcasting can be so vividly alive. It is his new Pye Portable—the portable supreme. Entirely self-contained—ready always for immediate use, anywhere. Glorious in tone, generous in volume, comprehensive in range of reception.

The Pye Portable is so well worth hearing that you owe it to yourself to go to your radio dealer at once for a demonstration. He will tell you of the magnificent reputation of the Pye Portable and of the lasting satisfaction it brings to its users.

The finest quality radio in the World—now so easy to buy! The Pye Portable can be yours for the first of 12 monthly payments of 35/- (The cash price is now only £19 . 19 . 0.)

Dual wavelength range; single dial tuning with fast and slow motion control calibrated in wavelengths. A wonderful receiver in a beautifully hand-polished walnut cabine'.

PYE ALL-ELEC-TRIC 3. No batteries no mains hum. Highest selectivity Maximum amplification. £15 or 12 monthly payments of 44/-

PYE SCREENED 4. The battery-operated alternative; £19.10.0. or 12 monthly payments of 34/6

PYE

THE BRITISH CHARACTER
LOVE OF OPEN-AIR SPORTS

'I don't know why the doctor recommended this Rugger to me. It seems most boring stuff.'

Critics of radio complained that British football fans were turning into 'fireside footballers'. Yet not all listeners were in danger: radio sport could bore as well as inspire. The criticisms fanned out to cover reading and learning:

'It is now an aspect of national character "that listening to the wireless is meritorious but reading a novel is a waste of time"' (E. M. Delafield, 1936).

'The radio is our servant, not our master, and should be used exactly as we please, . . . from the canon who writes his best sermons while hearing dance rhythms to the schoolboy who cannot do his prep if his parents turn the wireless off, brainworkers on all levels use their sets to help them with their work.' 'Yet university authorities are convinced that background listening is pernicious. Oxford has banned radio sets and most colleges allow only restricted use.' (Charles Wintour in *The Radio Times*, 1938.)

'Wireless femininities'

(title of weekly column in *Wireless Magazine*, 1925)

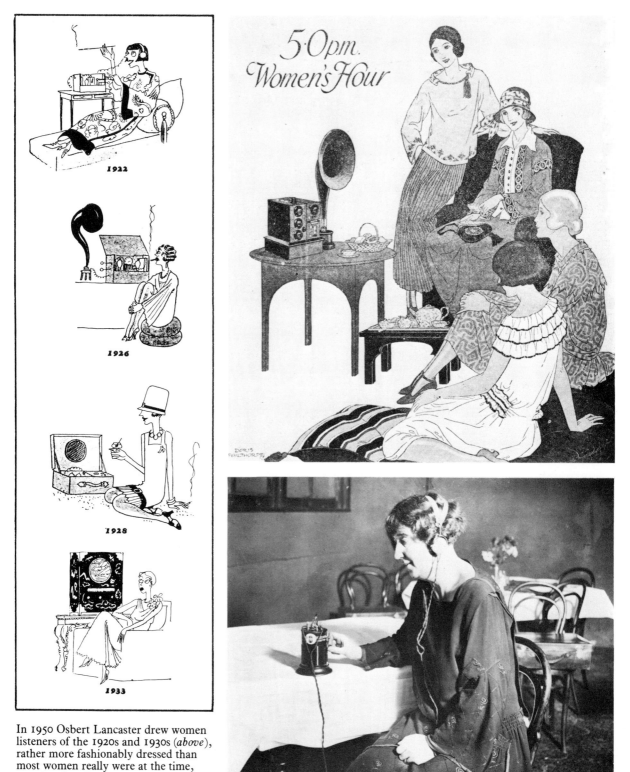

1922

1926

1928

1933

5·0pm. Women's Hour

In 1950 Osbert Lancaster drew women listeners of the 1920s and 1930s (*above*), rather more fashionably dressed than most women really were at the time, even in advertisements.

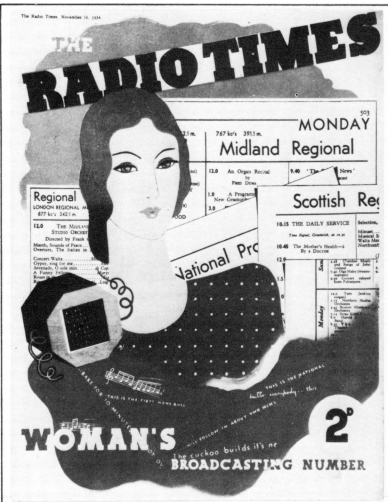

From the start, men patronised women listeners. 'It is the little things that so often influence the mind of a woman,' wrote Sinclair Russell in 1922: she appreciated being able to 'listen to musical entertainment without going out on a wet night in a new frock and run up expenses for taxis and high-priced seats.' For the debutante stuck in a traffic jam on the way to the Palace, a wireless helped pass the time (1930) (*left*).

For Lady Ossulton home listening meant 'loudspeakers arranged in bedrooms so that women could listen to the news while bathing and dressing for dinner', and then talk 'glibly and intelligently' to their male dining companions. Lady Ossulton observed that there were few houses 'where the wireless has not been laid on to the servants' hall also'.

'A Daily Woman' told *The Radio Times* in 1934 how much she enjoyed listening, though *her* old wireless set only went 'by fits and starts'. She was not keen on symphony concerts but liked a good play 'if my husband will keep quiet'.

Wireless helped to keep men at home:
'As a single man I strolled about
    and freely spent my tin
But now I'm wed I stay at home
    and simply listen in'
and one advertisement (for light fittings) in 1928 addressed 'The Women of Britain': 'The Radio has undoubtedly helped you to keep your husband and boys away from the club and kept them at home where they thus experience the benefits of your gentle charm and influence.' Yet marriage could be threatened, it seemed, by diverse listening tastes. 'Let each member of the family choose, in a spirit of accommodation, the items he or she *specially* wants to hear,' wrote ex-Labour Minister Margaret Bondfield, in 1937, 'and *turn off all the rest*'.

The young Godfrey Winn, who already liked to speak for the majority of women, asked in 1938 in *Radio Pictorial* 'Do women listeners get a square deal? . . . If I were a woman . . . I should feel that I had a justifiable grievance against the BBC', with too many 'too heavy' programmes and talks with titles like 'Vegetable Pies and Puddings'.

Yet for some women, wrote Filson Young in 1933, radio was a 'brook by the wayside . . . a milestone of joy . . . once their brief youth was over and the road of life offered little prospect of development except "toil and sorrow".'

'Music to while away...

Songs across the sea: broadcast links between liner and home.

Salmon-fishing to wireless music: a "cast" and a "broadcast".

Christmas cheer in adversity: radio for travellers in distress.

"Music wherever we go". A broadcast concert in a train.

The Illustrated London News, a keen supporter of Broadcasting in the earliest days, thought there should be 'Music Wherever we Go' (1923).

...the hours of travel'
(title of *Radio Times* article, January 1931)

Bright Assistant (*helpfully*). "AND THE GREAT ADVANTAGE OF THIS PORTABLE SET, MADAM, IS THAT YOU CAN CARRY IT ABOUT WITH YOU."

'Bit of luck I brought the umbrella!'
Specially drawn for 'The Radio Times' by Bert Thomas.

Portable wireless sets (and the word 'portable' was relative) first appeared in 1929 and 1930 – 'mains transportables' to move around the home, in the words of an advertisement, 'dispensing with battery worries for ever'.

Wireless sets for the open air (complete with batteries) came a little later ... and car radios later still. The Prince of Wales was a pioneer; *Radio Magazine* reported admiringly in July 1934 that 'the Prince's latest motor-car radio outfit is absolutely reliable, cannot run down and has no batteries. It is connected direct to the big battery built into his car.'

'My newly installed car radio was relating the story of the second day's struggle in the Lord's Test Match,' wrote another enthusiast, pioneer radio critic L. Marsland Gander, in 1938. 'Two hundred odd miles away Hammond and Paynter were piling up runs, retrieving a disastrous start by England. It was fitting that the voice should be that of Howard Marshall, lover of the English scene. . . . Everything, to our infinite content, toned into the picture.'

'Which shall we take, the car or the wireless set? We can't take both.'

JEALOUSY
A Suburban Tragedy

Along my little garden plot
  My ancient aerial stretches ;
But O ! it now profanes the spot
  And little joy it fetches.
I view it with a jaundiced eye,
  With sounds uncouth and snortable ;
It darkens my suburban sky
  Since Smith acquired a portable.

Like one who sees his neighbour gain
  A newer car and fleeter,
While he himself must still retain
  A secondhand two-seater,
Wild moods of envy and regret
  Surge in on me, unthwartable ;
I cannot bear my crystal set
  Since Smith acquired a portable.

Wireless frolics

W. HEATH ROBINSON'S IDEA OF A HAPPY RADIO FIRESIDE

Heath Robinson's idea of a 'radio fireside' (*above*) was radio in the open air – with the moon shining not on the fields or the river but on the streets. Other people's open air seemed made for wireless (*opposite*, *The Illustrated London News*, imaginary riverside radio party, 1923). 'Why not fit your canoe with a receiver?', asked *Popular Wireless* in June 1922. 'A sure way of increasing your popularity in a sports club is to run your radio receiver along to the club-house in your car,' wrote *The Broadcaster* a year later. *Punch* took the outdoor theme into the age of the battery portable (*bottom right*, August 1936). By 1938 there were warnings as well. 'Be moderate in volume and quantity. We have spoken.'

Of course, if you had your own specially built 'Listen-In Villa' (*below*, recommended by *The Broadcaster* as early as 1923), you did not have to worry.

Recreation, Relaxation and Western Electric WIRELESS RECEIVING APPARATUS

JUST FOR A CHANGE!

THE UP-RIVER DANCE TO BROADCAST MUSIC: A NEW RADIO JOY.

WITH A "SUIT-CASE" RECEIVING-SET AS BAND: AN AL FRESCO DANCE TO BROADCAST MUSIC BY THE RIVER SIDE,
WHILE ANOTHER SET IN A PUNT "PLAYS" THE IDENTICAL TUNE IN UNISON.

'Consoling voices of the air'

'Wireless is a new gift of God to the sick and the aged,' wrote *The Radio Times* in 1924, adding 'And what a blessing, a deep blessing it is to the blind'. *Punch* took up the theme eight years later:

'. . . *consoling voices of the air*
Soothing the sightless, cheering the bedridden.
The lighthouse-watchers, men who bravely bear
The burden of captivity unbidden –
Voices that calm the heart and ease the strain
Of those who lived in loneliness
     or pain' (11 May 1932)

Among the sick and the blind were ex-soldiers who were 'blasted by the war, broken bodily, and almost broken in spirit', and to them and others wireless reached out 'a friendly hand' (*opposite*, 'brightening the lives of the aged poor' in an institution and in hospital).

St Dunstan's encouraged blind patients to listen to wireless programmes (*top right*, 1927) and *The Radio Times* was published in Braille for blind listeners, who did not have to pay for wireless licences. Sir Ian Fraser, the blind MP, actually resigned his parliamentary seat to become a BBC governor in 1936, and Winston Churchill gave a rare broadcast on Christmas Day with the biblical-sounding theme 'Let the Blind Hear'.

'Broadcasting', it was claimed, 'brings . . . curative powers within the range of sufferers of all ages in hospitals and homes throughout the land.' For one listener, at least, it was 'a second doctor – and a good one, whose fees are very small'. A doctor claimed it was especially useful before and shortly after operations: when a patient was listening through headphones the pulse was more even.

The aged also expected – and received – wireless 'consolation', whether in institutions or in homes. 'As we older folk sit around the fire these winter evenings listening to the broadcast programmes,' wrote Edwin Pugh in 1927, 'the young people will not begrudge us, I hope, our rapturous enjoyment of old-time songs and music . . . Let them cast aside their headphones in disdain and . . . be off to the more stirring delights of the dance hall and the cinema'. The BBC provided Mr Pugh and his contemporaries with special 'Old Folks' programmes (*bottom right*, *The Radio Times*, April 1924).

'FOR THE OLD FOLKS'
The Midland Wireless Chorus and Orchestra, conducted by JOSEPH LEWIS
STUART ROBERTSON (*Baritone*)
STUART ROBERTSON, Chorus and Orchestra
Here's a Health unto His Majesty .. *Saville* (1670)
ORCHESTRA
Country Dances :
Come, Lasses and Lads .... } *Old*
Roger de Cover.ey. .... } *English*
STUART ROBERTSON and Chorus
Five Plantation Songs
     arr. Stanford Robinson
ORCHESTRA
Selection of Sullivan's Songs
CHORUS
Only to see her Face
     again *James Stewart*
Pelle Mahone
          MacNaughton
STUART ROBERTSON
and Orchestra
They all love Jack
          Adams
Widdicombe Fair
          Old English
ORCHESTRA
March, 'Boys of the Old
     Brigade' *Myddleton*
TONIGHT AT 8.35

'The healing power of radio'

(title of early *Radio Times* leading article)

'You think he's improving, nurse?'
'Oh, rather! He complained twice yesterday about the wireless.'

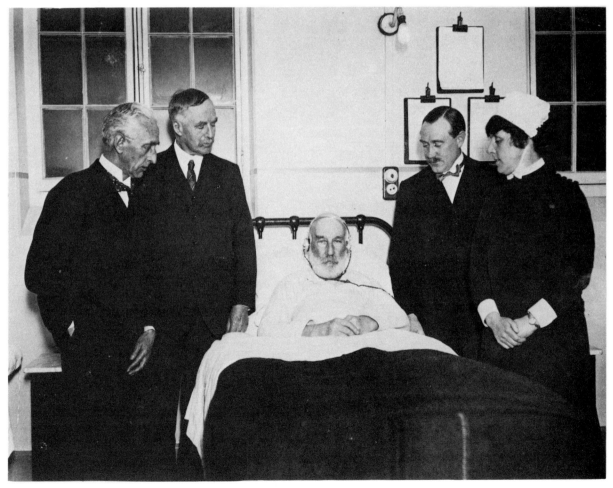

November 21, 1923.] PUNCH, OR THE LONDON CHARIVARI.

A LOST ART.

THE DINNER-PARTIES OF OUR ANCESTORS WERE EMBELLISHED WITH SPARKLING CONVERSATION—

BUT NOWADAYS THE TALKING IS DONE "OFF."

Punch's Almanack for 1925.

HEAD OF THE HOUSE. "MARY, GO AND TELL THOSE WAITS TO GO AWAY. THEY'RE MAKING SUCH A ROW WE CAN'T HEAR THESE CAROLS."

Early radio was blamed for a multitude of social sins. 'Broadcasting is the death of conversation and repose,' wrote E. V. Lucas in 1924, reminding readers of Herbert Spencer, the philosopher, who invented protective ear-pieces to cut out boring conversation at dinner parties. Lucas was amused that 'a similar arrangement should now be eagerly donned' with the opposite purpose of picking up conversation. *Punch* agreed (*above*, 21 November 1923), and so did the Ladies' Correspondent of the *Wireless Magazine* in February, 1925. 'Listening-in interferes with talk and companionships: it's hush-hush! all the time,' she complained. Fourteen years later a Bristol housewife complained, 'When Mr Middleton's on, you mustn't breathe,' and another woman, 'a witty raconteuse', grumbled, 'When I start to tell my family anything now, they say "O, hush! we want to listen to this". I reckon that the wireless has taken half the life out of me.'

...their manners'

(title of *Radio Times* article, August 1930)

'Would any of us, interrupted in the most thrilling passage of an interesting book, hesitate when someone drops in to see us?' wrote Mark Sesselle in *The Radio Times* in August 1930. 'Can there be any question as to whether we would put the book down? It is a great effort to disconnect the wireless as soon as anybody arrives, but it is certainly the thing to do.' The small Bert Thomas cartoon (*bottom right*) shows a listener 'forgetting her manners'.

Other listeners 'forgot' their ten-shilling wireless licences despite constant BBC reminders (*centre left*). One Cricklewood listener wrote indignantly to *The Radio Times* in February 1930: 'A lady was talking to me the other day about broadcasting and she told me that she and a large part of friends in her village had had a discussion as to how on earth the BBC paid its way. I told her about wireless licences and she actually said to me it was the first time she had ever heard of them. ... I know this sounds quite incredible, but can assure you it is a positive fact...'.

In October 1932 the GPO started a new campaign to catch licence dodgers (*top left*, one of the latest wireless detection vans with postal workers at Newgate Street, London).

Other anti-social listeners forgot to check their wireless sets for interference (*opposite bottom*, an early Radio detective Ford car of February 1926 equipped to detect radio interference).

Some listeners simply forgot to go home (*bottom left*, advertisement for Mullard valves, January 1931).

One famous listener avoided the problem of radio bad manners by staying at home by herself. Rebecca West wrote in 1929 of the 'ultimate of luxury' – listening to the opera in bed, in the dark 'when one has retired early and ... dined off a boiled egg on a tray'.

"Don't switch the radio on or they'll never go home!"
–it's irresistible through **Mullard**
THE·MASTER·VALVE

No wireless receiving apparatus, crystal or valve, fixed or portable, or in the form of a radio gramophone, may be installed or worked without a Post Office licence. Such licences may be obtained at any Post Office at which Money Order business is transacted, price 10s. Neglect to obtain a licence is likely to lead to prosecution.

What's the good of trying to talk to a person who is listening to a good comedian on the wireless?

Wireless associations

Advertisers for all kinds of products were attracted by wireless associations. 'Switch off the wireless – it's an Oppenheim' (publisher's slogan, 1929); 'Everybody Calling' (cigarette advertisement, 1929, *below*).

Although advertisers could not reach their customers directly by (BBC) wireless, as in the United States, they relied on the printed word. Ford Motors hoped to impress customers by comparing itself with the BBC (*opposite top*, 1936). Cadburys persuaded customers, 'This is the chocolate to eat at Home by the wireless set. . . . What could be better than a cheery fire, a comfortable chair, a good programme on the wireless, and a delicious Milk Tray to pass around?' (1939). Spratt's customers (*opposite*) had their own message (1937).

Incongruities

BY FREDERICK PARKER

"LISTENERS(IN) NEVER HEAR . . . ."

"'Urry up wiv' that beer, Em! We're bein' put through to the Savoy Hotel!!"

'Do you mind if I make it just a teeny bit louder, dear,
there's someone going to talk about Freedom?'

Not everything toned into the listening picture. There were curious incongruities – both of listeners and of broadcasters – which made good magazine pictures.

BROADCASTING AT THE CLUB.
Voice from 2 L.O. "HULLO, PETS!"

'Step on it, John, or we shall miss Larry the Lamb'

"ON BEHALF OF THE BOYS AND MYSELF, GOOD-NIGHT T'YE!"

leo Newman

"FOR WE'RE TOUGH, MIGHTY TOUGH, IN THE WEST."

Fine old English Listener (after a surfeit of Hill-Billies). "GUESS I'LL BE HEADIN' FOR BED, OLD-TIMER."

'Unbusinesslike listening'

(title of *Radio Times* article by Dr Percy A. Scholes, December 1937)

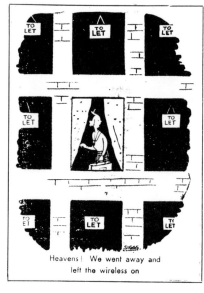

Heavens! We went away and
left the wireless on

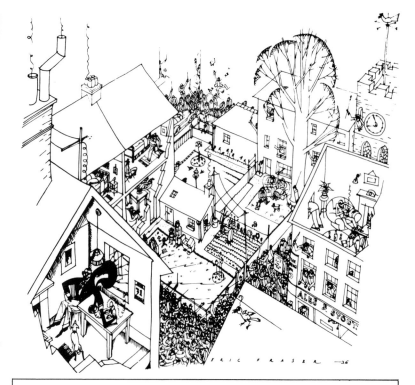

The fact that everybody was listening in did not please everyone. There was almost as much talk about the 'Loudspeaker Nuisance' (*above*) as there was about BBC programmes. 'A good Earfull' was too much. 'Be fair to your wireless set – and to your neighbours,' *The Radio Times* advised in 1933.

Be fair to the musicians also, it added, and make allowances since all 'artificially reproduced music becomes distorted when heard even at a short distance from the source of musical reproduction'. Above all, people should *listen* (*below right, Punch* on 'background listeners', September 1939).

When there was talk as early as 1923 of introducing wireless sets into London taxi-cabs *The Bystander* felt that the peace-seeking public would now have no alternative but to 'visit the National Gallery or go down a mine'. Ten years later silence itself seemed to be the main victim of broadcasting.
V. H. Friedlander's 'Progress' (July 1931) summed it up (*right*).

Another occasional victim of early broadcasting was common sense. Father Ronald Knox's 'News Bulletin Burlesque' of 1926 'scared a nation' when he 'reported' that 'a mob had set Savoy Hill on fire and was advancing on Whitehall'.

~~~~~ *PROGRESS* ~~~~~

There was a time when peace at evening
Flushed like a flower along the sky,
And majesty, on darkening tree-tops,
Went soundless by.

Now, when the sky's a red rose falling,
Switches release on garden dews
Adjacent blarings of loud-speakers,
And substitute, for rapture, news.

V. H. FRIEDLAENDER

THE BRADSHAW OF BROADCASTING

Hullo, Everyone!
    We will now give you *The Radio Times*. **The Good** *new*
    times. The Bradshaw of Broadcasting.
    May you never be late for your favourite wave-train.
    Speed 186,000 miles per second; five-hour non-stops.
    Family season ticket: First Class, 10s. per year.

The Radio Times p.1, no. 1, Vol. 1

WITH such forced joviality Arthur Burrows, the BBC's first Director of Programmes, greeted in characteristic fashion readers of the first issue of *The Radio Times* on 28 September 1923. The first real Bradshaw railway timetable had appeared in 1839.

True or misleading though the parallel may have been, *The Radio Times* at the start read more like a timetable than *The Times*. A quarter of a million 'passengers' rushed to buy the first edition of the new guide to their 'favourite wave train'. Railway metaphors abounded in this early phase of broadcasting history: 'station announcers' gave information (about 'signals') over loudspeakers, while 'land-lines' linked up 'stations', and like the railways, the BBC even provided a special (reduced) Sunday service.

Burrows's Bradshaw metaphor had its genuine point, of course, since, to quote Reith, the primary object of *The Radio Times* was to display clearly 'the programmes of all stations for the ensuing week'. Burrows was in a special position to know: he was briefly joint editor of *The Radio Times* with Leonard Crocombe, Editor of *Titbits*, and in this editorial capacity wrote his contribution to the first issue. Evidently given to analogy, Burrows mixed his metaphors and likened No. 2 Savoy Hill, the early headquarters of the BBC, to 'the biggest jigsaw puzzle yet invented'.

The facetious tone did not last long. Soon Reith, still plain Mr J. C. W. Reith, Managing Director of the British Broadcasting Company, was himself writing editorials and shared with *The Radio Times* readers his weightiest thoughts on the philosophy of broadcasting. When the journal reached its first birthday, in 1924, Reith presented what was called an appraisal of the

> *Rates of Subscription to 'The Radio Times' (including postage): Twelve months (Foreign), 15s. 8d.; twelve months (British), 14s. 6d. Subscriptions should be sent to the Publisher of 'The Radio Times,' 8-11, Southampton Street, Strand, W.C.2.*

function of *The Radio Times*. It had by then already established a circulation of 600,000.

The Radio Times was very much Reith's idea. In February 1923 hostile and jealous newspapers, fearing the competition of the new medium of broadcasting, decided to boycott the printing of the wireless programme, and Reith had told Burrows that because of the boycott, the BBC itself would issue a daily programme sheet to be 'worked up' as soon as possible into a weekly magazine. The press boycott only lasted one day, but the idea of the weekly journal swiftly turned into a reality. Thereafter the new magazine never looked back. As early as 1924, Reith, in his book *Broadcast over Britain*, could write of the success of *The Radio Times* as being 'without parallel in journalism'. He did not even mention the story of the boycott. History had made it irrelevant.

Reith believed that

... the bare programmes were not going to be sufficient. Comment on the programmes and news of the Company's activities were obviously demanded. This journal of ours is, we consider, of the greatest importance to the success of British broadcasting. It should be the connecting link between the broadcaster, individual or corporate, and the great listening public. We do not wish to feel that the magazine is bought in such large numbers entirely on account of the programmes. These will naturally remain the paramount appeal, but that is not good enough. If the broadcast service is to attain the maximum efficiency, and the listener to reap the greatest benefit, it can only be secured through a considerable degree of intimacy and understanding between the two parties concerned in the undertaking.

Not only have we provided in great detail and in a pleasing form the full programme of all our stations, but we have compiled a journal of universal appeal and of no mean literary standard.

The appeal of *The Radio Times* was not quite as universal as the appraisal suggested, however. There were outposts of resistance to the new journal in the oldest universities. Professor T. H. Pear, then of Manchester, who, as a psychologist, was interested in broadcasting techniques (and was later to write much about them), told a story of a visit to a Cambridge High Table in the twenties, quoted in *Who's Listening*, by Robert Silvey, the BBC's first Head of Listener Research. Pear had been describing to the dons the work he was carrying out on Voice and Personality (the title of his book). 'Someone further down the Table intervened with a question: "Excuse me, but I could not help hearing what you were saying. Have you by any chance published your results anywhere?" "As a matter of fact," said Pear, "I have – in *The Radio Times*." There was a pained silence for a moment; "Then I wonder," came the rejoinder, "whether you as Sherlock Holmes observed in *The Valley of Fear*, the language of Bradshaw was 'nervous and terse, but limited.' It is at this point that *The Radio Times*- Bradshaw analogy breaks down. The early *Radio Times* was wordy and, in scope and scale, almost unlimited. As the first *BBC Hand Book* put it in 1928: 'The programmes themselves are fully annotated with notes and pictures that are designed to awaken the interest of the reader and to aid his understanding and enjoyment of the programmes.' Reith's own views were an important feature, and there were copious annotations and illustrations relating to the personalities of artists and speakers. The Archbishop of York, Mr G. K. Chesterton, Sir Richard Terry, Sir Walford Davies, Sir John Squire, Mr Hilaire Belloc, Mr John Hilton and Professor E. J. Dent were amongst the outstanding contributors of 1935. And there was leaven too. In the words of the *BBC Year Book* of 1936, 'The Radio Times is lightened by humorous features, of which one, "Samuel Pepys, Listener", is now a firmly rooted institution.' Outstanding contributors had in fact written for *The Radio Times* since its earliest days – Compton Mackenzie and Virginia Woolf, H. G. Wells (who disliked broadcasting) and G. K. Chesterton (who liked it, with some characteristic reservations). Scientists such as Sir Oliver Lodge, physicist and spiritualist, also contributed to *The Radio Times*,

would be so good as to let me know when they will appear in a rather more accessible publication?".' At the time the circulation of *The Radio Times* was approaching one million.

Arnold Bennett, too, resisted the appeal of *The Radio Times*. Asked in 1927 to contribute to the Beethoven Centenary Number, he wrote to his nephew as follows:

I must write 500 words on Beethoven for *The Radio Times*. I know nothing about Beethoven but the RT and its organization seem to be making a great fuss about Beethoven this centenary year. I refused this request for an article. They re-requested . . . Shaw is the other star contributor. What is *The Radio Times*? I've never seen it.

With or without Bennett, *The Radio Times* by 1927 was already a national institution, so secure in its success that it could afford these occasional quirkish failures and even to laugh about them. In January 1925, when it was only just over a year old, it published the following letter from a listener:

Dear Sir, It may interest you to know that recently I went to a fancy dress ball as *The Radio Times* and got First Prize. The costume was home-made, and consisted of the following: Head, an aerial with *The Radio Times* top: centre-front, London programme for the day; centre-back, Manchester programme. The bottom of the dress consisted of front pages of *The Radio Times*. Yours, etc.

This was fame indeed. *The Radio Times*, its confidence boosted by such proofs of popularity, could afford to forget how fortuitously it had been born.

Bradshaw, too, had soon become an institution. Yet

which in 1925 published four of his learned broadcast lectures on 'Ether and Reality', more mystical than any Victorian writing on steam power. Such 'lectures' would at a later date have made their way into *The Listener*, to be established in 1929.

Fiction and poetry were commissioned too. In 1928 *The Radio Times* carried a long detective story in instalments by Margaret and G. D. H. Cole, while in the Christmas issue of 1931 there was a new Peter Wimsey Christmas detective story by Dorothy L. Sayers. To please readers, she gave the plot a suitable radio twist by choosing 'the Prime Minister's Wireless speech' as an object in a game of animal, vegetable and mineral played at a crucial time in the murder household. (Why no one guessed it was plain, for 'it was doubtful whether the object in question was of animal origin or a kind of gas'.)

Alfred Noyes's long poem about Nelson, *The Tale*, specially written for the BBC's Empire Day programme in 1924, was printed exclusively in *The Radio Times*, which devoted a whole column to it for three consecutive weeks. The following year Noyes was even commissioned to write an ode to Daventry to mark the opening of the BBC's new high-power, long-wave transmitter (see p. 20).

Serious music was always a favourite topic, and the distinguished musicologist Percy Scholes combined the roles of BBC Music Critic and Music Editor of *The Radio Times*. He once described *The Radio Times* as 'the music journal with the largest circulation in the world', and under his guidance the editor printed in 1929 a seven-page 'Miniature Dictionary of Musical Terms' which 'unabashedly translated foreign musical terms and titles of musical pieces since', as the *BBC Hand Book* for that year put it, 'few realise how great a barrier to musical appreciation these conventional foreign trappings have been'.

By 1937, three editors and fourteen years after its birth, *The Radio Times* could make a greater and more general claim. With the Coronation Number of 7 May the circulation exceeded 3½ million which was 'understood to be the largest ever recorded by a weekly magazine in any country'. Under the lively editorship of Eric Maschwitz (1927–33) and his art editor, Maurice Gorham, who succeeded him as editor, the best artists of the day were commissioned to design covers and illustrations. Every type of artist was represented, from Heath Robinson to Rowland Hilder; and from W. McKnight Kauffer, famous designer of posters, to Paul Nash and C. R. W. Nevinson, Official War Artist, who was responsible for the famous Coronation cover (see p. 23).

As the thirties went on *The Radio Times* grew in size

and scope as well as in circulation, and, not least, in advertising pages. The BBC kept advertising out: *The Radio Times* flourished on it, and when in 1942 a wartime reader of the shrunken austerity edition discovered in a pile of dusty salvage a faded copy of the 84-page *Radio Times* published in the Spring of 1938, he lingered over the advertisements as much as the programmes themselves. There was an 'abundance of commodities', with 'food, tobacco, chocolates, clothing, and cars . . . vividly displayed and commended to the reader'.

Bradshaw might not have approved of the inclusion of so much advertising and other 'irrelevant' material along with the timetable, but in one respect *The Radio Times*, by the outbreak of war, was growing increasingly like him. Patterns of broadcasting – the same programme at the same time every day, every week, every year – were emerging, and like the early railways were influencing the way in which people divided up, and even thought about, time. Wireless provided a fixed framework of life, what Filson Young called 'a thread of continuity'. The time of your favourite programme mattered to you as much as the time of your morning commuters' train. Just as the seasoned traveller following familiar routes did not need Bradshaw except when the timetables were changed, so a regular listener might almost do without *The Radio Times*.

Children, however, it was suggested, might be encouraged in good habits of punctuality and regularity by listening for the wireless time signal, noting the timing of programmes and by learning to use *The Radio Times* intelligently. 'The celerity with which today's child will find you any item in the programme pages of *The Radio Times* would put to shame the railway clerk looking out your connections to Nether Stopham on the 4.15,' wrote Elizabeth Cowen in *The Radio Times* in 1932, following the Bradshaw analogy.

Few listeners needed a timetable for the most regular services of all. 'There are more sets switched on at 6.30 p.m. and 9 p.m. than at any other time of day, for at those times the News Bulletin and Weather Forecasts are broadcast from all Stations. These services have a wider general interest than any other broadcast programmes.' So stated the *BBC Hand Book* of 1928, commenting that 'the desire for news is fundamental in humanity . . . and the desire for news about the weather is common to everyone in these islands, which are not gifted with the regularly fine weather of more southerly climates'.

By 1933, according to the *Hand Book*, the position of the News Bulletins was even more entrenched:

. . . their place, space, order and presentation in the programmes have been little affected by the experiments and reforms which have beset the rest of the programmes. They have sailed a relatively smooth and uneventful course, while all about them the waves of fresh ideas have reared their crests, subsided and been replaced. You might quite excusably have felt cheated and indignant if you had turned on the National Programme at 9 p.m. any night and had not been greeted by the dispassionate accents of the Announcer offering, without comment, items of the day's news for a quarter of an hour and no more.

In 1936 the immutability of the News was even celebrated by *The Radio Times* with a set of verses:

> *Some go to lunch at midday,*
> *And some at half-past one;*
> *While some, for a penny, consume at any*
> *Old time, the egregious bun;*
> *And tea-time may be five-ish,*
> *Or four-ish, as you choose,*
> *But all must agree with this firm decree –*
> Everything stops for the News.
>
> *Then Cook throws down her thriller*
> *And Jean, her homework sums,*
> *And Dad takes off his specs, to cough*
> *And arrange his elbows and thumbs:*
> *And Pussy looks up from her washing*
> *And Mum from her crossword clues*
> *And, eyes a-glisten, we settle to listen —*
> Everything stops for the News.

Everyone was prepared to 'stop for the news', but for many listeners there were too many other fixed points in the BBC's timetable. Announcing programme changes designed to make the schedule more flexible, the editor of *The Radio Times* wrote, in July 1936, 'The "lay-out" of the weekday evening programmes has always been based upon the disposition of those necessary fixed points, the News Bulletins.' He went on: 'The period from 6.30 to 8 p.m. in the National Programme has long been occupied by routine items, service talks (such as those on gardening, the cinema, and books), language lessons, talks for discussion groups, and the Foundations of Music. The fixed timing of these items has formed a block, which has made it difficult to develop this early-evening period along lines acceptable to the majority of listeners.'

Hilda Matheson was one of the listeners who did not find the BBC's fixed schedule acceptable. Several years earlier in her book *Broadcasting* (1933) she had grumbled about 'the necessity of remembering successions of exact hours and minutes, which produces the restless state of mind of those who are perpetually catching trains'. The original Bradshaw would not have sympathized. In June 1932 *The Radio Times* itself pointed out the drawbacks of the fixed schedule of programmes: 'A day-to-day service, such as Broadcasting offers,

tends, through its very regularity, to become accepted as a matter of course. In this lies a grave danger to Broadcasting which depends so largely for its effectiveness upon the selective concentration of its listeners.'

Highbrow listeners, sceptical about the likelihood of 'selective listenings', sometimes complained that too much broadcasting inevitably meant worse. In an article called 'From Morn till Midnight' in *The Radio Times* of 27 April 1928, Victor France, the novelist, recommended the following: 'Broadcast less – that is my advice to the BBC – and give yourselves and your listeners a chance . . . it would be better for you and for them, if . . . there were only four hours' broadcasting each day (instead of roughly, twelve), from 7 p.m. until 11 p.m., and that those four hours were filled with the very best you can give us. . . . ' Predictably *The Radio Times* correspondence columns carried storms of protest from affronted listeners of all types – invalids, housewives, night-nurses and so on – during the following weeks, including this plaintive one from 'Six Children': 'If the BBC follows Victor France, what about us and our Hour?'

Indeed, the Children's Hour, 'that memorable phrase', to quote the editor of *The Radio Times* in March 1934, 'announces one of the few programmes that you find at the same time every weekday, and of which you can be certain what to expect.' In fact, the timing was as important as the mood and contents of the programme. As Longfellow's words decreed, Children's Hour *had* to be during that pause 'Between the dark and the daylight when the night is beginning to lower.'

Just as regular and as important as these daily events were what a *Radio Times* editorial of March 1934 described as 'Peaks of the Week'. 'That's Sir Walford,' said a village woman to Hilda Matheson in 1933, as of a familiar friend. 'I always knows it's Tuesdays when I 'ear them sounds. You never 'ear 'em like that any other day.' Unlike Miss Matheson, she obviously appreciated schedules.

For millions of listeners like the village woman the week was measured out in familiar series of programmes. 'Series' could be very serious, like 'Foundations of Music', which ran for nine years from 1927 till 1936, and the Bach Cantatas (every Sunday afternoon from 1928 to 1934), or they could be very trivial – the lightest light music or the most popular variety. Particular programmes were associated with particular days of the week. For serious music lovers Wednesday was BBC Symphony Orchestra night, while swing enthusiasts could listen to their favourite dance band on regular nights of the week. In March 1933 *The Radio Times* printed this helpful schedule for them:

YOUR DANCE MUSIC
Monday
HARRY ROY and his BAND, from the Café Anglais
Tuesday
LEW STONE and the MONSEIGNEUR BAND, from Monseigneur
Wednesday
ROY FOX and his BAND, from the Kit-Cat Restaurant
Thursday
THE BBC DANCE ORCHESTRA, directed by HENRY HALL
Friday
GERALDO and his ORCHESTRA, followed by THE SAVOY
ORPHEANS (from the Savoy Hotel London National, 5.15 to
6 p.m.)

For many listeners Saturday night meant 'In Town Tonight' (first broadcast on 18 November 1933) at 7.30 p.m., followed by 'Music Hall' (from 1932) at 8 p.m. The regularity was part of the pleasure. When, in 1936, the BBC suggested changing the time of 'Music Hall' to 9.20 p.m. there was a national outcry. 'Switching on at eight o'clock on Saturday night has become a national observance,' wrote Kenneth Baily in a 'letter' to the BBC, printed in *Radio Pictorial*. 'Of all your "Hits" this was a sure favourite of which listeners would never tire.' Monday's favourite programme was actually named after the time it went out: 'Monday Night at Seven' (later 'Monday Night at Eight'). Its familiar signature tune reinforced the cosy and reassuring message:

> *It's Monday Night at Seven*
> *Oh, can't you hear the chimes?*
> *They're telling you to take an easy chair*
> *To settle by the fireside,*
> *Look at your* Radio Times
> *For Monday Night at Seven's on the air.*

That was the rhythm of the week. The seasons were part of the BBC's thinking, too. In this respect the 'Bradshaw of Broadcasting' came closer to being an

almanack than a timetable, though the railways, of course, had their summer and winter seasons. The BBC also published *Hand Books* to provide thoughtful listeners with year-long perspectives and, in Ivor Brown's words of 1934, 'to link up the listener not only with the machine but with the minder of the machine'.

Autumn was the peak broadcasting season bringing, as in academic life, new programmes, new voices, new ideas after the summer holidays. 'When autumn settles down on Britain, then is the time to settle down to listening', began the editorial of the Autumn Number of *The Radio Times* in October 1937 and it went on, 'With the long evenings the home and the fireside come into their own, and with them comes the radio; in summertime it may have been a luxury, now it is a necessity. No more casual switching-on when you have a minute to spare. You want to plan your listening as far ahead as you can. . . . The long evenings will hardly be long enough.' Sometimes, to maintain the autumnal mood, the word 'harvest' would appear in relation to 'a good crop' of programmes. There were visual images too. A familiar *Radio Times* autumn and winter illustration, repeated many times and in many versions over the years, showed a cosy hearth, father, mother and children sitting by the fire, listening to the wireless, the weather comfortably at bay outside drawn curtains.

In radio terms (as in Press terms) summer was the 'silly season'. 'Silly' was certainly the appropriate word for some of the outdoor settings for wireless imagined by enthusiasts in the earliest days of broadcasting. 'How greatly radio is going to brighten Summertime: on the river, in the garden, or at the seaside . . . making happy outdoor hours happier still', gushed the advertising copy for one lightweight radio set in 1924. Other advertisements and illustrations showed tennis parties, fishing and motoring expeditions all 'brightened' by radio. An idyllic picture, also of 1924, and illustrating the 'Portable Ethophone', shows a punting party complete with resplendent horn loudspeaker . . . the river rippling and glistening . . . the soothing whisper of soft summer breezes; and now a new source of pleasure is added . . . a pleasure which is always different, is provided by the marvel of the age, broadcasting . . . .

By the thirties more realistic attitudes prevailed. As the novelty of wireless wore off, so did the silliness of listeners. By 1933 Filson Young was writing soberly:

> To me there is a great difference between listening in summer and listening in winter, chiefly, perhaps, because I regard broadcasting as essentially an indoor affair . . . I definitely do not want to listen much to talks in summer . . . nor to operas or oratorios or to anything that requires sustained care. I have a general wish to slack off in every direction and I believe the majority of my readers feel the same . . .

I am not one who takes a portable set when I go out in my motor car or in my boat; and I hope that those who do are in a very small minority.

Young subsequently became involved in an esoteric and unprovable argument with Hilda Matheson who thought that 'since people's habits of listening is founded deeper than their daily habits, which change with the seasons, there is probably very little change in the use to which the receiving set is put between winter and summer'. She would have approved of the spirit of Henry Hall's *Radio Times* lyric (quoted on p. 8) extolling the virtues of wireless 'in Winter-time or Summer-time'. Garry Allighan, editor of the *Radio Magazine*, took up the theme in 1934:

Summer-time is radio-time. So is winter, and autumn, and spring. Because all time is radio-time. It has ceased to be a seasonal entertainment, to be put away with overcoats and heavy underclothing when we put the clock forward the Willett way.

That is where radio asserts itself with a supreme distinction among the arts of entertainment. Cinema-goers either have to stew in the heated atmosphere of the theatre or go filmless for the summer months. Ditto theatre-goers.

Whatever Miss Matheson and Garry Allighan thought about regular listening habits there was one time of year which was very special. 'Every year broadcasting sees further expansion in the Christmas programmes,' claimed the editor of *The Radio Times* in 1933, and every year bumper Christmas editions of *The Radio Times* advertised them. From Christmas 1932 King George V, with his annual message to the Empire, 'brought a new meaning and interest into Christmas Day for us all', as Leslie Baily put it. Sometimes Christmas imaginations became maudlin. A last-minute hole in *The Radio Times* of Christmas 1930 was filled in with a ballad whose refrain went as follows:

> *Don't switch off the wadio, Daddy,*
> *'Cos Mumsie loved it so.*
> *She stwuggled to buy us a licence,*
> *And she is gone, you know.*
> *But I 'spect she is listening, Daddy,*
> *In the heavenly mansions above:*
> *It's not only London that's calling,*
> *But Mumsie and Christmas — and Love.*

No wonder Young told *Radio Times* readers to 'cheer up if they suffered from a time of reaction after Christmas. After all,' he went on, 'Spring is coming, the season when every free moment calls you outdoors to the festival of renewing life . . . but,' he warned, 'do not be deceived into thinking that you will never need indoor solace and entertainment again.'

There was a new indoor solace and entertainment to stimulate jaded appetites. Television programmes first appeared in *The Radio Times* in 1930, when Baird's experimental programmes were announced. When a regular scheduled television started, for London only, in 1936, it was as if Bradshaw had included a supplement on travel by air. Reith would have approved of this particular metaphor more than he would have approved of Burrows's original railway one, for in 1938 he left the Director Generalship of the BBC to become Chairman of Imperial Airways.

'Wireless and wild weather'

(title of *Radio Times* article, February 1925)

WINDS N·E·
& SOME RAIN
IN SOUTHERN
DISTRICTS

THE
METEOROLOGOMETER FOR TESTING THE ACCURACY OF WEATHER REPORTS

Workers and idlers alike listened to the weather forecasts at 6.30 and 9. Yet the *BBC Yearbook* for 1928 suggested that farmers, sea captains and holiday makers were only a minority among listeners. 'There are few other listeners who do not indulge the national complex and switch on the loud-speaker or pick up the headphones with an unspoken prayer that they may not hear that another 'deep depression' is in the offing.'

There was a practical side also. Stove manufacturers complained to Reith in 1936 that BBC forecasts of a mild spell immediately reduced sales, while a Yorkshire innkeeper complained: when 'wireless said it were gwine to rain o' coorse, t' farmers won't stir oot o' doors'.

For more distant listeners the BBC weather forecasts provided a comforting link with home. In 1933 a Marconiphone booklet imagined 'an obedient servant of England in the British Consulate at Iquitos in Peru 2,200 miles up the River Amazon . . . who can now sit down before his Marconiphone and hear perfectly the voice a world away: "This is the National Programme from London. Here is the weather forecast for tonight and tomorrow. A deep depression . . ." But for the listener, no longer . . .'

'The Air Ministry, which prepares the broadcast Weather Forecasts, describes the weather as "rather warm", "warm", or "very warm". It does not use the word "hot". (*The Radio Times*, 1937.)

"Wireless says the fog'll be widespread to-day, Mum, so perhaps it won't be so thick."

82

THE DECLINE OF LOCAL PROPHECY

"*Sky be very bad to-night, Jarge. What do that mean?*"
"*Can't tell 'e. 'Erbert. Us'll 'ear it on wireless later.*"

F. SOUTHAMP. 28

F IS FOR FORECAST

The Farmer with his weather-powers
Can always, within certain hours,
Read England's Weather at a glance—
But not the Weather out in France.

Behold! the Broadcast Forecast came
To birth! and those who cast the same
Sweep the Horizon news to win
For Farmers who are Listening-In.

And now the Farmer knows what feast
Of sun is coming from the East,
Knows when his furrows will be blessed
With feeding rainfalls from the West;

He from the Forecast now will know
When broadcast he his seeds may sow,
When it is wise to cut his hay,
And when to cart the corn away.

"*An anticyclone is approaching from the west and fine weather will spread slowly over the British Isles, so need I wear my wellingtons, Mum?*"

There were popular complaints in early broadcasting days that 'we cannot hope for any decent weather so long as this wireless goes on'. *The Radio Times* was scarcely reassuring: 'Both the atmosphere and the ether receive such a shaking up every night whilst broadcasting is in progress that positively anything may be expected to happen.'

Weather might deteriorate, but the quality of weather reports improved. Shepherds (*above*) and verses from 'A Broadcasting Alphabet' by Eleanor Farjeon, 1927 (*bottom left*) treated them as supplements to and substitutes for traditional weather lore; children picked up weather jargon (*left, Punch*, May 1938). For radio critic Filson Young, weather reports were 'a daily reminder that we live not merely in houses but in that punctual and ordered world of nature where cause and effect circle visibly and invisibly about us'.

Thanks to *The Radio Times*...

Mervyn Wilson solves another domestic problem

1931

1936

1936

1938

Radio hearths

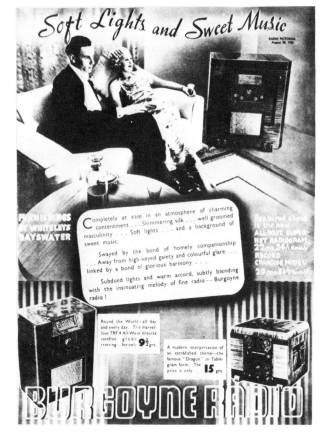

"Imagine her . . . . sitting by the little open fire on which she cooks her meals, with the receiver over her ears, her eyes closed for rest."

'Broadcasting . . . brings the noblest and best to your own fireside,' claimed the Marconi Company in 1923. It united families too: 'Many of the older people regret the scattering of the young folk to their various occupations and amusements, and think sadly of the old-fashioned "family" evening. But Broadcasting has brought this back again.'

The 'radio hearth' was a constant and ever-varying image in broadcasting literature. *The Broadcaster* featured happy radio hearths – occasionally outdoor ones – on its front covers in the early 1920s (*opposite*). *The Radio Times* showed poor old grannie (*left*, September 1924). In the mid-1930s wireless advertisements included Curry's cosy middle-class radio hearth (*top right*, *c.* 1934) and Burgoyne's couple listening in evening dress (their 'furnishings' by Whiteleys of Bayswater) at their all-electric hearth (*top left*, Radio Pictorial, 1936).

'Here is the News'

(title of a special *Radio Times* Supplement, 3 February 1939)

The most regular 'trains' in the Bradshaw of Broadcasting, the News Bulletins, ran in the earliest days at 7 p.m. and 9.30 p.m. No news 'trains' ran before the evening, and even then their contents were provided exclusively by the four News Agencies.

In 1922 the bulletins were read twice, 'first rapidly, and then slowly to enable the listeners-in to take notes', and the BBC's 'positive policy' was 'to give clear, accurate, brief and impartial news from the great world, in a form that will not pander to sensation and yet will arouse a continuing interest', as Reith himself explained in 1928.

By then, for some listeners, at least, what the BBC broadcast was *the* news, immutable and (preferably), like a train, unmissable. Throughout the 1930s the 'timetable' was steadily enlarged as the number of daily News Bulletins increased (although that national institution, the Nine o'clock News, was not established until 1938). 'This is an Age of News,' declared Sir Stephen Tallents, BBC Controller of Public Relations, in 1937, and *Punch* acknowledged BBC supremacy in the field (*bottom right*, Mansbridge cartoon, September 1938).

H. G. Wells, for many years lukewarm about radio, was never converted to broadcast news and time signals, which 'could be sent into a house far more conveniently if there were a silent recording apparatus such as the ticker,' he wrote in 1932. 'Broadcasting shouts out its information once and cannot be recalled. If you miss a word that word is missed for good. . . . It is absurd to suppose that science and invention could not furnish us with a silent recording set as cheap and controllable as the listening set.'

Wells left out the News Announcers. Nameless, yet widely known, they conveyed authority and dignity as well as information, and *The Radio Times* often featured them (*top right*, McKnight Kauffer's front cover, May 1929, and *opposite top*, Eric Fraser's front cover, February, 1939).

The announcer's dinner jackets were said to be more than symbols of authority – or snobbery. They were defended as 'a courtesy to visiting broadcasters' since announcers were expected to welcome to the microphone 'dinner-jacketed gentlemen' straight from their West End clubs.

Announcers were expected to make announcements as well as to read news bulletins, and these ranged from police

Radio Times, May 17, 1929.   Vol. 23.   No. 294.   [Registered at the G.P.O. as a Newspaper.]   SOUTHERN EDITION.

PROGRAMMES FOR MAY 19—MAY 25

THE RADIO TIMES

NEWS

WHITSUNTIDE

E. McK. Kauffer.

CONTENTS

2d   STORIES   BY   ELINOR MORDAUNT
VERSES   LIAM O'FLAHERTY
AND   COMPTON MACKENZIE
ARTICLES   RALPH DE ROHAN
              HARRY GRAHAM Etc.

ALL THE WHITSUN HOLIDAY PROGRAMMES

"WE'VE MISSED THE NEWS, EDITH."

'Perfect gentlemen'

(phrase of listener's letter to *The Radio Times* praising announcers, March 1939)

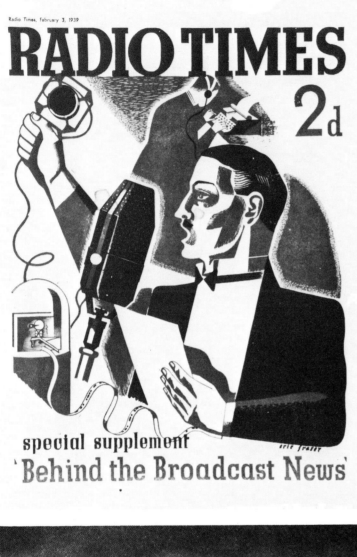

Radio Times, February 3, 1939

RADIO TIMES
2d

special supplement
'Behind the Broadcast News'

'I say, I'd rather not broadcast this police message'.
'Whyever not?'
'Well, it's me they're after'.

'PLEASE INFORM . . . IS DANGEROUSLY ILL'

and SOS messages (*above*, *The Radio Times*, March 1934; *bottom left*, *BBC Annual*, 1936). There was no place for triviality here either. Nearly 2000 announcements *not* broadcast included two 'designed to obtain matrimonial partners' and requests for the return of an umbrella lost on the Underground and for a pet bird called 'Billy Boy'.

Although news itself came direct from the agencies, the BBC (with few journalists of its own) was still blamed that too much news was bad. After all, as one listener complained in 1938, 'tragedies . . . do not constitute more than a fraction of one per cent of normal life'. Another listener suggested that the BBC 'take a complete rest on the Sabbath Day from disquieting communication'. Mr X, the suburban husband in Auden and Isherwood's *The Ascent of F6* (1937), expressed the problem more tersely: 'Night after night we have listened to the ignoble news.'

As the real news became steadily more 'ignoble' during the late 1930s, the BBC prepared for war: 'People would be getting home at all hours of the day, and the first thing they would want to do would be to hear the latest news,' wrote a BBC official in July 1939. 'Not listen to the News!' exclaimed one old lady, reported in a wireless survey in the same month, 'Why if we was to go to the war, the first you'd know of it would be the Germans marching up the street!'

Radio time

WHEN TO PUT YOUR CLOCKS RIGHT
TIME SIGNALS ON WEEKDAYS

STATION	10.15 a.m.	10.30 a.m.	12.0 noon	1.0 p.m.	4.45 p.m.	6.30 p.m.	9.0 p.m.	10.15 p.m.	11.30 p.m.
2LO	BIG BEN	GTS	BIG BEN	GTS		GTS	GTS		
5XX	BIG BEN	GTS	BIG BEN*	GTS	GTS	GTS	GTS		GTS
5GB			BIG BEN*			GTS		GTS	
Provinces						GTS	GTS		

NOTE. G.T.S.—Greenwich Time Signal.　　*Saturdays excluded.

"That's a large wireless set you've got there."
"Yes, I find it handy for giving the right time."

BIG BEN

TIME for the Time Signal!
　　Speak, Big Ben!
Boom out the time
　　To children and men,
Over Great Britain's
　　Listening Isles
Send your voice ringing
　　For miles upon miles.
Children that listen
　　Will turn into men
Ere you cease telling the
　　Time, Big Ben.
Men that now hear you
　　Tell the time plain,
Ere you are dumb will be
　　Children again.
Britain is listening.
　　Wondering, When?
Time for the Time Signal—
　　Speak, Big Ben!

The nature of the BBC time signal always roused strong feelings. 'Two Staffordshire Listeners' wrote this letter to *The Radio Times*.

'May we offer a heartfelt appreciation of the beautiful Bow Bells interval signal, so inspiring after that awful "Ghost in Goloshes" sound? If it conjures up such delightful thoughts and visions to home listeners, what must it mean to exiles overseas? It is so typically *England*.'

ALL STATIONS SHEEM TO HAVE CLOSED DOWN-- MUSHT BE LATER THAN I THOUGHT!

HULLO
CHILDREN!

Between the dark and the daylight
When the night is beginning to lower,
Comes a pause in the day's occupations,
That is known as the Children's Hour.

LONGFELLOW, quoted in the first *BBC Hand Book* 1928
by the contributor of the chapter, 'The Children's Hour'.

'FOR the children nothing is too good,' wrote the most famous of all uncles, 'Uncle Mac', Derek McCulloch, summing up the general attitude of the BBC to children's broadcasting. The *BBC Hand Book* of 1929, already looking back across those seven years with customary nostalgia, described him as 'one of the founders of broadcasting, who constituted himself an "uncle" and amused the children with fun and frolic for half an hour or so.' In the early days of sound there were no educational psychologists or sociologists to assess in detail the impact of the new medium, but everyone in the BBC itself from Reith downwards turned to the children and set out, in his words, to 'consider what effect broadcasting is likely to have upon them'. 'What is going to be the attitude of the new generation when and if it begins to take broadcasting seriously?' asked Filson Young, in a book of his collected essays *Shall I listen?* published in 1933.

Young, like everyone else who wrote about the subject, distinguished between the pre-radio generation and children who grew up with the medium: 'to the licensees of the coming generation broadcasting will be no new thing. In their lives it will be among the things that have always been, like motor-cars and aeroplanes.'

He recalled 'a four-year-old applying the headphones to his ears, listening for a few moments and then replacing them with the remark "It's only the Children's Hour" . . . To that little mind . . . there was no miracle in the wireless.'

As early as June 1924 Reith had commented on how quickly children took for granted that miracle and consequently how necessary it was for the BBC to concentrate on the content and quality of the programmes,

'clean wholesome humour, some light music and a sprinkling of information attractively conveyed'. Reith believed that programmes must also stimulate the imagination:

With children we have often noticed that they begin to listen with extraordinary keenness. For the first few weeks nothing will drag them away from the head-phones. Then the interest to some extent flags, and though they are still proud of being the possessors of the apparatus, their listening is not so systematic as formerly. This is possibly because they lack the necessary ingredient of imagination. It may be claimed, however, that they will, after the first period of disillusionment, gradually find that their interest grows again, and grows to be a far finer thing than the mere excitement about a novelty. They are developing the divine faculty of imagination.

For Reith and others, cultivating 'the divine faculty of imagination' involved two kinds of development; first, the encouragement of the arts of discrimination and second, the fostering of the willingness of all listeners, young and old, to share the listening experience. As 'Uncle Mac' put it in 1936, 'many parents can and *do* listen with their children, and thus share a common interest . . .' 'Broadcasting has opened a new world to be shared by the whole family,' Elizabeth Cowen wrote in 1934.

The last generation, exhorted to be seen but not heard, has launched itself in maturity as the first generation to be heard but not seen, and the ten-year-old of today accepts the miracle – never having known the old regime – with equanimity if not with gratitude. No question now of waiting one's turn for the evening paper – we all hear the latest scores, the latest news, together, and resign ourselves together to the deep depression settling over the N.W. coast of Scotland.

Young and other observers usually had a further point in mind. They refused to treat all children as if they were alike. As the *Children's Hour Annual* put it in 1936:

Beryl in Blackpool may like stories, while Brian of Bournemouth has a marked preference for plays. Again, Anthony of Appledore may thrive on nature talks, while Anna of Arundel may live only for music and song. We cannot always give you your own particular likes, but must try to build up fair shares of everything, with a little of something for everybody.

The choice of Appledore and Arundel rather than Leeds and Liverpool is significant: the children the observers and the broadcasters understood best were well-brought-up middle-class children.

The aunts and uncles who figured in the earliest local programmes, some of them self-appointed, before the BBC developed a national service, always sounded comfortably well-off. Indeed they obviously felt com-

"Auntie Cyclone."—Glasgow Station.
(Kathleen Garscadden)

seclusion of its own nursery, the communal jollity of the Children's Hour may seem unattractive.' There was also the problem of the so-called 'modern child'. 'Boarding-school boys in particular grow up precociously,' wrote the contributor of an article in the 1929 *BBC Hand Book*, 'and if they are not really little men at ten or twelve they have to pretend to be. It is quite useless to expect the spirited product of the modern Preparatory school to listen to anything labelled as specially designed for children.'

Whether or not it was true that prep school boys were particularly resistant to the delights of Children's Hour, it was certainly true that the programme itself often sounded as if it were run by prep school masters. 'Uncle Mac' himself, much loved as he was, could both sound and read schoolmasterly and rather patronising, particularly when he wrote in the *Children's Hour Annuals*: 'The best enjoyment can be obtained from listening to wireless only if you are prepared to give an item your full concentration.'

Whatever the class bias, there was one commandment on which the BBC insisted. The Children's Hour *was* for children and not for adults: 'It is planned for children, and all the effort that is put into it is inspired by the determination that everything broadcast . . . shall be fit to appeal to the keen, fresh, unspoiled mind of the child,' wrote the editor of *The Radio Times* in 1937 in a special Children's Hour Number.

But what did the children like? 'One of the most difficult problems for the Children's Hour is to ascertain the real tastes of the children,' admitted the *BBC Hand Book* in 1929. One basic difficulty had been expressed by a contributor in the *Hand Book* of the previous year: 'First and foremost, what is a child from the Broadcasting point of view? Anyone who has had

fortably well-off too. As C. A. Lewis, the BBC's first Deputy Director of Programmes wrote in an article called 'The Fun of Uncling' in *The Broadcaster* as early as 1923: '. . . there are many advantages to being a Radio Uncle for one can talk to thousands of nieces and nephews at once and there is no fear of being interrupted.' The world of Uncle Caractacus, as Lewis dubbed himself, was unashamedly middle-class: 'I don't hear the cheerful but rather sleepy voices shout "Goodnight" over the bannisters when the evening's fun is over, or the shrill cheers when nurse agrees that there shall be one more game before bedtime,' he wrote.

The presence of nurse gave the game away. Yet Hilda Matheson, firmly middle-class in outlook but to the left in politics, could console herself that the Children's Hour might actually appeal *more* to poor children than to middle-class children since 'to the child brought up with many resources of its own, and accustomed to the

How do you listen to wireless programmes?

expertise of children knows that there is a wide gulf between a boy or girl of eight and one of twelve and the adolescent of sixteen.'

The BBC had always tried to find out what children liked long before there was any formal listener research. As 'Uncle Mac' wrote in the *Children's Hour Annual* for 1937: 'We welcome both criticism and appreciation alike, but,' he added sternly, 'it is not fair to criticise unless you have been prompted to do so as the result of selective listening . . . which means taking the weekly edition of *The Radio Times* and making notes about the programmes you really do want to hear. It may be, for example, that on Wednesday you find there is a play you particularly want to hear, but that you have a friend coming to tea – not a quiet friend, but one who simply must talk the hind leg off a donkey. Have him – or her – to tea, by all means, but cancel your proposed date with the loudspeaker, or, of course, cancel the invitation to your friend and arrange another day.' 'In Children's Hour we are intensely interested in your reactions,' Uncle Mac reassured his readers, 'but you can only put them forward to us if you listen along the lines I have endeavoured to describe.'

Children *did* put their reactions forward to the organisers of Children's Hour from its earliest days, and less self-consciously than most adult listeners. During the year 1926, the first for which records are available, the *BBC Hand Book* for 1928 informed readers that 'the number of letters received in connection with the London and Daventry Children's Hour had been 54,334. These concerned many subjects, but 8,810 of them contained expressions of approval of the work that was being done while only 22 contained adverse comments of any kind.' However, in the following year's *BBC Hand Book* the contributor of the chapter 'The Children's Hour' expressed some scepticism: 'Many hundreds of letters reach the BBC every week from the children, most of them written in childish handwriting, but it is impossible to say how many of these are prompted by adult taste, or even dictated by parental preferences.'

Sometimes 'parental', or at any rate adult, preferences on the subject of Children's Hour appeared undisguised in the correspondence column of *The Radio Times*, 'What the Other Listener Thinks':

THAT DREADFUL CHILDREN'S HOUR 21.6.29
Can anything be done even now to eliminate that present scourge of afternoon broadcasting – I refer to that dreadful 'Children's Hour'. In common with very many others, I have for a long time wondered to whom this is meant to appeal. Personally, I find it hard to imagine any 'normal' child listening to this inane drivel for nearly an hour. It is very disappointing to be suddenly switched off from, say, a variety or dance band programme at tea time just to hear that imbecile Aunty something or other. Do please stop it and cease torturing – *Five Bored Listeners*.

Much more typical was a satisfied grown-up listener who, *The Radio Times* reported in April 1932, 'was found listening to the Children's Hour . . . because he was sure of a period of good clean fun', whilst 'a working woman' interviewed at the same time, said she liked the Children's Hour best out of the whole day's programme. 'Her husband and all the children listened and she was sure of a time to herself to get on with the family darning.' (She did not report whether she herself actually enjoyed or even listened to the programmes.)

Between four and five hundred letters a month arrive at the BBC from Children's Hour listeners—and here is one, typical of many.

It was in the third number of *The Radio Times*, published in October 1923, that the words 'The Children's Hour' had been used for the first time to apply to children's broadcasting. The name stuck, outliving various rivals such as 'Kiddies' Corner' and 'Fairy Grotto', until by 1934, the editor of *The Radio Times* could write of the Children's Hour, 'that memorable phrase'.

As early as 1928, Reith had assessed the Children's Hour as 'a form of broadcasting art' which, 'wholly novel, leaped at once into its permanent place in the scheme of popular life'. It had leaped from small and unplanned beginnings, the 'happy inspiration' of Percy Edgar, head of BBC Birmingham who started a 'Children's Corner' a few weeks after the BBC was established in 1922. London and the other regions rapidly adopted the idea and by 1933 Hilda Matheson, the BBC's first Head of Talks, wrote enthusiastically of the Children's Hour whose 'tide of popularity has swept round the whole globe, and little Chinese, Japanese and Indian children share in the broadcast version of this very Western Institution – the daily migration from nursery to drawing room of the correctly brought-up Victorian child'.

Inside and outside the BBC there were sharp critics from the beginning who shared Hilda Matheson's view that the 'light-hearted informality' of Children's Hour could 'degenerate sometimes into a studied facetiousness . . .'. Miss Matheson believed that 'A skilful and intelligently conducted Children's Hour does not need to depend upon condescending heartiness nor silly puerility to be popular.' It was not that she, or indeed any of the controllers of the BBC, thought that the Children's Hour should be solidly educational in mood and content. Longfellow's verse, quoted at the beginning of this chapter, was extremely apt. The Children's Hour *did* provide 'a pause in the day's occupations' for the children who were said, by a contributor to the first *BBC Hand Book* in 1928, 'to view with distaste a type of programme definitely and obviously educational – school out of school . . . The accepted principle is therefore that the purpose of the Children's Hour is mainly recreation and not instruction or moral improvement.' The problem was how to keep the 'fun and frolic' under control: the programme could 'no longer be left to the chance inspiration of the moment because in reality, though they may not realise it, people are demanding a higher standard of technical accomplishment'.

As the BBC grew and broadcasting jobs became more specialized, people expected and on the whole received those higher standards. Yet as the thirties went on, some older members of staff looked back with

'Aw, the old man won't wallop me — he's been listening to those child psychology talks.'

regret at those distant days when anyone 'who had any contribution to make to the pleasure of child-listeners co-operated very willingly. In their service he put aside pressing problems, urgent tasks and official staidness, braced himself to overcome the fatigue that results from a strenuous day, and established a tradition that . . . almost anybody "on the strength" will give to the Children's Hour any assistance that lies within his power.' Clearly, Longfellow's phrase applied as much to the timetables of those early wireless 'uncles' and 'aunties' as to those of their listening 'nephews' and 'nieces'. One member of staff commented in 1929: 'In the Broadcasting environment this period was a pause in the day's occupations in the truest sense.'

Eventually those early frolicsome 'uncles' and 'aunties' themselves grew up, in step with their original 'nephews' and 'nieces' who, as the editor of *The Radio Times* pointed out in 1934, were 'already adults, licence-holders, citizens'. Their programme had matured too: 'The Children's Hour has grown up with broadcasting,' the editor continued, and 'the spontaneous fooling of the Aunts and Uncles has given place to programmes that even the precocious child can enjoy. The Children's Hour has shown that broadcasters can enjoy broadcasting without being undignified.'

Children at the microphone

Children broadcast – and were broadcast to – both inside and outside school.

There was scope for many talents. Sir Walford Davies, soon to become a top BBC favourite, conducted the Temple Church choirboys in the first schools broadcast in April 1924 (*above*), while ten years later a very different group, 'Hughie Green and his Gang', were already 'hardened broadcasters'. Green was fourteen in 1934 (*bottom left*) and by then had already impersonated Maurice Chevalier, talked on *In Town Tonight* and played in *Emil and the Detectives*. 'He is not tough or cute or knowing, and he doesn't talk in wisecracks', was one contemporary verdict on him.

Children's Hour sometimes gave unknown child artists their chance. *The Radio Times* in March 1938 (*bottom right*) devised an all-children programme which Uncle Mac hoped would have the salutary effect of showing children just how difficult broadcasting was.

This afternoon at 5.0 *young listeners* are to hear a programme by *young artists*

Favourite characters

'Uncles' and 'Aunts' prided themselves on their informality. They did not want to be like school teachers. *Children's Hour* was conceived by Reith as 'a happy alternative to the squalor of the streets and backyards' (*above*, 'favourite characters' of the programme in 1934, *left to right*: 'Elizabeth', 'Stephen', 'Mac' and 'Barbara').

The best-known Uncle of all time, 'Mac', is shown (*centre*) with the equally well-known David Seth-Smith, the 'Zoo Man', in 1937, who had first broadcast five years before on 'animals in captivity', a popular *Children's Hour* theme.

In *Toy Town*, based on the models and stories of S. G. Hulme Beaman (and the longest-lived of all *Children's Hour* programmes), Uncle Mac played Larry the Lamb for thirty years ('Please, Mr. Ma-a-yor, sir, I'm only a little lamb!'). Other characters (*bottom left*) included comic-guttural Dennis the Dachshund, stolid Ernest the Policeman and pompous Mr. Mayor.

Playing at broadcasting

A WIRELESS UPSET

We made a wireless set to-day
*   With Nurse's work-box on the floor*
(Well, yes, she chanced to be away!)
*   We stretched her wool from door to door*

To make the aerial. But, oh!
*   It tangled up and broke instead,*
When Nurse came back this vexed her so
*   She said 'You'll listen-in – in bed!'*

Some critics thought that wireless had a bad effect on children's manners. *Punch* suggested a new way of answering back (*top right*, August 1923).

'Playing at broadcasting' became a favourite new game, both at home (*above*, poem in *Wireless Magazine*, February 1925, and *bottom right*, page of *Hullo Boys! Annual*, 1924) and at school (*below*, letter from a Manchester teacher to *The Radio Times*, March 1934).

Father (*making exit at conclusion of lecture*). ". . . So now you understand that I will not permit children of mine to behave in so unladylike a manner."
One of the Girls (*aside*). "2LO now closing down."

HOW BROADCASTING STARTED
WIRELESS PROGRAMME
ILLUSTRATED

1.0 [Dinner] Time Signal

3.30 An Hour of Melody

The Wireless Trio.

7.0 Local News

Fat Stock Prices

This is the first news copyright reserved Here are the fat stock prices

fat pigs all weights 1/2 lb
wild goose 1/- a
feather

In order to get my class of Standard IV boys and girls to talk easily, I asked them to give half an hour of broadcasting to the rest of the class. Two nine-year-old boys arranged the programmes entirely alone, and this is part of their work. It so amused me that I asked for their notes and promised to send them to you. Above is a reproduction from one of their exercise books. The Fat Stock Prices actually were said in the following order (with a serious voice, of course):—

Fat pigs—all weights	..	1/2 per lb.
Fat cows	.. ..	5/- per oz.
Horses ..	.. ..	2/6 per cwt.
Fat pigs with small noses	..	8/6
Chickens	.. ..	5/- per chick.
Wild Geese	.. ..	1/- a feather.

—Harold Radford, West Didsbury, Manchester.

Hello ! Boys, Hello ! Girls.

T HIS is the Chilprufe Company calling. To-night we are going to tell you all about those wonderful little garments you wear called CHILPRUFE, or, to be exact, CHILPRUFE FOR CHILDREN, because, do you know, kiddies, that when Mr. John A. Bolton first invented and designed these little garments, he insisted that only children's garments should be made, but when all the Mummies saw what beautiful stuff it was, well, of course, they wanted Chilprufe too, and then the Daddies wanted Chilprufe, so to-day it is really Chilprufe for Children, and also for grown-ups.

Well, kiddies, do you know that in Australia special sheep are kept which produce much finer and softer wool than is found anywhere else, and even then, these sheep produce two or three qualities. That which is cut from the sheep's breast is much softer and silkier than the rest, and it is only this particular quality which is used in making Chilprufe. Of course, it is much more expensive than the other kinds, so if you ever hear your Mummies mention that Chilprufe is expensive, you will be able to tell her why it is.

Children of all ages could learn the radio alphabet provided in *Radio Magazine* in 1934 by Archie de Bear, Radio Critic of the *Daily Express*.

A is the Aerial, right up above;
B is the Broadcaster some of you love;
C is the Concert-Hall – entrance is free;
D, Colonel Dawnay, the Programme O.C.
E is the Ether on which you're a rover;
F is the Fade-out before it is over ...
G's Gramophone, with Chris Stone to entrance;
H, Henry Hall, to lead you a dance.
I's Interference you cannot cut down;
J is the Joke that you wish it would drown. ....
K's for King-Hall and the Kids in his spell;
L is the Listener – Licence as well.
M's Eric Maschwitz, Variety chief;
N is the Nonsense that passes belief.
O is the Opera the Orchestra plays;
P is the Programme that sometimes gets Praise.
Q is Queen's Hall, with the Queues in its teeth;
R – like the rest of the staff – stands for Reith.
S is for Siepmann, initials C. A.;
T for the Talks he directs every day.
U's the Utopia all listeners crave;
V is the volume; W the wave.
X, unknown quantity, up in the air;
It takes a YZ to locate what is there!

Visitor. "HOW NICE FOR HIM! NOW HE CAN LISTEN TO ALL THE BEST MUSIC."
Fond Mother. "YES—AND IT'S SO GOOD FOR HIS EARS—THEY DID STICK OUT SO."

'A spoken fairy-tale'

(Reith's description of the *Children's Hour* in 1924)

Bedtime Stories !

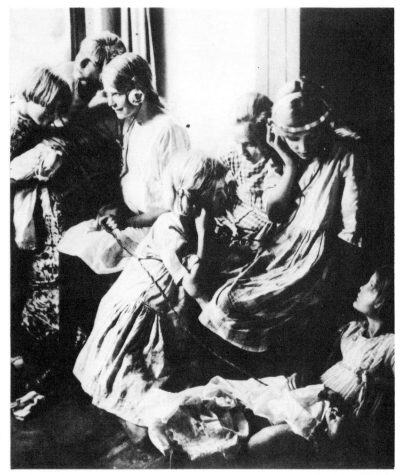

In the earliest days of broadcasting tiny tots were often photographed gravely listening-in (*above, Wireless Magazine*, February 1925). *The Illustrated London News* showed slightly older children, 'spellbound by a broadcast fairy tale', and commented that 'the new magic of science makes for contentment in the nursery' (*top right*, November 1923). For some parents, too, the 'new magic' was a godsend (*bottom right, Punch* cartoon, September 1926).

Before 1929, when the BBC started the Radio Circle, the well-behaved little children shown on these two pages might well have become Radio Sunbeams, each one promising 'to do all I can to keep cheerful and healthy, to do my best in delighting the lives of other children, to be kind to animals, to try to make my home, school and surroundings beautiful, and certainly not to throw any rubbish such as crockery, tins, paper, etc., into the streets about my home or in the countryside. To look for beauty in books, pictures, and in all things of our daily life, and to be allowed a member of the ring of Radio Sunbeam.'

WHAT IS HOME WITHOUT A RADIO ?

Mother (to nurse): "Let the little darling listen to the Children's Hour, and then, when he's had his supper, the Radio Dance Band can play him to sleep."

The BBC thought that good programmes helped to make good children (*bottom left*, W. Heath Robinson's idea for nursery audience research). Stephen King Hall, popular broadcaster to children (and others) on current affairs in his series, 'Here and There', was one of those who believed there was a link between broadcasting and behaviour (*top and centre*, King-Hall's famous 'signing-off' words, here used as end-papers in the 1935 *Children's Hour Annual*).

[Young Listeners today] 'are confronted by an opportunity undreamed of by earlier generations, of sampling Life – Life as understood and appreciated by grown-ups, with all its varied interests and delights,' wrote Elisabeth Cowen in 1932. When the children were not listening to the radio, the grown-ups encouraged them to read about it.

Above, illustration 'The Head Listens-In' from a typical radio story in a boys' annual, called 'The School Technician or the Amateur Announcer, a tale of dirty work in the Fourth Form.'

'Happy girls and boys'

(line from the Ovaltineys' song)

"Ise so glad I'm an Ovaltiney"

OVALTINEYS are very lucky boys and girls, with the Ovaltineys' Own Comic published specially for them and their own Concert Party broadcasting every Sunday afternoon. And there's lots of fun with secret signs and mysterious code messages known only to members of the League of Ovaltineys.

THE BRITISH BROADCASTING CORPORATION

Telephone TEMPLE BAR 8400 BBC *Telegrams* ETHANUZE, LONDON

SAVOY HILL. LONDON W.C.2

When replying please quote PK./LHH.

23rd April, 1929.

Master Raymond Mander,
72, Cambridge Road,
New Malden,
Surrey.

My dear "Member,"

Thank you very much for your card of April 19th and the badge, certificates, and Radio Circle subscription.

We all want to congratulate you on having won six competitions, and if you will let us know when you could come to the Studio to receive your silver badge, we will send you a ticket of admission. Perhaps you would mention two or three days, as there are certain days when we don't have visitors.

If it isn't convenient for you to come to the Studio at all, we will of course send you the badge by post, instead.

With best wishes from us all,

Yours sincerely,

Alan Howland, ("Columbus")

P.S.   We are returning the certificates herewith.

The Radio Circle was the BBC's own club for young listeners. Members received 'dainty' membership cards (*opposite*) and personal replies to their letters from the BBC 'uncles' (*top right*, 1929 letter from 'Uncle Columbus' to Master Raymond Mander, later to become, with Joe Mitchenson, co-founder of the famous Theatre Collection. His ninepenny 2LO Radio Circle badge is photographed lying on the letter). Members were entitled to have their birthdays called out on *Children's Hour* until 1933 when sheer numbers made it impossible to continue ('Many happy returns of the day to Johnny Green of 21 Manor Road, Harbourn, and if he will look in the coal scuttle he will find a present').

In 1938 the BBC started the radio discussion 'Under-Twenty Club' (*bottom right*, members with their chairman Howard Marshall). In good BBC style it claimed to 'mix entertainment with education'.

The 'Ovaltineys', under *their* Chairman, The Chief Ovaltiney, attracted as many 'happy girls and boys' to Radio Luxembourg as to Ovaltine in the late 1930s (*above*, *Radio Pictorial* advertisement, July 1936).

DOROTHY HUTTON

THE · BRITISH · BROADCASTING · CORPORATION
IS A MEMBER OF THE
RADIO CIRCLE
FOR THE YEAR
1930

THE BRITISH BROADCASTING CORPORATION
IS A MEMBER OF THE
RADIO CIRCLE
FOR THE YEAR
1931

A 1920s radio party, from *The Illustrated London News*.

WHAT ARE THE WILD WAVES SAYING?

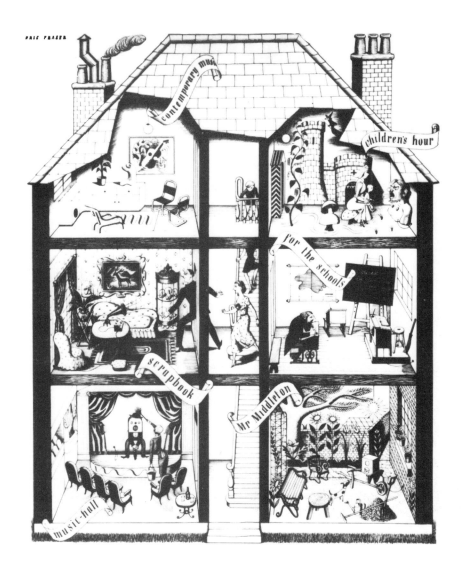

What are the wild waves saying
Sister, the whole day long,
That ever amid our playing,
I hear but their low lone song?

JOSEPH Edwards Carpenter's poem was written long
before the discovery of the wireless wave – by Hertz
in 1889 – made broadcasting possible. Yet the first line
was used as a slogan for Igranic wireless coils in the
early twenties, and figured, slightly adapted, on a wireless stall at a church fête in the pre-BBC summer of
1922 when 2LO, the station of the Marconi Company,
was broadcasting from London, largely to listeners
with homemade sets.

Carpenter's poem – like Mabel White's sculpture,
L'Onde Hertzienne, exhibited at the Paris Salon in 1928
– maintains the uplifting theme. His last lines claim
'something greater that speaks to the heart alone':

The Voice of the Great Creator
Dwells in that mighty tone.

This was the unconscious prelude to radio, and the
quality of the verse did not improve as the range of
radio programmes broadened. Radio became a medium
of communication and the chorus of the theme song of
Radiolympia in 1936 ran as follows:

Oh! Oh! You radio!
Oh! what I owe to you my radio:
I listen in and you dispel the gloom,
For you bring all the stars into my room;
Oh! Oh! You radio!

You're the most entertaining friend I know,
You give me music, dancing, joys I never knew
Oh! radio I'm radiating thanks to you.

Listeners were wisely recommended to learn these
words in the bath!

W. H. Auden and Christopher Isherwood were less
grateful and flattering to radio in their play the *Ascent of
F6* in 1937. Mr A., the ordinary suburban husband and
listener, resists the sensational radio promotions and

The wireless stall set up by Mr Norman McKee at a church fête in 1922.

L'Onde Hertzienne (The Hertzian Wave), a sculpture by Mabel White symbolising the Wireless Wave; it was exhibited at the Paris Salon in 1928.

propaganda of the magnate, Lord Stagmantle. He instructs Mrs A:

> *Turn off the wireless; we are tired*
> *of descriptions of travel;*
> *We are bored by the exploits of*
> *amazing heroes;*
> *We do not wish to be heroes,*
> *nor are we likely to travel;*
> *We shall not penetrate*
> *the Arctic Circle . . .*

Yet Auden and Isherwood recognised that listeners nonetheless had a choice:

> *Turn off the wireless.*
> *Tune in to another station;*
> *To the tricks of variety*
> *or the rhythm of jazz.*
> *Let us roll back the carpet*
> *from the parlour floor*
> *And dance to the wireless*
> *through the open door.*

From the pre-BBC start of broadcasting there were different kinds of radio programme, but musical evenings came first and foremost. Dame Nellie Melba, sponsored by the *Daily Mail*, sang from Chelmsford in June 1920 in what was later described as 'a great initiating ceremony of the era of public amusement'. The BBC included sections on all its range of programmes in its *Hand Books* which first appeared in 1928: sections which recorded in considered language what was later called the 'programme output' of the year, and which had been presented weekly in *The Radio Times* from September 1923. Broadcasts from commercial stations were conveniently recorded in *Radio Pictorial* after they became popular in the middle-thirties, yet the 'wild waves' were neutral in the competition between

the BBC and stations like Luxembourg and Normandie, and they brought with them a strange confusion of foreign sounds as well – the Tower of Babel in the sitting room.

Music was a universal language, 'the common language of Paradise', as Reith called it in his book *Broadcast over Britain* in 1924. It was no accident that a musical event had been chosen by the *Daily Mail* to 'initiate the new era of public amusement' when Melba sang in 1920; nor that the first BBC Outside Broadcast was a transmission of an opera, *The Magic Flute*, from Covent Garden, in January 1923. One typical day's complete programmes in November 1922, during the first week of the BBC's life, consisted of nothing but music:

MARCONI HOUSE
TRANSMITTED ON THURSDAY NOVEMBER 16th 1922

From 7 o'clock to 8 o'clock
1. Mr Leonard Hawke .... BARITONE
    (a) Drake Goes West
    (b) Tick Tock
2. Mr Bruce Maclay .... TENOR
    (a) 'Andante'   *Anderson*
    (b) 'Serenade'   *Goodall*
3. Mr Glyn Dowell .... SOLO FLUTE
    Selected
4. Mr Billy Beer .... HUMORIST
    (a) 'I knew there was a catch in it'
    (b) 'The Parish Magazine'
5. Miss Lily Clare .... CONTRALTO
    (a) 'A Summer Night'   *Goring Thomas*
    (b) 'A Little Silver Ring'
6. Miss Dorothy Chalmers .... SOLO VIOLIN
    (a) 'Hymn to the Sun'   *Rimsky Korsakof*
    (b) 'Rosamund'   *Schubert*
At the piano . . . . . Mr L. Stanton Jefferies, ARCM

In 1928 the first *BBC Hand Book* gave the figure of 62 per cent for the proportion of music in all programmes during 'a typical winter month', and in May of the same year, perhaps overwhelmed by incessant broadcast music, *Punch* posed 'A Wireless Problem':

> *Music, when soft voices die,*
> *Vibrates in the memory.*
> *But where on earth does music go*
> *When I switch off 2LO?*

One of the answers to this metaphysical puzzle was: to the legendary errand-boy whistling the Bach theme which wireless had taught him. 'Wireless,' declared the great contralto, Dame Clara Butt, in 1927, 'is helping to build up a vast new body of intelligent listeners. It is educating them by giving them the finest music.' Dame

Clara robustly welcomed the radio as the enemy of dreary musical parties in the drawing room. She wrote in an article in *The Radio Times* in 1925: 'As long as the wireless set brings first-class music into the home, musical people will not permit themselves to be troubled with indifferent amateur performances – except as a social necessity.'

The BBC took seriously its self-imposed duty of giving listeners a thorough musical education, based firmly on the Foundations of Music. In these daily twenty-minute programmes, which began in 1927 and continued for nine years, the BBC declared its worthy intention of giving 'lovers of music an opportunity for the synoptic study of standard works under the conditions of a sound performance by a first-class artist'. The BBC's decision to take over the almost moribund 'Proms' in 1927 and the formation of the BBC Symphony Orchestra in 1930 increased opportunities for listening to first-rate performances after the listeners' BBC homework – 'the synoptic study' – had been virtuously done.

Hilda Matheson told a story of a descendant of Mendelssohn who was stopped by a London policeman for a minor motoring offence. 'When the offender gave his name the policeman stopped writing in his note-book: "Not a relation of the Mendelssohn we hear on the wireless, sir?" and, on hearing that this was indeed the case, he waved the great man respectfully on.' She also reported that she had heard that 'in the out-patient department of a large women's hospital in a poor quarter of London, which dealt with a considerable charwoman population', many were discovered to be ardent subscribers to the sixpenny opera libretti published in English by the BBC to help listeners.

The poet Wilfrid Gibson was moved, when he observed the inspiring effect of wireless music in humble homes, to write these verses for *The Radio Times* in December 1926:

MUSIC STOLE IN . . .

MUSIC stole in; and all the idle chatter
Of gossip tongues was stilled; and for an hour
Our hearts were held by the ethereal power
Forgetful of the long day's fret and clatter.

No longer in a narrow track of duty
Each life moved dully in its little round:
Released from servitude by magic sound,
Our hearts were one with the eternal beauty.

Turning from verse to prose, there were certain perennial musical themes, variations on which helped over the years to fill the correspondence columns of *The Radio Times*. One very basic criticism advanced by several sophisticated writers was that 'too much music

may be worse than none', to quote Edward Crankshaw in *The Radio Times* in 1932. He denounced 'music all the year round, or even all the day round' as 'the height of inanity'. 'Far too many listeners,' he complained, 'have not shown the faintest capacity for employing the wireless and have debauched themselves with broadcast music . . .'. Crankshaw was generous, however: 'The BBC cannot be blamed for this, any more than the wine-growers can be blamed for drunkenness in London.'

Less sophisticated critics continued throughout the whole period to resist the BBC's attempts to educate their musical taste. A Bermondsey reader of *The Radio Times* in June 1932 wrote:

I feel that I must write and express my opinion of your radio programme. . . . If ever I have wasted ten shillings, I think I have by paying for a licence to hear such stuff as you are giving us lately, to say nothing of paying six pounds for the wireless set. As a man who has to work for a living, I was never schooled to hear such beautiful classical music as we get from all those musicians with fancy names and cosmopolitan titles to their music. As you have Daventry and London Regional, why not have a lively programme on one and classical music on the other to suit either the lively ones or those who want to have a quiet existence? I might say that I am voicing the opinions of many more, and when my licence is run out you can have my set for a mere song if your programmes do not alter. Mournful music is not very appetising for anyone to listen to after a hard day's work. The best parts of the day's programmes are during the day when most people are at work, and late at night when it is time to be asleep.

Another endless conflict took place between the 'pro-' and the 'anti-moderns' in musical taste. The BBC felt it had a duty, 'by virtue of the invention which it employs, always to be a little ahead of the times', as Percy Scholes put in in 1929. 'Anything less', he said, 'would be an insult to the imagination of the general public.'

Scholes sometimes over-estimated that imagination, however. After the English première of Berg's *Wozzeck* – proudly presented by the BBC in 1934 – Ashley Sterne, author of light-hearted revues for the BBC, damned the opera with faint praise: '. . . though I am not exactly humming its melodies today, it didn't bore me in the least. I was quite "interested", though I cannot help thinking that so many of the Modernists in music are pursuing vain gods. Their stuff never goes to your heart; and what is the good of that?' Complaints about 'Schoenberg's Sheer Decadence' and 'the discordant cacophonies inflicted by the BBC' were very common, and eventually even the BBC had to admit that 'a great deal of modern music is not "everybody's meat" ' – words written in *The Radio Times* in 1936, the very year that the familiar words, 'Foundations of Music', disappeared from the BBC's programmes for ever.

Chamber music was not 'everybody's meat' either. 'To my mind the people who say they like it are relics of the past Victorian era,' wrote one reader of *The Radio Times* in 1929, going on (inconsistently) to ask for Gilbert and Sullivan and *The Mastersingers*, 'music worth listening to'.

Most savage of all, however, was the campaign – sometimes expressed in moral terms – of the jazz-haters. Often, jazz broadcasts stirred up ugly racist attitudes, as they did, before they were banned, in Nazi Germany. An Aberdeen listener wrote to *The Radio Times* in October 1928:

I wish to register an emphatic protest against the continued and continuous infliction (by the BBC), upon sensitive ears, of that type of so-called music which is broadly termed Jazz. This horrible cacophony can only be regarded as a hark back to primeval savagery and appeals only to the lower or more primitive instincts. It is usually accompanied, in part, by 'singing' of a negroid nasal nature, the words being, almost invariably, asinine in form and, not infrequently, sensual in motive. It is true that I have it in my power to switch off whenever Jazz is broadcast. But I fail to see why I should have to exercise that power. I have paid for my licence.

Dance music did not raise such violent passions, and some dance-band leaders became genuine family favourites 'in houses where no one has ever "twinkled" or "hesitated" or "glided" or "dragged"', as the *BBC Hand Book* for 1929 picturesquely put it. It also observed that 'dance fans' were not the only listeners to welcome Jack Payne and his men when they started regular broadcasts in 1928: 'The Dance Orchestra which Payne formed and which he himself directs has taken a sure and permanent place in the affections of listeners,' said the BBC, in much the same tone and language as it adopted about the radio preacher.

Henry Hall, who succeeded Jack Payne as leader of the BBC Dance Orchestra in March 1932, was given a similar seal of approval: he had the honour of giving the very first broadcast from the new Broadcasting House in May 1932. Official approbation could hardly be more explicit, and the following year *The Radio Times* commented: 'Henry Hall's band has become as accustomed as the six Greenwich pips; no one gets mad about it any more.'

What the BBC really wanted was listeners who did not get mad about anything; who were 'not only tolerant but eclectic in their tastes . . . who can listen to and enjoy either Bach or Henry Hall'. So wrote the editor of *The Radio Times* in March 1935 in an editorial which, with no sense of bathos, celebrated jointly the 250th

anniversary of the birth of Bach and the beginning of the fourth year on the air of Henry Hall and the BBC Dance Orchestra.

Another four years later – at the end of the period covered by this book – *The Radio Times* printed a letter which must have gladdened the heart of the BBC: 'I am only a member of the ordinary working class, and am seventeen years old, but I have always enjoyed a good symphony. . . . If a few more people listened to such music Britain might be able to appreciate the works of the masters that will live for ever.' This listener did not mention Henry Hall.

There were as many 'works of the masters' in the BBC's drama programmes as there were in its musical output. Indeed, the first wireless drama programme to be broadcast, on 16 February 1923, consisted of three scenes from Shakespeare, the first of which was the quarrel scene from *Julius Caesar*. Shakespeare seemed to have written his plays in order that they might be broadcast, for, as Reith put it, 'They fulfil to a great extent the requirements of wireless. . . . He had little in the way of setting and scenery, and relied chiefly on the

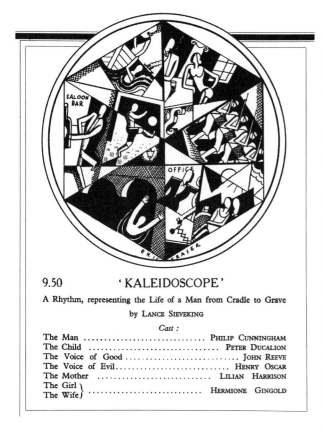

9.50 'KALEIDOSCOPE'

A Rhythm, representing the Life of a Man from Cradle to Grave

by LANCE SIEVEKING

Cast :

The Man	.... PHILIP CUNNINGHAM
The Child	.... PETER DUCALION
The Voice of Good	.... JOHN REEVE
The Voice of Evil	.... HENRY OSCAR
The Mother	.... LILIAN HARRISON
The Girl } The Wife }	.... HERMIONE GINGOLD

vigour of his plot and the conviction of the speakers to convey his ideas.'

As the twenties went on, the work of other great playwrights was adapted (which usually meant cut) for broadcasting. They were staple fare, and there were complaints in the thirties when the proportion of newly-commissioned radio drama had greatly increased. 'Just think of the good old days when Val Gielgud produced the fascinating plays of Chekhov, which were *not* specially written for broadcasting,' wrote one nostalgic London listener to *The Radio Times* in April 1939.

Back in 1929, in the heyday of the Great Plays, it was suggested in the *BBC Hand Book* that the wireless transmission of past masterpieces offered

a bridge over the gulf . . . between the business theatre of today and the national theatre of tomorrow. . . . Broadcasting, not being swayed by narrow financial considerations, may let a million serious listeners hear Strindberg, Ibsen, Euripides, Shakespeare, Sheridan, spoken by the most accomplished players (from the vocal point of view) and yet not be haunted by the awful possibility of being forced to close its doors because the play has not drawn the public.

Reith, himself an enthusiastic actor in BBC staff productions, grasped the importance of radio drama as an art form in itself and wrote earlier and far more intelligently on the subject than many professional theatre critics. He always urged listeners to take radio drama as seriously as if they were in the theatre: '. . . much of the success of the radio play depends on the listener,' he wrote in 1924. 'His imagination must be in full exercise and his attention concentrated . . . if people are moving about the room, or the telephone rings . . . the play has simply no chance.'

There were business as well as domestic obstacles to the transmission of radio drama in the earliest days of broadcasting. The managements of commercial theatres feared that the public would not come to see plays and musical comedies which they had heard, even if only in part, on the wireless as 'outside broadcasts'. The theatre critic of the *Illustrated London News*, J. T. Green, pointed out as early as 1923, at the height of the boycott of radio by hostile theatre managements, how mistaken this attitude was: 'For the listener-in, having read the description of beautiful spectacles, will not rest content with the mere hearing.' Furthermore, Green warned, by persisting in the boycott managements risked facing 'the most disastrous competition in their history . . . for . . . the BBC is a powerful growing concern; it commands great resources.'

The first full-length play, specially written for radio, was *The White Chateau* by Reginald Berkeley. It was broadcast in 1925, as if in defiance to the action of the Theatre Managers' Association, which in that year acted as a body in opposition to the claims of broadcasting. As Green had predicted, the boycott merely encouraged the development of radio drama as a separate form, and by the late twenties the BBC was presenting genuinely experimental radio plays which used – some critics thought over-used – all the exciting effects made possible by the Dramatic Control Panel newly installed at Savoy Hill.

One early *avant-garde* radio play was Lance Sieveking's *Kaleidoscope* (1929) 'a play too purely radio to be printed for reading'. It had a cast of over a hundred in eight studios, and some listeners thought the effects were overdone. A Surbiton listener wrote to *The Radio Times* in November 1938:

I am writing to you because I so very much appreciate the plays that you include from time to time . . . I do want to say, however, that almost all the plays have been rendered less enjoyable because the impossible has been attempted. I mean this. I feel that introduction of noise effects and, to some measure, the intonations and inflexions of the voice, which are in place on stage, are not successful when broadcast.

Such criticism was perfectly fair and well-balanced, but other writers felt real excitement at the possibilities of radio drama. 'The rising of an Ibsen of the Ether may happen and give us great things,' wrote Dallas Bower in *The Radio Times* in 1929. He went on to suggest the unlikelihood of such a phenomenon 'unless a mercenarily disinterested genius can be found'.

That genius was not found, but progress continued so that 'Astyanax', dramatic critic of *The Radio Times* in the late twenties, could write '. . . radio drama is no longer the Cinderella of the stage. It is finding its own art-form, and it is making its own "stars". It is worth attention and criticism. . .'.

Such critics suggested that the absence of the visual might even be an advantage, with H. G. Wells arguing from the sidelines that radio drama was 'a new and useful art, if only because it teaches us what life must be for the blind'. 'I do not think it can be put sufficiently strongly,' wrote Astyanax in 1928, 'that the broadcasting play has – or should have – nothing to do with visualisation. It has to do with the ear – not the eye.' Not everyone agreed, however: from 1923 onwards there were critics and listeners who could hardly wait for the advent of television. 'Before many years,' a Wimbledon listener wrote in 1924, 'we shall not only listen to broadcast plays, but be able to witness them, on a screen in our own homes. The argument that the listener cannot see the facial expressions, the scenery, the colouring, the light, and all that goes to contribute to the joys of the theatre, is absolutely true. There, indeed, lies the invitation to make good the deficiency.' Charles Morgan, the novelist, looked forward to television also. He believed that 'until it is reinforced by television, the scope of the wireless as a vehicle for drama . . . must be a narrow one'.

Radio drama, although it continued to raise heated arguments throughout the twenties and thirties, actually accounted for a very low proportion of broadcasting time. In 1926 the *BBC Hand Book* gave the figure of only 1·69 per cent, and ten years later the figure was still no more than 4·3. In the grand BBC scheme of things Drama was merely part of the Spoken Word, which above all, meant Talks.

Talk, of course, could be of all kinds, from the lightest and earliest – the famous 'How to Catch a Tiger', broadcast on 27 January 1923 – to the most serious political talk, only possible after 1928 when the original ban on controversy was lifted, and still closely circumscribed thereafter. In an 'Open Letter to the Listener Who Hates Talks' in a 1930 *Radio Times*, Douglas Woodruff recalled for his readers that broadcast talks had taught listeners 'How bats sleep; Where papier mâché comes from; Common faults in hum-

ming; Secrets in sardine tinning; the Evolution of Braces, and other useful things. No one pretends that acquiring information is particularly useful or pleasant, any more than physical jerks are particularly pleasant.' The mythical BBC professor discoursing on earth worms became a familiar figure of fun.

'Listeners Who Hated Talks' were not just those who resisted information. Some loathed what they thought was the high percentage of 'highbrow' talks. 'One would suppose, to judge by the programmes,' wrote a critic, C. Henry Warren, in *The Radio Times* in 1933, 'that the "average listener" envisaged by the Talks Department of the BBC lives mainly on a diet of great thoughts.' The position seemed to be worse than it was in either music or drama. 'Whatever your taste in music, you cannot complain that the BBC ignores you.' Warren went on, 'From Ketelbey to Stravinsky, all kinds of music find their way into the programmes at some time or another. For those who like to relax to music there is *Danny Boy*, and for those whose enjoyment is more self-conscious there is *Le Sacre du Printemps*. Which is all as it should be.' In talks, however, the diet of culture and information was unrelenting. The light-hearted 'tiger' seemed to have left few descendants.

Certainly the Talks Department of the BBC treated the possibilities of the talk as an art form as seriously as the Music Department treated the possibilities of the sonata, or some people in the Drama Department the possibilities of the feature. The BBC soon found out – in some cases by bitter experience – the qualities of the Ideal Broadcast Talker. 'Sincerity, tolerance, humanity, vitality and a sense of humour, seem to be among the positive virtues in this connection,' decreed the *BBC Year Book* for 1931, '. . . and pomposity, superiority, and a didactic or dry-as-dust manner, to be among the positive vices. Listeners are quick to recognise those who can, as it were, enter their room as a friend might enter it, and talk to them as a friend might talk.'

Rebecca West wrote eloquently of her difficulties as a Broadcast Talker. The Talks Studio at Savoy Hill was so depressing that she referred to it as the 'morgue' and to talks as the BBC's 'morgue work'. In any case she feared that 'a talk coming so evanescently from the wireless cannot stamp itself and its implications on the mind with anything like the impressiveness of the black words on a white page, that can be referred to again and again'.

Some wireless talks set out to supplement the black words on the white page with a sense of white chalk on a black board: these were the talks for schools. In the middle twenties *The Radio Times* began to carry articles with titles like 'The School of the Fireside' and even 'The University of the Air' (although, as one critic acidly pointed out, 'a university implies every kind of cultural influence that broadcasting is not'). The first broadcast talk – indeed possibly the first broadcast – definitely addressed to schools was given by that great talker, Sir Walford Davies, in April 1924, but M. Stéphan's French lessons had begun two years earlier.

'A Wireless in Every School: Radio as the Teacher's Ally', was the suggestion of Arthur Greenwood, the Labour MP, in an article in *The Radio Times* in March 1925. He advised 'mobilising the World's Brain Power, scientists and historians, poets and musicians, travellers and inventors behind the teacher in the classroom.' He was careful to point out that this would merely reinforce the teacher and not replace him.

In the early days of Schools Broadcasting some teachers regarded the new medium as a rival. To quote 'A Wireless Schoolmaster' in *The Radio Times* in 1933, 'There was a notion that somehow it was the thin end of a wedge, and that if it was successful the teaching profession would dwindle into a select visiting staff at Broadcasting House.'

The 'Wireless Schoolmaster' should have substituted the words 'Savoy Hill' for 'Broadcasting House', and the past tense for the present, for by 1932, when the BBC moved house, broadcast lessons had long ceased to be either a novelty or a threat; they were simply a useful tool to aid the harassed teacher. The tool had to be used in moderation, however. Filson Young issued a stern warning in *The Radio Times* in March 1932.

If you can imagine a person isolated from the rest of the world and given no education whatever except what can be got from broadcasting, can you imagine what his mind would be like, if he had a mind at all? For hours every day he would be receiving a mass of miscellaneous education passing him by as swiftly as the landscape passes the eyes of the traveller by train.

Yet not all critics adopted such a pessimistic view. By 1939 A. C. Cameron, Secretary of the Central Council for Schools Broadcasting, wrote that through Schools Broadcasts 'children are learning to listen; indeed the ordinary child of today who has been brought up with broadcasting . . . can probably listen more intently to a talk, and pick up more points, than his elders.'

The BBC always hoped that the educational influence of broadcasting would not be confined to a pigeonhole marked 'Education'. A St Pancras cleaner, Mrs Florence Knightly, interviewed by *The Radio Times* in March 1939, after the BBC had begun to take listener research seriously, declared herself an enthusiastic listener:

I think radio's a proper education. People can go to the pictures or the dance halls for their fun, but it's not all of us have got the time or the energy to go out and study. Wireless makes learning easy. The people talking might be in the same room.

You can have your Band Waggon; give me the symphony concert on the other wavelength every time; and what I say about Band Waggon goes for crooners and jazz too. Not that jazz music is bad; it's the instruments that muck up a good thing. I like good music with my dinner, and afterwards there's the schools talks. Who wouldn't be a kid these days? Then later on there's the news, and the talks by famous people about what is going on in the world. You can't believe half what your newspaper says, but you can always believe the wireless. Twenty years ago a woman like me wouldn't know anything about politics, but thanks to the radio I can hold my own quite well.

Mrs Knightly spurned Band Waggon, one of the most popular radio shows of the day – and a show which pointed the way to many radio shows of the future – but many listeners moved easily from talks to patter and back again. Radio was establishing its own comedy tradition. Variety was always more popular than talks, even though the patter could not be accompanied by 'the false nose, the slipping trousers, the crushed top hat, or the upset chair', a list of non-available radio props published in the *BBC Year Book* for 1933.

Four months before its first programme of dance music, the BBC had presented its first variety programme, in January 1923. Friction between the BBC and the management of music-halls restricted the radio contracts of stage and variety artists even more than those of professional actors in serious drama.

Even if managements were willing, however, something was missing – the greasepaint – and what was always present was the inhibiting sense of the fireside. 'Not everything . . . can be successfully brought to the fireside. I realised that the other night when I listened in to a variety programme,' wrote J. B. Priestley, summing up the difficulty in *Apes and Angels* (1928).

I have no fault at all to find with the programme itself. All the people were good of their kind, and their kind was that of the music-hall. They had better voices than the average music-hall singer, and I have no doubt that their jokes were really very good jokes. Yet the fact remains that, to one listener, at least, that entertainment seemed as dead as mutton, whole worlds away from the genuine variety show. What killed it was the fireside.

The fireside was where the family gathered, and in the family circle both the smutty and the sophisticated were ruled out. Kenneth Baily, writing in *Radio Pictorial* in 1936, was relieved that 'in the privacy of the home' it was 'difficult to indulge in a robust Falstaffian orgy'. Furthermore,

the fact that all types of people, holding all kinds of beliefs, suffering from all kinds of deformity and disease, and going through every type of trouble and distress, were listening to every comedian who opened his mouth before a microphone, was a fact that could not be ignored.

Anywhere, at any time, someone is listening whose own personal circumstances may be exactly those poked fun at by the broadcasting comedian.

The reasons for such 'moral' censorship were valid, but there were many listeners who wanted more variety with more spice in it. There was always a sense of censorship, thus Tommy Handley, long before he became famous as a broadcaster, wrote in *The Radio Times* in 1928 that 'the choice of material is, of course, extremely restricted: many everyday happenings, the foibles of politicians, the advertisement columns of the newspapers, many tried and trusted sources of inspiration for comedians are closed against the broadcaster, and it is a well-recognised fact that many of the songs and much of the patter which cause paroxysms of mirth in the music-hall or theatre fail utterly to amuse the

listener at home.' Interestingly, he thought there was plenty of fun in the BBC and in wireless itself:

. . . if jokes grow whiskers, millions of gags must by now have grown cat's whiskers! . . . listeners, too, are interested in the *personnel* of the BBC, hence the Announcer is a constant figure of fun to all outside the studio; within that grim chamber the Announcers must be taken seriously! I have found also that the public enjoy good-humoured skits on the more serious educational features of the programmes, and I have even had the impertinence to discourse on such subjects as voice culture, music, and dietetics. In this connection I might mention that Sir Henry Walford Davies did me the honour of mentioning my ridiculous remarks on music in one of his ever-popular talks a few weeks ago, and a quip of mine regarding a method of decarbonising the tonsils attracted the attention of one of the motor journals.

It was generally recognised that broadcasting made heavy demands on the broadcasting artist. 'If he is to come frequently to the microphone and to establish a reputation he must be constantly in search of new material, a new experience for the stars of music-hall who, owing to the widely scattered nature of their audience, had been accustomed to make gags, business and songs last for years.'

Gags quickly made their way through the country. They were quoted at the factory and in the street, particularly in the late thirties, just as the latest songs were hummed or whistled. It was Radio Luxembourg rather than the BBC which made the most of what later came to be called pop music, but the BBC remained supreme in variety. By 1934 Eric Maschwitz, who moved from *The Radio Times* to widen the range of BBC variety programmes, maintained that:

. . . the much-vaunted 'war' between Broadcasting and the Music Hall is at an end. Whenever it is possible to do so, music-hall proprietors and managers are most helpful in providing facilities for the BBC to broadcast their artists from the studio and in allowing microphones to be installed in their theatres; Broadcasting, in its turn, is each month contributing more artists and material to the programmes of the music-halls.

Maschwitz was happy that the 'war' had been won, and he was soon on his way to fight other battles in Hollywood. Yet Reith and his senior colleagues still wanted the BBC to provide more than entertainment. In 1925 J. C. Stobart, Director of Education and much else besides, had noticed how radio was appealing to 'people of a type who would hardly be found in any such place as a theatre'. The Wireless Wave penetrated far beyond the footlights. The BBC's programmes were like life: 'sometimes they give us one experience, sometimes another'.

Most broadcasts came from the studio, even the Last Post in 1923 (*top right*), which 'a pompous and pernickety official' would not allow Reith to broadcast direct from Whitehall. Listeners seldom visited studios, though the BBC often reminded them of the care programme builders took to inform and entertain them. As a *Radio Times* reader put it:

They have a task of vastness that bewilders,
A few short hours, a million minds to please . . .
  (1932)

The perils of 'the other side of the microphone' were best known to the broadcasters themselves. 'All the terror of the unknown was upon me,' wrote Mabel Constanduros in 1925, when she found herself in 'a drab-hung empty room', and was told simply, 'There is the microphone; please begin.' She did not know how. 'Where should I stand? How loudly must I speak; And what should I say?' Three women broadcasters – Rebecca West, Beatrice Webb and Cynthia Asquith – shared this sense of 'the ordeal of the microphone', although Fougasse (*below*) and Bateman (*opposite, bottom*), depicted male victims.

PAINFUL ORDEAL OF EMINENT ACTOR OVERCOME BY STAGE FRIGHT
AT HIS FIRST EXPERIENCE OF BROADCASTING.

...in coelum est'

('Who knows what the evening may bring?' – Livy, quoted in wireless advertisement, 1924)

The Studio

Sound proof Double Window

Chimes

Red Light

Red Light

Organ

A Performer

The Announcer

the Microphone

Fan Switches

Switches for Studio Lights

Sound proof Double Window

DO NOT TALK LOUDLY

ENTRANCE FORBIDDEN RED LIGHT SHOWING

Five Layers of Fabric

Showing red light over a studio doorway and a bit of the studio wall in part section

"Quality" Signaller – Operator who listens in to broadcasts as heard by the public, and who signals, if necessary, to the announcer to correct the position of the performer in relation to the microphone.

The Green Room

" The microphone is ready for your broadcast, Miss Robinson "

The Radio Times summed it all up well – if long-windedly – in September 1930: 'The task of exciting, and therefore delighting, a million people with an entertainment coming via an unresponsive microphone and devious mechanical routes from a shrouded studio is no mean task. For the broadcaster to be able to triumph over the remoteness, the lack of contact, the physical strain inseparable from studio work, and still retain enough vitality to titillate a public which, from the casual circumstances of its listening, is even less receptive than a theatre or a cinema audience, implies qualities which are not easily found, but which, when found, are quickly recognisable on the other side of the microphone.'

'Pity the broadcasters,' commented one sympathetic listener far more succinctly.

THE COMEDIAN ON APPLYING FOR & BEING GIVEN AN ENGAGEMENT TO BROADCAST

AND ON COMING FACE TO FACE FOR THE FIRST TIME WITH THE ALMIGHTY "MIKE".

'Radio at its best'

Picture in Sound

How a feature programme comes to the microphone

In the following pages you will see how a programme is built, from the conception of the idea right up to the broadcast performance. The programme that you will follow is an imaginary 'feature' calling on the varied resources of broadcasting—'actuality' recording, special music, and a live cast.

The original idea for this programme comes from a writer outside the BBC, who suggests a broadcast giving a vivid sound-picture of a great system of docks. Laurence Gilliam, chief feature producer, likes the idea, and writes to the author telling him so. They will meet and at a later stage collaborate in writing the radio script.

Photographs specially taken by Bernard Glemser

No other broadcasting organisation in the world made as much as the BBC did of its 'features'. These drew together the distinctive arts and techniques of broadcasting, at their best creating a new artistic genre.

Lance Sieveking, the radio and television producer, described the features programme in 1934, when the *genre* was already established, as 'an arrangement of sounds which has a theme but no plot'. Six years earlier Cecil Lewis had dubbed the first features 'radio at its best'.

Features could cover anything, past or present. One of Sieveking's own feature programmes, 'Crisis in Spain', was broadcast in August 1934 (*above*). The Spanish Civil War was soon to divide poets and writers, but this programme was praised as 'the first English example of the reporting in Radio form of contemporary events. The crisis in Spain . . . is presented in terms of news items printed and broadcast at the time all over the world.'

Picture in Sound (*top right*) was the subject of a whole *Radio Times* Supplement (December 1938) which described the making of a feature on Southampton Docks and how Laurence Gilliam, prince of features, had first approved the idea, and how researchers, scriptwriters, engineers, producers – and real-life people – had collaborated successfully.

The *Voice of Paris* (March 1939) describing the State visit of President Lebrun (also the subject of a prominent television 'O. B.'), was one of the last peace-time features.

The story in words, music, and recorded sound of twenty-four hours in the life of Paris—broadcast tonight at 8.0 in celebration of M. Lebrun's arrival in England on his State visit

The Spoken Word

For some listeners (and critics) all that you needed in broadcasting was words. Talk was obviously 'the best of radio' – whether serious or funny, learned or topical, simple or profound.

The Talks studio at Broadcasting House, unlike any other, was decorated in traditional style. It was lined with books and the microphone stood out over a lectern. There was thus a link between bookmanship and the art of the formal talk, carefully scripted, vetted and delivered live. There was a picture of George Washington above the fireplace, reminding the broadcaster never to tell a lie. Both books and fireplace were, however, fake.

There was little satire in the Talks (always, like the Spoken Word, spelt with a capital letter), though 'Nat' and 'Reg', the studio hounds (called after the National and Regional programmes) introduced some gentle humour (*bottom left*, January 1939) and cartoonists at least could make fun of rather too eloquent broadcasters of Talks (*above*, Watts' maiden lady talking on 'Babies and how to rear them').

'There's a lot of talk in a wireless set,' wrote Auden and Isherwood in *On the Frontier* (1938), 'and a lot more promised than you'll ever get.'

Ordinary voices *were* sometimes heard, separately, of course, from the voices of the great. A popular series of talks on 'The Day's Work' in 1930 demonstrated that people were 'keen to hear what the Covent Garden porter, the steeplejack and the postman had to tell'.

For listeners who did not like talks – and there were many – there was ample advice. 'Don't let us worry about the height of our brows: we are concerned with life, and the future is ahead of us.' (*BBC Year Book*, 1931.)

NAT and **REG** — The Studio Hounds

No. 24–'MOTHER AND DOCTOR'

'This afternoon Dr. Dalmatian is going—

—to talk about Children's Ailments . . .

Good heavens, he's got measles!'

A "MYSTERY" SOLVED: WHERE THE "WIRELESS" APPLAUSE COMES FROM.

DRAWN BY OUR SPECIAL ARTIST, C. E. TURNER. (COPYRIGHTED)

BROADCASTING VARIETY FROM 2 LO (LONDON): A PRIVILEGED AUDIENCE IN A B.B.C. STUDIO APPLAUDING A SINGER AT THE MICROPHONE AFTER HER "TURN"; AND TECHNICAL LISTENERS IN A SOUND-PROOF CABINET BACKGROUND.

'The Music Hall of the Air'

(title of *Radio Times* article, April 1928)

Fougasse

"WHAT I SAYS IS, MRS. JONES, THERE'S TOO MUCH OF THIS HERE VARIETY AND MOST OF IT'S ALL THE SAME."

The British public (*left*, as seen by Fougasse, *Punch*, February 1935) was always said to love Variety: certainly it was usually placed first in the popularity polls run by newspapers.

Behind Variety was the tradition of the music hall, though the absence of stage and footlights provided a new challenge. A substitute had to be found for 'the silver tissue of the leading lady and the funny hat of the comedian', wrote the *BBC Hand Book* for 1929, when radio was already far more influential than any music hall. Radio was felt to offer a nostalgic 'refuge on the ether' for displaced personalities of the halls, but it was, of course, building up new personalities and a new audience at the same time. Magazines like *The Illustrated London News* stimulated as well as satisfied the public's appetite to know what went on behind the scenes at Savoy Hill (*opposite*, 'Broadcasting Variety from 2LO', *The Illustrated London News*, 1929).

Class still came into it, as it had done in the music hall. So, too, did nationality. Variety was not cabaret, nor was it American show business. When Maschwitz ran light entertainment he was told squarely it was only 'right and fair' that the 'shirt sleeves and carpet slippers' public should be as entertained as the public listening in boiled shirts.

Vulgarity was outlawed from the earliest days of broadcasting; a card was handed to new BBC artistes saying, 'No gags on Scotsmen, Welshmen, clergymen, Drink or medical matters. Do not sneeze at the microphone' (*c.* 1925 onwards).

YOU NEVER KNOW

My wife has just remarked: 'Band Waggon is on at a quarter past eight'. 'Yes,' says I, 'and also *Judas Maccabæus*.'

'Who's he?' asks my wife. 'Is he in Band Waggon?' – *F. G. Partridge, Newbury, Berkshire* (letter from *The Radio Times*, 16 December 1938).

'Stageless drama'

(title of *Radio Times* article on radio drama, 1931)

'Radio is going to give the artist the greatest opportunity to express himself he has had since the days of Homer,' wrote Compton Mackenzie in September 1929. Mackenzie, of course, was thinking of the 'spoken word' rather than the range of novel sound effects made possible by the BBC's exciting Dramatic Control Panel in Savoy Hill and used in plays like Charles Croker's 'tragi-comic radio fantasy', *Speed* (*bottom right*, panel in *Radio Times* programme page, 2 April 1928). The artist Eric Fraser presented his own picture of the new-style radio producer who could 'mix at will the output, in speech, music and effects, of 8 studios'. (*Opposite, bottom*, 28 August 1931, *The Radio Times*).

By the early 1930s critics of radio drama were insisting that technological gimmicks were not enough – though they might be fun. Even *The Radio Times* admitted in 1932 to 'the enthusiastic mistakes of experiment ... an over-indulgence in the mechanical element at the expense of the human'. Filson Young summed up the problem and the challenge to the listener. 'The voice, and the voice alone, has to carry the whole burden of dramatic expression. There is no scenery ... no gesture, no visual beauty of voice or form ... [yet the listener] can people the darkness with pictures, more real, more vivid and more beautiful than any you can see on the stage.'

Radio drama had its enemies, too, like C. Whittaker Wilson, who thought that the very idea of 'aural spectacle' was a contradiction in terms and that it was time the BBC realised that 'people like to buy chocolates and sit on tip-up seats to eat them' (*The Radio Times*, December 1938).

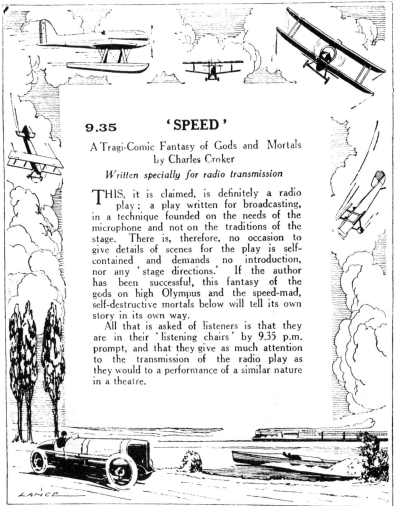

9.35   'SPEED'

A Tragi-Comic Fantasy of Gods and Mortals
by Charles Croker

Written specially for radio transmission

THIS, it is claimed, is definitely a radio play : a play written for broadcasting, in a technique founded on the needs of the microphone and not on the traditions of the stage. There is, therefore, no occasion to give details of scenes for the play is self-contained and demands no introduction, nor any 'stage directions.' If the author has been successful, this fantasy of the gods on high Olympus and the speed-mad, self-destructive mortals below will tell its own story in its own way.

All that is asked of listeners is that they are in their 'listening chairs' by 9.35 p.m. prompt, and that they give as much attention to the transmission of the radio play as they would to a performance of a similar nature in a theatre.

'Effects'

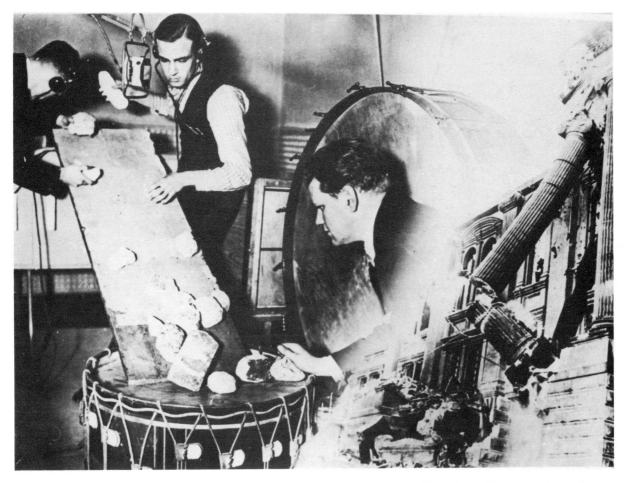

From the earliest days artists and writers found radio drama 'effects' an intriguing (and easily illustrated) topic. 'The story-writer for the broadcast must, I think, keep us engineers busy,' wrote Captain Eckersley in 1923.

'... Scene 8 is the home of the dandy, and one must hear the creak of the trouser-press and the clank of the manicure-set. The villain dashes away by the Scotch express. Our microphone must hang in the rheumy, echoing vault of a main terminus.... Background is the thing!'

Nine years later Broadcasting House had its own sophisticated 'effects' studio on the sixth floor. Leslie Baily compared it with 'some fantastic futuristic torture-chamber, furnished ... with grotesque machinery in chromium and grey, with switches, wheels, fans, chains, heavy bolted doors, drums, whistles, mallets, swords' (*above*, photo montage of BBC effects, January 1933).

'Shall we sell the air?'

(title of *Radio Times* leading article, July 1929)

TRAGEDY AT THE BIG HOUSE

" They caught him listening to Radio Luxembourg "

LUXEMBOURG CONCERTS YOU SHOULD NOT MISS
1293 M.

SUNDAY, SEPTEMBER 13

BROADCASTING PRECAUTIONS OF THE FUTURE

ESCORTING A BROADCASTER TO THE MICROPHONE.

NOT ACCORDING TO PLAN!

USE TOOTSICUM'S TOOTH PASTE!

TAKE HIM AWAY!

AN ANNOUNCEMENT.

THE LECTURE ON SEA-SHELLS IS CANCELLED, AND YOU WILL HEAR A LITTLE MUSIC INSTEAD.

Will the B.B.C. be able to stop a sham Professor of conchology—let us say—from advertising something else in which he happens to be interested?

Straight from the Prairie!

"HEAR ME ON THE AIR!"

Says OLD HETHERS

The BBC's great rival, Radio Luxembourg, went on the air in 1934. It was almost as easy to make fun of as the BBC itself. In some ways it was an anti-BBC, offering highly selected (popular) rather than balanced programming and depending on advertising revenue.

From the start the BBC feared the competition of commercial radio (*opposite, top left, Radio Pictorial* cartoon, August 1937) and it made the most (or worst) of American broadcasting as ammunition with British listeners. *The Radio Times* quoted a cautionary joke from *Life* magazine:
FIRST COLLEGIAN: 'What's the correct time?'
SECOND COLLEGIAN: 'I don't know exactly, but I think it must be about half-past the balloon-tyre hour.' Even children got the message: 'Uncle Caractacus' explained in *Hullo Boys* (1925) that 'we British have the world's best broadcasting service because *we* learned from American mistakes'.

In the mid-1930s new gossipy radio magazines covered Radio Luxembourg and its stars. They also reinforced in print radio advertising campaigns (*left* and *above, Radio Pictorial*, 1937 and 1936). Meanwhile the *Daily Mirror* joined in the debate with its cartoon fantasy, 'Broadcasting precautions of the future' (*opposite, below*, 1934).

The virtues of BBC music, old and new, were proclaimed in the language of Shakespeare as well as of Reith:

And those musicians that shall play to you
Hang in the air, a thousand leagues from hence,
And straight they shall be here; Sit and attend.

Under Adrian Boult's baton, the BBC Symphony Orchestra, formed in 1930 (*opposite, Radio Pictorial's* photo montage, 1934, 'Music Makers All'), set out to provide music not only for the concert-going public but for listeners who were 'prevented from concert-going by lack of means or opportunity or by personal preference'. The Promenade Concerts, taken over by the BBC in 1927, provided conveniently for both.

Good composers were given almost as much attention as their compositions. Wagner, who might be murdered by an early wireless orchestra (*below*, comment from a listener to *The Radio Times*), divided the public, and an early cartoon shows one listener anxiously asking another 'er – is that Wagner or only Oscillation?' Beethoven, however, always towered large, not only in the famous *Radio Times* front cover by Batt (*bottom right*, 28 April 1939) ('copies on good quality paper, price 6d, post free'), but in the Boult – and Proms – repertoire. Friday night *was* Beethoven night.

Bach had friends and enemies, and of Handel one jaded listener was driven to write 'when are we to be delivered from the eternal Handel's Largo? . . . .'

That was one problem about BBC music, a greater daily output of music than in any previous period of history – meeting resistance yet exercising an irresistible influence on listeners of all types.

Grandpa. "MINE'S DOING 'FAUST.' WHAT'S YOURS DOING?"

BEETHOVEN
THE MAN AND HIS MUSIC

In memory of
TANNHAUSER
Murdered by the
London Wireless Orchestra
19th September 1923

...shall be filled with music'

(Longfellow, quoted by Arthur Burrows as a goodnight to 2LO listeners, 1922-3)

RADIO PICTORIAL
June 11, 1937

The flute section, showing Robert Murchie, principal flautist.

Trumpets and trombones in full swing

Sir Adrian Boult, the Symphony Orchestra's renowned conductor.

Eugene Cruft, principal double-bass.

View of the second violins.

The violas bringing sweet music.

Paul Beard, quiet, earnest, much respected leader.

Radio gardeners

"I EXPECT YOU REVEL IN THE WIRELESS GARDEN TALKS, MR. SPUD, WHEN YOUR DAY IS DONE."

"THIS AFTERNOON MR. MIDDLETON IS GOING TO TALK ABOUT THE CACTUS."

Mr C. H. Middleton's wireless talks gave a great boost to gardening as a hobby from 1936. In March 1937, when the BBC asked delegates to a conference of listeners 'Who are your favourite speakers?', Mr Middleton was one of the top two. In the same year the BBC (then becoming involved in listener research) even held a 'Middleton poll', when the great gardener himself asked listeners which of two times they preferred for his weekly talks. 'The BBC want to please you and I am quite prepared to do what I'm told as far as I can and to give you what you want.' Armchair gardeners flourished and *Punch* had his own views on them (*top right*, 21 September 1938 and *bottom right*, 24 September 1937). Real gardeners also felt the bracing effects of radio talks (*top left*, *Punch*, 5 May 1937).

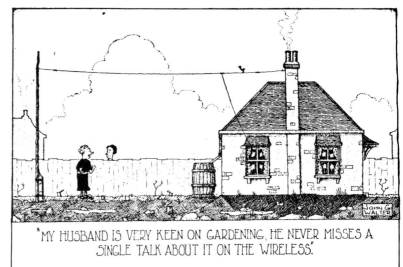

"MY HUSBAND IS VERY KEEN ON GARDENING, HE NEVER MISSES A SINGLE TALK ABOUT IT ON THE WIRELESS."

A Bridge four

"THE BRIDGE-HAND INTERRUPTED TO LISTEN TO A BROADCAST TALK"

SUNDAY BRIDGE
"Do you mind if we have the Archbishop during this rubber?"

'... IT IS ABOMINABLY RUDE TO LISTEN WITH ONLY HALF AN EAR.'

Bridge was another special interest which the BBC had covered from the earliest days (*top left*, broadcasting Bridge from 2LO. Players: Viscount Massereene, Viscount Castlerosse, the Countess of Ossery, and Viscountess Massereene, *BBC Year Book*, 1928). Sometimes the game provided an interruption to good listening rather than the subject of it. C. Whittaker-Wilson complained in 1934 of the 'habitual playing of Sunday-night Bridge through a broadcast service, a symphony concert, and the Epilogue. Calling "Three No Trumps" against the Apostles' Creed or the César Franck Symphony appears to me as idiotic as trying to read a novel against the Nine o'clock News. Yet half London does it.'

The violinist, Kreisler, who disliked broadcasting and 'one-eared people sitting in their carpet slippers and turning a knob', reported that in New York, when he had been out playing Bridge at the house of friends, they sometimes said: '"Let's turn on the radio and hear Toscanini with the New York Philharmonic" – the world's greatest conductor and one of the world's greatest orchestras. Presently, he added, some person would exclaim, "One heart", and another respond with "Two Spades", and the bidding would go on until someone would say, "Turn that thing off." And off goes Toscanini' (*Radio Magazine*, 1934).

The family approach...

From *The Radio Times*, 27 April 1928

PERSONALITY PARADE

For many years broadcasting artists, announcers and speakers remained rather mysteriously aloof – in the air, as it were! Now, however, these 'Stars of the Air' are becoming better known to listeners. They bring to the microphone so much more than a mere accomplishment or voice – they bring a personality; and it is often this personality which interests the listener and makes a 'Radio Celebrity'.

S O BEGAN the introduction to an album of cigarette cards of 'Radio Celebrities' issued by Wills in 1934. From the earliest days of broadcasting, the notion of a radio 'personality' had intrigued listeners and the BBC itself. What qualities made a 'personality' on the air? Were the same qualities needed to succeed on the wireless as on the cinema screen or on the stage?

It was the sense of the disembodied voice which generated interest in these questions, just as pictures without sound had generated questions about the cinema in the silent days of the screen. When the new medium of television added pictures to the disembodied broadcast voice, these questions were no longer asked, just as the equivalent questions ceased to be asked when the 'talkies' added a sound track to the silent image.

A few entertainment celebrities conquered each of the media in turn, adapting their talents from stage to silent screen; from wireless to 'talkies' and, ultimately, to television. Gracie Fields, Jack Hulbert and Cicely Courtneidge, 'Gert and Daisy' and a few of the dance-band leaders fell into this elect group.

The BBC was all in favour of mixing the media in this way. 'Welcome to Film Stars!', encouraged *The Radio Times* in January 1935. 'It is right that the film star in London should be invited to broadcast,' it stated, '. . . for, in the cinema, appearance is everything, and lack of intelligence can be covered by elegant movements. But the radio demands personality, without aid from smiles or dresses. To confront it is the ultimate test of the film stars; if they can hold their public on the microphone, they are something more than a nine days' wonder.'

Not all stars passed the test, whether they came to wireless by way of the cinema or the stage. Some did not even want to try the test; they stolidly refused to broadcast from choice. Sir Thomas Beecham originally turned up his nose at the idea, but later capitulated. Sir Henry Wood, whose name later became synonymous with popular classical music when the BBC took over the 'Proms', also stood aloof from broadcasting for the first few years.

As late as 1934 – the year when the Wills cigarette-card album came out – *Radio Magazine* featured, in an article called 'Why Don't They Broadcast?': 'three stonewallers; Serge Rachmaninoff, pianist; John McCormack, tenor; and Fritz Kreisler, violinist'. McCormack was reported to object to broadcasting 'because he is convinced it depreciates his value as a public entertainer'. Kreisler refused to broadcast, *Radio Magazine* reported, because he disliked the idea of 'playing to people who, sitting in their carpet slippers and turning a knob, would use his music only as a background to cards or conversation'.

For similar reasons some old-style comedians disliked broadcasting: they objected to using up all their gags on millions of listeners simultaneously. The best new wireless comedians were those, like Clapham and Dwyer and Flotsam and Jetsam, who, as *Radio Magazine* put it, 'could perennially find new and scintillating material for the audience of the New Age'. The search for new laughter-makers was to continue in each generation and was to lead before 1939 to Arthur Askey and Richard Murdoch.

In the beginning adaptability was almost everything, and the composition of the cigarette-card album itself revealed the mixed media in which 'radio celebrities' operated. The fifty stars (in a few cases, double acts) comprised:

> Two Announcers;
> One Station Director;
> Two Sports Commentators;
> One presenter of record programmes;
> One Children's Hour 'Uncle';
> One Children's Hour 'Aunt';
> Two 'Talks' experts;
> Fourteen serious musicians;
> Five stars of musical comedy;
> Six comic 'double acts';
> Seven solo comedians;
> Eight dance-band leaders.

Two types of 'radio personality' were missing from the album – the radio preacher and the politician. The BBC had, however, years before analysed the qualities required of them. The preacher was to be a man whose 'tone of voice' was that of 'the intimate and sympathetic talk'; he should 'introduce the address in a "human"

overleaf *A cartoon by Sherriffs, from* The Radio Times, *1 March 1935, showing fifteen 'singers of popular melodies'. Extreme left: Joe Crossman; top three, left to right: Brian Lawrence, Elsie Carlisle and Sam Costa; below them: Gerrie Fitzgerald, Les Allen, Harry Bentley and George Barclay; front: Sam Browne, Harry Roy (with saxophone), Peggy Dell, Nat Gonella (with trumpet) and Phyllis Robbins. Girvan Dundas stands behind the microphone and extreme right is Peggy Cochrane.*

Radio Celebrities

(from a Wills cigarette-card album, *c.* 1934)

SIR HENRY WOOD

DR. ADRIAN BOULT

B. WALTON O'DONNELL

CHRISTOPHER STONE

GEORGE F. ALLISON

JEANNE DE CASALIS

CICELY COURTNEIDGE

CAPTAIN H. B. T. WAKELAM

JACK AND CLAUDE HULBERT

GILLIE POTTER

TESSA DEANE

CLAPHAM & DWYER

way'. Preachers who had 'won a pulpit reputation by literary skill in the use of epigram' were warned, in the *BBC Hand Book* of 1933, that the microphone was 'a pitiless revealer of any hollowness that lies behind their tinsel'. Not many preachers had the personality of the Gospeller, Gipsy Smith, who could 'project his smouldering fires across the ether': most would aim humbly at the quality of 'audible sincerity'. One of the most successful radio preachers, the Reverend W. H. Elliott, was said to have 'the power of projecting himself into the home and, as it were, taking husband and wife or son and daughter as they sit by the fireside and speaking into their ears and into their very hearts'.

When the 'son and daughter' of the mid-thirties were not deriving spiritual comfort from the radio preacher, they were likely to be sitting by the fireside reading one of the new 'human-interest' radio celebrity magazines. Modelled closely on the film magazines of the late twenties, they were quite unlike the first wave of wireless journals of the early and middle twenties, which had concentrated on the science and gadgetry of the new and 'miraculous toy' rather than on the 'personalities' of broadcasting.

The first and most popular of the new-style journals was *Radio Magazine* – later overtaken by *Radio Pictorial* – whose editor was Garry Allighan, subsequently Reith's biographer. In his first editorial message he announced his aim: 'to concentrate all the accumulated human interest of radio entertainment within two covers'. It would not, however, be a 'fan' magazine since, Allighan flattered his readers, '"Fan" is short for fanatic, and this magazine is not going to cater for fanatics. . . . The average cultural level of the regular radio listener is . . . heightened by broadcasting more than the average cultural level of the regular cinema-goer is heightened by screen entertainment. . . . *Radio Magazine* will deal, in an intelligent manner, with intelligent matters for intelligent people.'

Despite Allighan's avowed aims, his paper immediately settled into the comfortable chatty routine of a typical fan magazine. Articles 'revealing the personalities of broadcasting' appeared in every issue: there were titles like *Backstage at a Broadcast,* describing 'the magic and mystery of radio performances'; *Eavesdropping in Radioland*, 'intimate gossip about star-life in the studios' by 'Man o' the Mike'; *Stars in their Gardens*, 'down the garden path' with (among others) Mabel Constanduros, Charlie Kunz and Commander Stephen King-Hall; *The Man Who Oils the Wheels at Broadcasting House* (he proved to be not Reith, but the chief superintendent of Broadcasting House, 'a very human being'). There was even an attempt to put glamour into the unexciting BBC staff

cafeteria with an article called *Feeding the Stars at Broadcasting House*. 'Eating is the great leveller – Producers, Stars and High Officials meet at the tables!' The article even went on to describe Reith himself at the self-service counter '. . . He picked up a tray, slithered it along, paid his bill, and carrying a vegetarian meal of beans and potatoes before him, walked down the room until he found a table . . .'

The subject of radio 'personalities' and 'radio personality' was not, however, confined to the gossip columns of popular magazines: it had attracted serious academic attention long before it was exploited by gossip columnists and cigarette manufacturers. In 1931, Professor T. H. Pear published a fascinating study, *Voice and Personality*, in which he set out 'to examine the extent to which a voice heard on the wireless can reveal its owner's personality'. 'How many persons, when they hear a voice "on the wireless",' Pear asked, 'visualise or guess at the speaker's appearance and personality?' In his experiment, carried out in Manchester in 1927, with the enthusiastic help of the local BBC station, 2ZY, Pear tried to find out. Nine unidentified speakers were asked to read the same passage from *Pickwick Papers* (selected as being 'a midpoint of literary taste: a passage to which the "lowbrow" would not, and the "high-brow" dare not, object'). The nine speakers were a policeman, a secretary, a clergyman, a business woman, an army officer, a judge, an electrical engineer, Mr George Grossmith, the famous humourist and actor-manager, and Professor Pear's eleven-year-old daughter. Listeners were invited to enter on a simple questionnaire-form, the sex, age, occupation, power of leadership, place of birth and place affecting speech of each speaker. Nearly 5,000 reports were received; the results were interesting, but on the whole indeterminate.

One appreciative reader of Pear's study was Hilda Matheson. As the BBC's Head of Talks from 1927 until 1932, she had more than an academic interest in the idea of radio 'personality'. Early in her career, she had concluded that her speakers would project their personalities 'naturally' only if, paradoxically, they used a carefully prepared and timed script. 'What was natural had to become artificial before it would sound natural again,' commented one of Miss Matheson's colleagues, summing up her methods. There was also the question of quality of voice: 'Why is it that some people, with voices like corncrakes or like sparrows, can hold the breathless attention of a vast audience?' she asked. 'Why should countless listeners write to a particular broadcaster to describe the help and comfort of her "kind" voice?' Such unanswered questions continued to puzzle Hilda Matheson after many years of experience and even after she had left the BBC.

Many writers on radio tried to pin down the elusive question of 'voice personality'. In December 1930 Charles Jones described, in an article for *The Radio Times*, his reactions as a listener to hearing for the first time on the wireless some of the most celebrated writers of the day, 'the Voices that Breathe o'er England':

Just as an expert will make clear the expression of character in handwriting, so a man, his mood and temper, are revealed to the painstaking listener by his voice. . . . Perhaps the most astounding voice heard by wireless is that of Mr H. G. Wells. . . . It sends one's eyebrows up. Is that squeaking, petulant thin cry the voice of the modern prophet? Mr Wells has written of himself in 'First and Last Things': 'Such a man as myself, irritable, easily fatigued and bored, versatile, sensuous, curious and a little greedy for experience . . .'. The rising note of curiosity, the avid haste of versatility, the impatience and emphasis of irritability are in the voice. No full sonority could carry this complex burden of endearing, human character. It is above all a human voice, not detached or aloof, but ardent with the boon tones of close acquaintance; the voice of the novelist rather than of the collaborator in the 'Science of Life'.

Another collaborator in that ambitious work, Professor Julian Huxley, possesses a voice of more assured quality. He is the specialist, as compared with the excursionist, in learning. His voice, unlike that of Mr Wells, is not a clash of overtones, seeking to be all things at once, but a confident and calm vehicle of declaration, with the sinewy utterance of authority. The sound of it is the stuff of persuasion. One feels the power of certainty in a voice which expresses the clear conviction of a searchlight mind operating in a chosen province.

Mr Compton Mackenzie brings to the microphone the lilting, careful voice of the artist. With him the idea never clamours to break the bonds of words, but seeks to settle itself comfortably into rhythmic speech. We have heard him speak of Manx cats in sleek, soft-padded prose, melodious with mystery-making vowels; of butterflies in flight with vivid arpeggii of fast-spoken words; of a leisured island in a lonely sea, with plaintive sentences like sustained chords, or the breath of a slow wind. . . . One is curious about the voices of great or well-known men, just as one is curious about the beauty of famous women. One collects such impressions as autographs are collected. These voices are, indeed, mental autographs, stored for remembrance.

Jones collected his 'mental autographs' exclusively from celebrities who came to the microphone with reputations made elsewhere. He might well have added the 'autographs' of politicians, that other category of celebrities missing from the cigarette-card album. Among statesmen Stanley Baldwin was the most successful broadcaster, the only one to grasp the importance of learning a new technique of speaking – rather than orating – in the studio. At the General Election of

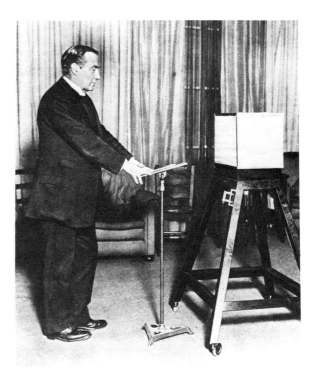

Stanley Baldwin reading his address to the public from 2LO on 16 October 1924.

October 1924, the first time that broadcasting was used for transmitting political speeches, only Baldwin accepted the invitation to give a special address from 2LO. The *Illustrated London News* reported that he did so 'with remarkable effect', whereas Mr Ramsay MacDonald (whose speech was merely transmitted from a public meeting in Glasgow) 'did not "broadcast" well, owing to his oratorical devices of raising and lowering his voice, turning from side to side and striding about the platform at various distances from the microphone'.

By the late thirties most politicians had some experience of broadcasting, and in an interesting article in *The Radio Times* in January 1937, the journalist Hamilton Fyfe looked back on the election broadcasts of 1935. In Fyfe's opinion, Baldwin was still in the lead of political radio 'personalities'. In the 1935 election broadcast

. . . he alone talked; the others orated. They wrote out speeches and delivered them in a platform tone. From a platform they would have sounded well. The audience would have collaborated. Cheers and laughter and interruptions would have helped the speakers out. Without such aid they sounded lamentably thin and dry.

Attlee read his at breakneck speed, as if he feared he might not get it all in – and finished five minutes before he need have done. Mr Greenwood was too statistical, Mr Lloyd George too emphatic, Mr Herbert Morrison too cocksure. Sir John Simon's tone was conversational, but his matter was not. Mr Baldwin would have done even better if he had been less resolutely political; but he was, in spite of that, far and away the most ingratiating. His effort came near being a chat, while the rest were – just speeches.

Fyfe went on to account for the success of Hitler as a radio 'personality', despite the fact that the Führer, unlike other successful political broadcasters, including President Roosevelt, did not adjust his usual ranting style of speech-making to the special conditions of the studio. The reason, Fyfe wrote, was that:

His broadcasts are listened to, wherever this can be arranged, by masses of people standing or sitting close together, thus creating in some degree the mass-psychology which a speaker requires. . . . Now we have in use a method by which those who seek to be leaders can put across to a whole People, not merely their proposals, but their personalities. By the voice more than by anything else is personality indicated. . . . You may train your features, even your eyes, to conceal what you think and feel. You cannot so control your voice. The blind judge people by their voices, and scarcely ever misjudge them.

A BBC publicity photograph c. 1930. The caption read:

Their pronunciation of the King's English must be faultless, whilst each must possess an adequate knowledge of the principal European languages – not least of their qualities is an abundance of tact and courtesy which makes artistes feel at home in the atmosphere of a Broadcasting Studio and helps novices to overcome the terrors of the microphone.

They are (clockwise from top left): Godfrey Adams, Freddie Grisewood, John Snagge, T. C. L. Farrar and Stuart Hibberd.

The blind listener had always won praise for his sensitivity to the nuances of voice; now the wireless gave him new scope for analysing personality as well as the companionship which friendly broadcasters could bring into the home. 'Even the occasional broadcaster, heard for the first time may establish intimacy,' wrote the blind Sir Ian Fraser, MP, Chairman of St Dunstan's, in *The Radio Times* in August 1934. '"Did you hear so-and-so the other night? What was he like?" "Oh, he didn't say much, but he was a friendly sort of chap." How often has this, or something like it, been said? Does it not go to prove that it is not always the matter, but more often the manner which contributes most to the successful broadcast? . . .'

For the blind listener what counted was the personality rather than the celebrity of the broadcaster, and for every famous name who featured in Charles Jones's 'mental autographs' there were brand-new radio 'personalities' who made their names on the wireless. Often they were much more effective broadcasters than the great established names from outside. The BBC itself was well aware that 'broadcast speakers, once in the studio, are broadcast speakers and not "eminent authorities",' as the *BBC Hand Book* put it in 1931, going on to observe

. . . it is personality at the microphone that counts, far more than names or deeds or elocutionary attainments. Yet each year as the power and uses of broadcasting are more fully realised, the harassed members of the BBC staff are more and more bombarded by those who sit in high places and upon committees, and who claim that Lord This or Professor That must alone represent their views at the microphone. It is a dangerous tendency, for the whole fabric of broadcast talks may crumble under the continued assault of speakers who do not possess sufficient personality to interest the public and whose aim is always to instruct and never to entertain. On the other hand, personality by itself clearly won't do: the speaker who puts rubbish and inaccuracies over the microphone with conviction and charm is an even greater menace than the dull and careful statistician. Somewhere between the two, between the dull authorities and the racy liars, the ideal race of broadcasters has to be discovered.

For many listeners the 'ideal race of broadcasters' had already been discovered. They were the BBC Announcers, quintessential 'radio personalities', yet anonymous. The BBC even brought out a group photograph of them – still individually unnamed – in *c.* 1930. Paradoxically, they were to be featured like celebrities and yet to remain nameless. 'This photograph will give many listeners their first glimpse of the Announcers, whose friendly voices are heard daily by millions the world over,' ran the caption to the photograph, 'a particular request by the BBC prevents us, however, from completing the introduction by publishing their names.' It was to take the threat of a world war to reveal the not-very-well-guarded secret of the Announcers' identities: on security grounds they revealed their names before each news bulletin. They also discarded their pre-war dinner jackets.

The identity of other radio personalities was never in any doubt. Among them were Christopher Stone, the BBC's first disc-jockey (an expression which had not yet been invented), A. J. Alan, the great teller of tall stories; the first sports commentators, Captain Wakelam, George Allison, the manager of Arsenal and the young John Snagge; Mr Middleton, the gardening expert; and Alistair Cooke, lately down from Cambridge and described by *The Radio Times* in June 1936 as 'that young man with a flair for talking'.

There were older men, also, who possessed that flair – eminent figures, distinguished in their own professions, but who were not widely known to the public until wireless turned them into 'personalities'. Sir Walford Davies, with his brilliant programmes on classical music, and Sir Oliver Lodge, the eminent scientist, both became popular with millions rather than the few thousands who would have known of them before broadcasting.

Rebecca West, the novelist and critic, described her attitudes to hearing on the wireless the voices of such celebrities in *The Radio Times* in December 1929. She could imagine vividly the physical presence and personalities of broadcasters even when she had never met them.

When I went into a room recently, knowing that Mr Vernon Bartlett was one of a large number of persons present, I was able to pick him out without difficulty, though I had never seen him before. I had not been deceived in the cherubic charm the wireless had suggested. . . . a talk records the personality of the speaker as a similar number of printed words could not do. I find that I do not remember what Virginia Woolf said in her biography of Beau Brummell the other night with anything like the detail with which I would remember anything that she had written; but while I was listening to her I got almost as vivid a sense of her as if she was standing in the room. From the tones of her voice one realised her fineness, her fastidiousness, her inheritance of a great cultural tradition and, over and above everything else, the light grace with which she can run on ahead of the ordinary person's understanding and point out some new aspect of reality, which raises her from the category of merely charming persons to that of the great creative artists.

The miracle is that, on the wireless, one could 'see' Virginia Woolf so plain; and that one can see various other personalities so plain, I cannot help feeling that if one had never met Miss Sackville-West one would know from her talks on the wireless that she was tall, and dark, and brooding, slow-moving and graceful; and that when Mr Harold Nicolson

Alistair Cooke with the American ambassador, Robert W. Bingham, introducing 'The American Half-Hour' in 1936.

pops out of the wireless, as he seems to at each of his talks, not like a Jack-in-the-box, but like a chicken out of an egg, one could be certain, even if one had never seen him, that he was a masterpiece of elegance. And the other night I was listening to Mr George Bernard Shaw's 'Point of View', when I remembered something about him that I had forgotten for years. He is to us nowadays a white-haired G.O.M., but when I heard that proud, challenging voice, that was plainly spoiling for a fight, I remembered that he was born red-headed and had tawny streaks in his beard when I first knew him. And I am sure this power the wireless has to evoke personality is not effective only with people one knows, is not merely a matter of reviving associations by reproduction of the similar speech.

Rebecca West was hardly a typical member of *Radio Magazine*'s 'audience of the New Age': she herself was already a 'personality' when she wrote her article in 1929. Ten years later, the 'ordinary listener' was beginning to claim a place in *Personality Parade*: if radio created or magnified 'personalities', it was also being claimed by 1939 that it was affecting the personality of regular listeners. In one of the few pieces of direct social research carried out in the thirties on the role of broadcasting in everyday life, Hilda Jennings and Winifred Gill of Bristol University concluded their survey with these words:

The present inquiry shows that broadcasting is already helping to develop personality, fostering critical and creative powers, strengthening and broadening the basis of home life, and helping to bring about that breadth of outlook and knowledge of affairs which become daily more necessary for responsible citizenship.

'This announcing business'

(title of *Radio Times* article, June 1939)

Proud of his versatility, the announcer was 'a man of many roles, a host, an adaptable speaker, often something of an actor and always a reservoir of fact'.

At first announcers, 'garrison troops of the studio', were anonymous, but in December 1936 *The Radio Times* revealed their identities. 'You know their voices, but you may not know their names: so we give you also dates and times when you may hear each of them announcing during Christmas week.' They were (*clockwise from top left*): Stuard Hibberd, Alvar Liddell, Frank Phillips and Freddie Grisewood. Losing anonymity did not mean abandoning authoritative Spoken English, very different from the English most people spoke, as Pont pointed out in *Punch* (*bottom right*, September 1936). 'Those blokes at the BBC 'ave all got such a saloon-bar voice, 'Enery,' a working-class woman complains in a very public-bar *Punch* cartoon of 1937.

THE BRITISH CHARACTER

INABILITY OF BRITISH BROADCASTING ANNOUNCERS TO SPEAK ENGLISH

'Dear men'

(heading of listener's letter to *The Radio Times* about announcers, March 1939)

POPULAR MISCONCEPTIONS A LONDON ANNOUNCER

'Say what you like, he's still my favourite announcer—
in spite of his photograph'

Pathetic scene in a broadcasting studio when a conscientious announcer
suddenly remembers that he forgot to say "Good-night, everybody," before
closing down.

WIRELESS ANNOUNCER

USED to worship actors,
Used to worship stars,
Used to wait at stage-doors
By their motor-cars,
Then I fell a victim
To a movie-man,
I became a raving, craving
Valentino fan,
Till I changed and made another choice—
Now it's not a Man, it's just a Voice.

Wireless Announcer!
Perfect pronouncer!
I worship you!
(*Voce, not out*, 2) HERBERT FARJEON

Radio artistes

The caption to Ginsbury's drawing of Mabel Constanduros (*bottom left*, *The Radio Times* 1928) described her as 'first among the stars whom broadcasting raised to their due place in the firmament'. *Below*: opening lines of a 'Mrs. Buggins' radio revue broadcast on 19 July 1929.

A VOICE: Mrs. Buggins! You're wanted at the BBC.

MRS BUGGINS: 'Ave I got to go now?

A VOICE: I'm afraid you're late as it is.

MRS BUGGINS: Can't I slip into my blue velvet?

A VOICE: They're waiting for you now—

MRS BUGGINS: Oh, well, it can't be helped, I s'pose – Alfie – if you so much as *touch* that pail of water while I'm away – I'll . . .

(Fade out Mrs. Buggins and fade in Opening Chorus.)

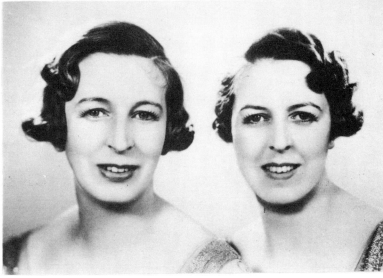

'By the term personality we mean today characteristics of a person that distinguish him or her sharply from other people,' wrote Eric Maschwitz, Head of BBC Variety, in *The Radio Times* in September 1935, boldly stating the obvious.

'If we say that Gracie Fields, for instance, is one of the outstanding personalities of the music-hall we mean that she possesses gifts, mannerisms and attractions which are peculiar to herself, The "personalities" of broadcasting are artists like Mabel Constanduros, Tommy Handley, Stainless Stephen, Claude Dampier, Arthur Marshall, Ronald Frankau, Gillie Potter, Elsie and Doris Waters, and Leonard Henry, whose performances are all highly individual; if you were to switch on your set during their performance you would have no difficulty in distinguishing at once who was speaking or singing.'

For many keen listeners merely 'distinguishing' between the voices was not enough and by the mid 1930s popular radio magazines were inviting readers to 'read about the stars you've heard'. As one 'Radio Who's Who' put it: '. . . the radio artistes are always shrouded in a veil of mystery . . . the public knows little of their "other lives" . . . [now] the veil is lifted. Many people who were just names will become realities . . .'

Geoffrey Edwards, Editor of the *News Chronicle*, described sitting 'in the Grand Hotel of Radio (Broadcasting House) waiting for the stars . . . But in this case the people who come and go are of far greater interest to me than hotel visitors.' The people Edwards saw 'come and go' might have included Harry Lauder (*opposite, above left*); the Western Brothers ('Cads Calling!') (*opposite, top right*); Stainless Stephen of the 'punctilious pronunciation' (*opposite, bottom right*); Henry Hall, leader of the BBC Dance Orchestra, first and most regular visitor to Broadcasting House (*top left*, appearing on an early Guest Night with Noël Coward, 27 October 1934) and Elsie and Doris Waters, popular and experienced radio performers, who were said to have been so nervous on their first broadcast that it made 'stern demands on the spurious mirth with which they essayed to conceal it' (*bottom left*, picture postcard, c. 1935).

Microphone talent

Maurice Winnick, Billy Cotton, Jack Jackson, Sydney Lipton, Lloyd Shakespeare, Marius B. Winter, Nat Gonella, Joe Loss, Lou Preager

'Day by day there continues at Savoy Hill the search for microphone talent,' claimed *The Radio Times* in 1928. 'It may surprise listeners to learn how small a percentage of those artists who come up for audition satisfy the high standard demanded by the BBC.' The artists on these pages passed the test. Many dance band leaders became radio stars, with a regular broadcasting time and a signature tune. In 1935 *The Radio Times* helpfully printed a list of them.

Harry Roy	Bugle Call Rag.
Jack Jackson	Make those people sway.
Roy Fox	Whispering.
Sydney Kyte	Tune in, keep listening.
Ambrose	When day is done.
Jack Payne	Say it with music.
Sidney Lipton	Medley, soldiers in the park.
Henry Hall	It's just the time for dancing.
Charlie Kunz	Here comes Charlie.
Jack Hylton	Oh, listen to the band.
Mrs Jack Hylton	This is the Missus.

Henry Hall also had a 'signing-off' tune, 'Here's to the Next Time'. He had left the BBC by 1936, the date of Sherriffs's 'band leaders of the air' (*top*).

'Can there be sex appeal on the radio, voices that allure?' asked one radio journalist. Vera Lynn provided one answer; aged nineteen in *Radio Pictorial's* 1937 photograph (*centre left*), she was then 'crooner' with Charlie Kunz (*second from right in Sherriff's drawing*). Gracie Fields (*centre right*), already an institution in the 1930s, received the Freedom of Rochdale in Coronation year and the BBC celebrated with a special programme, *Our Gracie*.

Tommy Handley did not become 'That Man' until *ITMA* started in July 1939, but he had been a radio star since the early days of 'Radio Radiance', a 1925 series of sketches and songs. *Right*, Tommy Handley with cast of the *How's That* Revue at Savoy Hill, 1926

Ambrose, Sidney Kyte, Jack Hylton, Carroll Gibbons, Roy Fox, Lew Stone, Herman Darewski, Harry Roy, Charlie Kunz, Geraldo

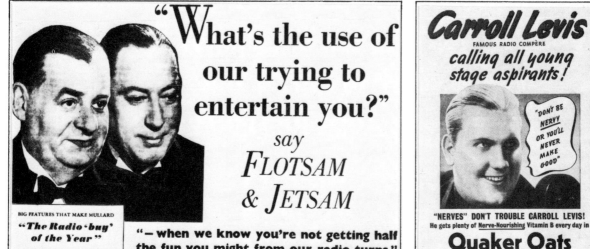

"**What's the use of our trying to entertain you?**" *say* *FLOTSAM* *& JETSAM*

BIG FEATURES THAT MAKE MULLARD
"The Radio-buy' of the Year"
"ACOUSTIC DESIGN." No unwanted

"— when we know you're not getting half the fun you might from our radio turns"

Carroll Levis
FAMOUS RADIO COMPÈRE
calling all young stage aspirants!

"DON'T BE NERVY OR YOU'LL NEVER MAKE GOOD"

"NERVES" DON'T TROUBLE CARROLL LEVIS!
He gets plenty of Nerve-Nourishing Vitamin B every day in
Quaker Oats

'Real radio personalities are as rare as buttercups in Iceland,' commented *Radio Magazine* in August 1934. Eric Maschwitz, Head of BBC Variety, who encouraged much new talent, would have agreed. So, too, would Carroll Levis (*above*), the Canadian presenter from 1937 of the long-running amateur 'Discoveries'. Frustrated performers often wrote to *The Radio Times*.

I wanna be discovered, Mr Levis,
Now don't you think I've got what it takes?
My family think I'm good, of course, that's understood,
But somehow I can never get the breaks!

Flotsam and Jetsam (*centre left*, Mullard radio advertisement, 1934) and Richard Murdoch and Arthur Askey (*bottom left*, broadcasting in *Band Waggon* starting 5 January 1938 from the imaginary flat in Broadcasting House) passed all the radio personality tests.

Voices to fill the hours

DAME NELLIE MELBA

MADAME TETRAZZINI

EVELYN LAYE

THE PRINCE OF WALES
left THE SITWELLS

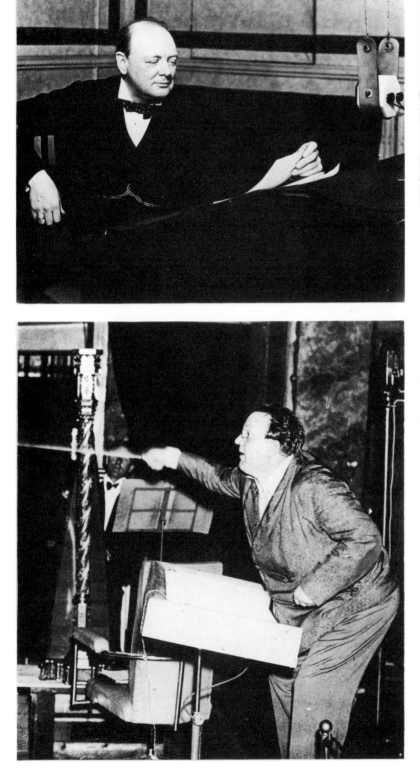

In the early days of the 'miraculous toy' many stars were happy to be photographed merely listening-in. Pictures of ear-phoned celebrities in the early 1920s (*opposite*) include opera singer Mme Tetrazzini and Evelyn Laye, musical comedy star.

Soon celebrities were lining up at the BBC's microphones, although theatre stardom was no guarantee of studio success. 'Personality has an almost uncanny way of revealing itself on the wireless, and of revealing its absence if it isn't there,' commented the *BBC Yearbook* for 1929.

Successfully revealed personalities included Dame Nellie Melba and the Sitwells (Osbert, Edith and Sacheverell), who broadcast together in August 1926 (*opposite*). *The Radio Times* was hardly referring to them when, in 1934, it said '[broadcasting] personality is not always individual, teams or congregations acquire it. Henry Hall's Band and St Martin-in-the-Fields may seem poles apart, but each is a composite personality. All these are friends: they keep you company . . .'. The Prince of Wales was featured as Number One in a *Radio Times* series of 1928, 'Masters of the Microphone'. Richard Tauber the singer (*left*) conducts a BBC rehearsal in June 1935; Winston Churchill (*top left*), as Chancellor of the Exchequer, delivers a Budget speech in April 1928. Sir Oliver Lodge the scientist (*above*) appeared on a list of favourite broadcasters of some East End factory girls in 1933. When asked the reason, they replied that although they couldn't understand what he said, 'he makes us think of queer things we hadn't thought of before'.

'Who's Who in the Broadcasting World'

(title of article in the *News of the World*, 18 November 1924)

The B.B.C. is always wrong.
"*I beg yours*"

'Flitting in and out of the rooms [of Savoy Hill] are some of the figures whose voices are familiar all over the United Kingdom.' *The News of the World* featured some of the flitting figures in words and drawings (*bottom right*) in November 1924. 'First and foremost' was Mr J. C. W. Reith, managing director and 'presiding genius' of Savoy Hill (*top right*, photograph of December 1926 when Reith's knighthood was announced and the BBC was about to become the Corporation). Other Savoy Hill personalities included Mr A. R. Burrows, 'Uncle Arthur', 'the original golden voice from 2LO'; Mr R. F. Palmer, 'Uncle Rex,' director of the London station and 'a fine baritone singer'; Mr L. Stanton Jefferies, 'Uncle Jeff', 'very popular among the young listeners-in' and 'possessed of a pleasant light vein of humour'; Captain C. A. Lewis, 'Uncle Caractacus'. Organiser of Programmes; the only full-time aunt, Miss Cecil Dixon, 'Aunt Sophie', said to be on the BBC staff 'to keep all the uncles company'; and 'last, but by no means least', Captain P. P. Eckersley, 'who combines with technical skill organising abilities and a delightful gift for entertaining . . . grandson of the famous Professor Huxley . . . he may be suspected of having inherited scientific genius'. By 1936 the tone of radio artists and journalists was more familiar. The title above Nicholas Bentley's drawing of Reith, from *Muddling Through* (1936), is 'The BBC is always wrong'. *Radio Pictorial* printed a chatty article by John Trent, 'BBC Bachelors on Parade' (1936), describing 'some of the men who have yet to tread the aisle to slow music' and 'to fall victim to Cupid's darts . . . Charming young men they are, with personality and good looks, yet they appear content with single blessedness.'

SOME PERSONALITIES AT THE B.B.C. LONDON STATION. BY OUR SPECIAL ARTIST.

QUAECUNQUE

DEO · OMNIPOTENTI
TEMPLVM · HOC · ARTIVM · ET · MVSARVM · ANNO · DOMINI · MCMXXXI
RECTORE · IOHANNI · REITH · PRIMI · DEDICANT · GVBERNATORES
PRECANTES · VT · MESSEM · BONAM · BONA · PROFERAT · SEMENTIS
VT · IMMVNDA · OMNIA · ET · INIMICA · PACI · EXPELLANTVR
VT · QVAECVNQVE · PVLCHRA · SVNT · ET · SINCERA · QVAECVNQVE
BONAE · FAMAE · AD · HAEC · AVREM · INCLINANS · POPVLVS
VIRTVTIS · ET · SAPIENTIAE · SEMITAM · INSISTAT

The statue The Sower *by Eric Gill and the inscription above it, in the entrance of Broadcasting House.*

This Temple of the Arts and Muses is dedicated to Almighty God by the first Governors of Broadcasting in the year 1931, Sir John Reith being Director-General. It is their prayer that good seed sown may bring forth a good harvest, that all things hostile to peace or purity may be banished from this house, and that the people, inclining their ear to whatsoever things are beautiful and honest and of good report, may tread the path of wisdom and uprightness.

THIS lofty inscription, in the original Latin, still meets the eyes of all who gaze upwards when they enter the vestibule of Broadcasting House. 'Sir John Reith, no doubt, ordered that it should be placed there so that it should confront every one of his staff every time they walked into the building,' commented Kenneth Baily in a critical article. 'Britain's Watchdogs of the Ether', in *Radio Pictorial* in 1937. The admonition 'Lift up your eyes' thus preceded 'Lift up your Hearts', not used as the title of a programme until December 1939, after the end of the period covered by this book.

In 1935, one Latin word from the inscription, 'quaecunque', had supplied the BBC with a new motto, vaguely pious and piously vague. It took the place of the by-then seemingly out-dated original motto, 'Nation Shall Speak Peace Unto Nation', the choice of one of the first Governors of the BBC, the strong-minded Labour pacifist, Mrs Snowden.

What were the 'things . . . beautiful and honest and of good report'? And who was to decide which 'things hostile to peace or purity' should be 'banished' from Broadcasting House? Reith, with God-given confidence, was sure that he knew the answer to both questions long before the new motto was coined. 'The Broadcasting Service should bring into the greatest possible number of homes the fullest degree of all that is best in every department of human knowledge, endeavour and achievement,' he had told the Crawford Committee in 1925. 'Rightly developed and controlled, it will become a world influence with immense potentialities for good – equally for harm if its function is wrongly or loosely conceived.'

Garry Allighan, Reith's first biographer, wrote that the first day Reith stepped into the lift of Magnet House, years before Broadcasting House was built, he felt he was on a divine mission. He knew, too, that he had the power to fulfil it.

In 1923 he had been reinforced in his beliefs – if he needed reinforcement – by no less a person than the Labour leader, Ramsay MacDonald, just as he was later to be reinforced by the Conservative Leader, Stanley Baldwin. 'Keep up the standard of your service,' MacDonald told him, as one Scotsman to another. 'Do not play down. Remember that the great mass of our people really want good things.'

In practice, the Reithian concept of 'service to the ideal of righteousness' involved the BBC in broadcasting not only what was 'best in human knowledge, endeavour and achievement', but also 'a thoroughgoing, optimistic and manly religion'. The *BBC Hand Book* for 1928 included the following:

In a national service to which nothing that pertains to the life of men is foreign, it was natural that from the beginning religion should find its place in British Broadcasting. It could not be otherwise. Even if the programmes aimed only at providing education and recreation, religion could not be denied a place; but when those who were responsible for Broadcasting set before themselves the object of raising the national standard of values and of a constructive idealism, it was obvious that the religious service should be one of the regular programme features.

Religious broadcasting began in the first months of the Company's existence. The Reverend John Mayo, Vicar of Whitechapel, preached the first radio sermon in December 1922. Ten years later he recalled his impressions of the occasion for the Tenth Anniversary Number of *The Radio Times*:

I approached the microphone on the Sunday before Christmas, 1922, with much trepidation. At 5.30 p.m. on that day I came up from Whitechapel to talk to the children, and after my evening service I hurried back to the Strand to address the grown-ups. Heavens! How nervous I was! A tiny room at the top of Marconi House – airless, heated, a watchful controller with an equally watchful engineer, and – yes! those awful dangling mouthpieces which were the 'mikes' of the period. I had numerous letters by Monday morning's post speaking in terms of warm (really warm!) approval; and I felt enormously relieved. Radio Religion, thus begun, has grown in volume beyond all imagining. There can be no question of its value. I do not believe that many people have forsaken church or chapel for the service of the parlour, but what I do believe is that a vast body of people who never heard a word connected with religion from one end of the year to the other, now listen Sunday after Sunday to sermons by wireless, which for eloquence, earnestness, and Gospel truth have never been surpassed. And in addition, they have found themselves praying with the prayers, singing with the hymns. I only ask this one thing of my executors – that they put on my tombstone: He preached the first broadcast sermon!

By 1932 'Radio Religion' had become far more than the broadcast sermon. The *BBC Year Book* for 1933, reviewing the first ten years of religious broadcasting, summed up the history:

The simple religious address of those first days soon developed into the Studio Service; this again was supplemented by the outside broadcasts of services from churches. To these were added in the course of time, first a

THE EPILOGUEMETER FOR TESTING THE PUNCTUALITY OF THE EPILOGUE

mid-week service and then a short daily morning service; other services and religious programmes, occasional or regular, find their places in the schedule; and lastly, there is the Epilogue, a form rather of meditation than of service, by which the Sunday evening's programme is closed on a note in harmony with the day.

As early as 1924, the Reverend 'Dick' Sheppard earned for St Martin-in-the-Fields the title of 'the Parish Church of Broadcasting'. 'I suppose no greater opportunity for evangelistic work was ever placed within the reach of a religious organisation in the whole history of Christendom,' wrote Sheppard in *The Radio Times* in 1932.

Certainly under Reith's leadership the BBC had attempted to appeal to vast numbers of Christians of most denominations. In his introduction to the first *BBC Hand Book*, 1928, Reith summed up the BBC's attitude to

that branch of work . . . which . . . rests upon an instinctive sense of fitness – broadcast religion. . . . The policy was initiated, and persevered in, of broadcasting a non-sectarian Christianity, confined, in respect of doctrine, to those simplest essentials to which all Christians of the West can adhere, and thus able, with a participant congregation of millions, to maintain the devotional character which differentiates a service from a mere intimate talk upon serious things. Even with no articulate support there would still be a dominating 'consensus' in the old sense of the term.

This 'consensus' approach produced a very different pattern of 'Radio Religion' from Catholic broadcasting in continental Europe or Gospel broadcasting on American commercial radio. Its main weakness was a

prevalence of platitude. For one critic, at least, radio preaching was 'anaemic', doctrine 'watered down', and 'exhortations confined almost to the generalisation: "Be good and you will be happy".'

Despite such criticisms, by 1932 the BBC's religious programmes had received the official blessing of the Church of England. The authors of the Canterbury Report on the religious value of broadcast services and their bearing on public worship set on record that in their

considered judgment the effect of religious broadcasting has been exceedingly valuable. It had recalled to the acknowledgement of God many thousands who had, from various causes, been out of touch with sacred things. The appeal of God has found its way into homes and into hearts untouched by organised religion. We have had abundant evidence from many sources of men (the sons of Martha no less than the sons of Mary) *doing the work of life* who have paused to listen and take heed to the message. It has brought religion once again into the market-place. Discussions spring up (on points made in the preceding evening service) between men descending in the cage, in factories, under the lee side of a hedge, in bars, and places where other songs and subjects are usually heard and discussed.

The Radio Times printed many letters which showed how much comfort the poor, the old, the sick and the isolated derived from religious broadcasting. In February 1930 'Two Young People, whose ages total 140 years' wrote from 'the fireside in a bungalow in Essex': 'On Sundays we always listen to the Children's Service, Lessons, and Night Service which we both enjoy. . . . The nearest church is four miles away and impossible to attend (that's where the wireless comes in). Before the bells leave off for the service the old lady says, "Put your pipe down, you don't smoke in church". Of course, being one of the dutiful, I obey. Now our only desire is that we may live some time to enjoy our only two possessions – our Old Age Pension and our humble crystal.' The letter was signed 'An Old Has-been'. The following January an eighty-five-year-old, 'constant listener to your Morning Service', wrote 'I do not get to church except for occasional Communion Services. I am sure a great many people like myself could pay the same tribute to its help.'

Several correspondents of *The Radio Times* reported radio 'congregations' in unusual places, like 'J.W.', who wrote in May 1924:

'Dear Sirs – While at Erith [Kent], the other day, I heard one of the wonders of wireless. While passing a public house, I was more than surprised to hear all therein joining in singing a hymn which was then being broadcast from London. Surely, the preacher never dreamt of such an audience?

Some radio worshippers commented on how much they appreciated being able to pray 'together' though many miles apart. 'After listening to the Reverend Pat McCormick's Sunday address I would like to express the great appreciation of our family of five sisters,' wrote an old lady from Herne Bay in February 1930, '. . . though married (except the writer) and living in homes in different parts of England we rejoice that we can still assemble at morning prayer together – household duties are laid aside for the time being and the family meets, as in days gone by when at one home, for prayer and praise.'

Unfortunately there is little surviving visual evidence covering such themes. It would have needed Victorian anecdotal painters to do justice to them. They would have done justice to the BBC Sunday also. Reith complained that the old Victorian Sunday had already 'come, in large measure, to be regarded as an archaic absurdity'. He wanted the BBC to revive it. 'There is no telling the effect,' he wrote in *Broadcast over Britain*, 'when for this brief period in a busy week the lamps are lit before the Lord and the message and the music of eternity move through the infinities of the ether, filling the whole earth with the glory of them, as once there appeared a glory in the cloud and a spirit moving upon the face of the waters.'

In the early days of broadcasting there were no Sunday programmes until about 8 p.m., and then usually only concerts of a serious nature with an address in the middle. On 6 February 1925 *The Radio Times* editorial consisted of 'An Official Announcement: The Religion that is Broadcast', which outlined the austere pattern of Sunday broadcasting: 'Normally there are no trans-missions during church hours. This rule is rarely broken, and then only when a complete religious service is being broadcast. There are two hours of specially chosen music on Sunday afternoons. Then in the evening at 8 or 8.30 a short religious service is sent out from all studios. Familiar hymns or metrical psalms are sung. Usually there is an anthem, and a fifteen minutes' address.' The editor added complacently. 'Our correspondence leaves no room for doubt that the distinctive character of Sunday programmes is widely appreciated and welcomed.'

The 'distinctive nature' of Sunday broadcasting was a perennial topic of letters – not all of them appreciative and welcoming – to *The Radio Times* and to the BBC itself. 'Why must Sunday programmes be so dull as Ealing is on Sunday?' complained one listener from London w5 in November 1928. 'My appeal to my radio is "I beg you take me from the sordid realities of earth into the realms of sweet make-believe, by the path that is called harmony." Pray hear my appeal lest I am again forced along the path of degradation by tuning in some joyous foreigner who was rendering "Ever so goosey" on the Sabbath!'

A more satisfied listener was W. S. Robinson of Wellingborough who wrote in 1929: 'With what pleasure I look forward to the church sermon on Sunday evening! I think myself, and no doubt many others too, that they bring back happy memories of choir days. On these Sunday evenings once again I am back in the old church of my native town singing the old hymns and wondering what has become of many old friends of twenty-five years ago. Many thanks to the BBC for these happy Sundays.'

By 1930 the pattern of Sunday broadcasting was beginning to relax a little. 'The BBC has always tried to frame these [Sunday] programmes in a way which might blend the maximum of wholesome brightness with the atmosphere of quiet leisure about the hearth,' wrote the music editor of *The Radio Times* in October 1930, when he introduced a series of Sunday evening orchestral concerts.

Gradually the BBC introduced more non-religious programmes on Sundays, but they had to be worthy of serious attention. 'From the very first, the Sunday programmes were something special,' wrote Filson Young in 1933 in the role of BBC spokesman rather than radio critic. 'The habit (by no means confined to England) of putting on better clothes than usual and having something special in the way of food on one day of the week is a very sound thing; and *broadcasting with us has always put on its best clothes on a Sunday*. Sunday afternoon is indeed a very suitable time for a programme of special interest. Outdoor occupations and amusements are limited. Sunday is still essentially a day devoted to the enjoyment of their homes by those who have them, and wireless is a very important part of the furniture of these homes.' Young went on to commend the weekly Sunday afternoon Bach Cantata programme and the Sunday broadcasts of Shakespeare plays.

The rules for Sunday broadcasting were subsequently further relaxed, but there were no Sunday morning programmes other than the Morning Service and the Weather Forecast until April 1938. Even then, the type of music programme transmitted 'represented the BBC's desire to lighten programmes without destroying the special nature of the day'. Radio Luxembourg was left to the bored and the ungodly.

The godly thought the BBC did not go far enough in making Sunday a special day. Others were shocked, before Radio Luxembourg and Radio Normandie started to cater for secular tastes, by continental stations accidentally picked up. One Coventry listener wrote to *The Radio Times* in March 1930: 'As I was adjusting my wireless set last Sunday afternoon to hear the beautiful Bach Cantata from the Daventry station, I inadvertently moved my indicator too far, when I was scandalised to hear syncopated dance music. I continued to listen until I had ascertained that it was not proceeding from any British Station. Could not the reception of profane music on the Sabbath be rendered more difficult by our British Stations causing "interference" on all the foreign wavelengths?'

After the relaxing of the Sunday rules in 1938 (which happened, incidentally, before Reith's departure) a Welsh minister wrote to *The Radio Times*: 'Being a lover of music I cannot help but appreciate Mr Charlie Kunz's ability as a pianist. But why do the BBC allow such an intrusion into the sanctity of the Sunday as that manifested on the morning of Sunday, October 16? Are not six days in the week sufficient to satisfy the needs of those who have a desire for jazz and dance music?'

Religious and aesthetic criticism often overlapped, a natural result of Reith's belief, shared by many serious listeners, that 'peace and contentment spring from the possession of adequate intellectual and spiritual resources and are not to be won to any permanent degree in any other way. They are the gifts of Jehovah-Shalom.' Writing less like an old-style religious prophet, Edward Crankshaw gave the same message in 1933, when he wrote: 'I don't know what impelled Marconi to strive for the perfection of wireless, but it certainly wasn't the conviction that men's houses should be filled with jazz and vaudeville.'

There was a direct link between religion and morality on the one hand, and aesthetics and self-improvement on the other. J. C. Stobart, the BBC's first Director of

'A writer complains that there is no great centre of culture and learning left in the world today. We trust that this tactless remark will not reach the ears of the BBC.'

Education, was also put in charge of religious broadcasting, thus helping to bring 'music, literature, art, horticulture, sport, science – indeed the whole domain of refinement and culture – within the radius of the humblest home', to quote a 'tribute from a Listener' in *The Radio Times* in December 1924. *The Radio Times* itself hailed Stobart's appointment as a proof 'that the BBC is not content to be regarded as a mere entertainer'.

'Entertainment' was a word which had already come under the severe scrutiny of Reith himself: 'A closer inspection . . . is sufficient to show how incomplete is the ordinarily accepted meaning [of the word],' he had written the same year in his book, *Broadcast over Britain*. 'To entertain means to occupy agreeably. Would it be urged that this is only to be effected by the broadcasting of jazz bands and popular music, or of sketches by humorists? I do not think that many would be found willing to support so narrow a claim as this. . . . Enjoyment may be sought, on the other hand . . . as part of a systematic and sustained endeavour to recreate, to build up knowledge, experience and character, perhaps even in the face of obstacles. . . .'

Obstacles there were in plenty, especially in attitudes to 'improvement'. It was permissible for Englishmen to be contemptuous in public of education in a way that was not possible with religion. Gordon Oakes went so far as to claim, in *The Radio Times* of 12 December 1928, that the average Englishman 'so loathes the word "education" that he is liable to knock one down if one mentions it'. One Sheffield listener who objected to this 'rather grandmotherly uplift-policy' – to quote a phrase of Norman Edwards, the editor of *Popular Wireless* – wrote a letter to *The Radio Times* in August 1928: 'We feel that the BBC is trying to educate us and we resent it. We want you to take a little more for granted; we should like to be treated either as educated people or irretrievably ignorant people. Give us all sorts of music and literature and jazz, and even talks, but please sugar the pill.' Edwards himself complained that most BBC talks seemed like 'the syllabus of a dry University Extension Lecture Course . . . lacking the most essential ingredient – popular appeal'. Another bored listener asked *The Radio Times* in July 1932: '*Must* truth speak as if from its boots?'

Punch had weighed in on this argument in January 1927 during the first days of the new Corporation. A facetious article called 'Trouble with the BBC' began:

There is much consternation, not to say perturbation, at Savoy Hill over the truculent attitude of the low-brow listener-in. The new BBC is determined, it seems, to supply the British public with mental uplift. The British public, on the other hand, refuses to be mentally uplifted. Whenever it finds that it is being mentally uplifted it complains that it is being morally let down. Shaking with rage, stern men from the outer suburbs write letters to the BBC complaining that an attempt is being made to educate them.

'Such an outrage on our liberties has never been attempted before,' they cry, 'and we do not intend to tolerate it now. Who may we ask, and what was DEBUSSY? Give us SOUSA every time.'

It was no accident that *Punch* chose music to demonstrate his theme. 'Music', as Reith had written in 1924, 'is the common property and common enjoyment of mankind. . . . Because of the very universality of its appeal a great proportion of broadcast programmes has been devoted to music. . . . It is an accepted fact that broadcasting has been the means of educating musically large numbers of people.' By 1932 *The Radio Times*, looking back on ten years of broadcasting, could boast that:

After ten years' experience we are at last seeing over here the results of the policy, so far as the broadcasting of music is concerned, of giving the public 'something slightly better than it thinks it likes': taste improves and with the improvement of taste comes increased enjoyment. There, we are convinced, lies the proper path along which the broadcasting of music must develop, if it is to take a place in the cultural life.

If music was the prime example of 'the things beautiful and of good report' solemnly commended in tablets of stone in the vestibule of the new Broadcasting House, what were 'the things hostile to peace or purity' which must be cast out? The 'peace' amounted in practice to the avoidance of controversy in topics of politics, religion and industrial affairs; the 'purity' amounted to the avoidance of improper behaviour in members of BBC staff. In an interesting article, 'That BBC censorship', in the *Radio Pictorial* of 17 August 1934, Oliver Baldwin, son of the Prime Minister, presented what purported to be a balanced view of a thorny subject:

Of course there is censorship in the BBC and it is very difficult to imagine how one could run a similar organisation without it, especially in these days of difficult foreign relations when any expression of opinion by a disinterested speaker may cause friction between two countries and lead to protests in the Parliaments of the respective countries.

Apart from censorship of talks on foreign affairs, there are other directions in which the blue pencil is used, and which are quite understandable and to be encouraged.

I refer to remarks on living persons calculated to bring those persons into disrepute or hold them up to contempt, which may fall from the lips of some hard-hearted speaker and legally be considered libellous.

There is the danger, in a vaudeville programme for instance, of some over-frank piece of humour that would upset the equanimity of any respectable member of the public and cause him or her to register a violent protest with the authorities.

There are sentences in some talks that have to come out because the speaker has seen fit to smile at that particular form of religious belief that is held by the majority of the public.

Ridicule of the medical profession or criticism of the forces of law and order make the hand of the censor shiver with apprehension.

Any attempt to advertise goods, private ventures or individual companies are naturally censored, since otherwise our radio entertainment would be worse than a walk in the country round suburbia, where hideous hoardings loom up on all sides of us and gawdy posters shout to us that we may – or even must – buy this and that and the other to enrich our homes, build our bodies or entertain our minds. . . .

Yet, Baldwin admitted, 'when an unemployed man's talk is so censored that there is no difference in the presentation of his attitude towards life from that of an employer of labour, it becomes extremely stupid'.

Reith himself had asked the Post Office to relax the ban on 'controversy' in political and religious matters. It was galling for him to be attacked for conducting a policy imposed on the BBC by the Government. 'The application of the present policy involves the neglect of many opportunities in forming public opinion in matters of vital importance,' he told the Post Office in 1928. Responding to this powerful argument, the Post Office agreed to withdraw the ban on 'controversy' in the light of 'the loyal and punctilious manner' in which the BBC had hitherto 'conformed to its obligations'. The BBC adjusted only gradually to the new freedom, remembering, to quote the *BBC Hand Book* for 1929, that programmes went 'direct into the homes of people of every shade of opinion, and it would [therefore] be a misuse of such a privilege to allow it to be the vehicle of unchallenged partisan statements. . . . The greatest care is taken to prevent listeners having conclusions thrust upon them.'

Some listeners thought that too much care was taken and charges of 'blandness' continued to be levelled at the BBC throughout the thirties. Charles Wintour, then a Cambridge undergraduate and later editor of the *Evening Standard*, wrote an article on 'Why under-graduates don't listen' for *The Radio Times* in 1937:

Another grudge against the radio which I often hear at Cambridge is really founded on dislike of our system of Government control of broadcasting. The restraint which the official position of the BBC brings in its wake is unpopular. The withdrawal of *Patriotism Ltd*, the fuss about Mr Muddlecombe, JP, being drunk, even the now long-past resignation of Vernon Bartlett, these are various instances of the too feminine delicacy with which the BBC has to pick its material. Undergraduates relish humour that bites – and the fangs of the BBC were all drawn long ago. . . . What would happen if someone could write radio plays in the manner of Low's cartoons? Or if some genius wrote another *Absalom and Achitophel* satirising, not seventeenth-century Monmouth and Shaftesbury, but two modern politicians? The BBC could not think of producing such plays however brilliant they might be. Talks and original drama are usually restricted to a lukewarm escapism and 'safe' ideas which dull the interest of a politically-minded undergraduate.

There was never any doubt about Reith's attitude to 'purity': all impropriety was 'banished from the House'. Every broadcasting artist had to agree to keep his or her material free from mention of 'marital infidelity, effeminacy in men, immorality of any kind'. This clause was part of the standard BBC contract. In 1936 the cartoonist of a leading daily paper took to drawing Reith as a straight-faced Mrs Grundy, complete with gamp, while in 1938 Herbert Farjeon, witty author of the lyrics for the revue, *Nine Sharp*, satirised the Reith regime (with no apologies to Gilbert and Sullivan):

DIRECTOR: When I was a bairn, I dwelt up north
In the Land o' the Leal and the Fairth o' Forth,
And a' through my youth in my ain countree
I polished up my English very carefullee.
CHORUS: He polished up his English very carefullee
DIRECTOR: I polished up my English sae carefullee
That noo I am the Ruler o' the BBC.
CHORUS: He polished up his English sae carefullee
That noo he is the Ruler o' the BBC.
DIRECTOR: I sent for some chaps to gi'e some chats,
And some aunts and uncles tae amuse the brats,
But the best of a' the folk I use
Are the braw bonnie laddies wha annoonce the news.

CHORUS: The braw bonnie laddies wha annoonce the news.
DIRECTOR: They say 'Guid nicht' sae beautiflee,
A' the lasses are in lo'e with the BBC.
CHORUS: They say 'Guid nicht' sae beautiflee,
A' the lasses are in lo'e with the BBC.
DIRECTOR: That nae man's morals should be lax or loose,
I decided when I built Broadcastin' Hoose,
So I summoned up my staff and said, 'Hoot, mon, hoot,
If I hear ye canoodlin', ye gang right oot!'
CHORUS: If he hears of us canoodlin', we gang right oot!
DIRECTOR: I sat upon canoodlin' sae successfullee,
There's never been a babby in the BBC.
CHORUS: He sat upon canoodlin' sae successfullee,
There's never been a babby in the BBC.

'Canoodling' meant, above all, being the 'guilty party' in a divorce case. The pioneer Chief Engineer of the BBC, Peter Eckersley, had to leave the Corporation after his divorce, even though he was a man of whom Reith had once said: 'His name and his genius are of

'That there is a Mrs Grundy at Broadcasting House is now held as a popular belief. Is it true?'

household repute.' In 1935 Reith received a letter signed by fifteen celebrities, including H. G. Wells, Oliver Baldwin, J. B. S. Haldane, Harold Nicolson, Vera Brittain and C. E. M. Joad, complaining about the BBC's 'undue regard to the private lives of its servants', and observing that 'not every departure from Victorian conduct may be legitimately considered to afford evidence of moral turpitude'. Reith, however, remained unmoved.

In his biography of Reith, published in 1937, Garry Allighan, editor of *Radio Pictorial*, reported that when he asked a BBC official for the reasons for maintaining these 'Victorian standards', he was informed that 'Sir John Reith's attitude to what are termed "moral delinquencies" on the part of his staff is due to the indisposition of which he would be conscious in inviting dignitaries of the church to broadcast if it was known that the "Directors" and "Announcers", who would have to deal with them in the studio, were "guilty parties".'

Meanwhile, in the Commons, Sir Stafford Cripps, himself later to be judged an austere figure, strongly criticised 'the position of the BBC's staff, whose private lives seemed to be subject to a dictatorial control and who suffered from restrictions far more stringent than those applied to Civil Servants while not enjoying the Civil Servants' advantages of security of tenure and definite system of promotion'.

Despite the so-called 'dictatorial control', however, there were always a few cranks who attacked the BBC for undue permissiveness, like a West Hendon listener who wrote to *The Radio Times* in February 1936, the same year as *Radio Pictorial*'s 'Mrs Grundy' cartoon:

The BBC, the strongest power in Great Britain, could exercise an influence to the good in the country; it has done nothing but perverting and corrupting the people's taste and I hereby express my contempt and abhorrence for the way the Corporation is managed. The BBC, always ready to encourage gross cruelty and never having a word for the other side, is a perfect disgrace to the country and directly responsible for most of the distress which is being experienced. I hope that sooner or later Broadcasting House will meet its reward by burning down to the ground: nothing better could happen to Great Britain.

Bad language and other kinds of coarseness which somehow slipped past the 'censors' of Broadcasting House, were another common source of complaint which helped to fill the correspondence columns of *The Radio Times*. 'I do beg you to keep out immoral plays, bad language and gluttonous drinking with hiccups,' wrote Miss Mortimer of Yorkshire a mere two months before the outbreak of the Second World War. She had an ally in another listener who was 'scandalised because the New Year [1939] was ushered in with the sounds of drinking and the coarse noises of the street'. He wanted church bells and an inspiring message. Reith had by then left the BBC but there had always been a small proportion of such 'offended' correspondents like the 'Disgusted Father' who wrote to *The Radio Times* in 1935:

When my boy was about eight years of age, some of his playmates asked him why he did not swear like they did. He replied, 'I am like my Dad; I can say all I want to say without that kind of language'. I wish that some of the artists who write and produce radio plays would learn the same lesson. Our English language is forceful enough, to those who know how to use it, without so much 'damn it' and 'go to hell'. Cannot somebody teach those fellows how to make language effective without making it offensive? Any man who habitually used such phrases would not be admitted into our house, and would be told why. But when I switch on the wireless he enters, and I am powerless. There are many parents who feel like I do; parents who want their children to appreciate the beauty of their mother tongue.

The 'mother tongue', spoken by millions who could not understand the meaning of 'Quaecunque', (and despite 'Disgusted Father's' low opinion of the BBC's standards), had in fact been a matter of constant preoccupation in the BBC from the earliest days of broadcasting. 'We have made a special effort to secure in our various stations men who, in the presentation of programme items, the reading of news bulletins and so on, can be relied upon to employ the correct pronunciation of the English tongue,' wrote Reith in *Broadcasting over Britain* in 1924. 'I have frequently heard,' he added, 'that disputes as to the right pronunciation of words have been settled by reference to the manner in which they have been spoken on the wireless.' Of course, Reith believed, the BBC's responsibilities in the matter were great, 'since in talking to so vast a multitude, mistakes are likely to be promulgated to a much greater extent than was ever possible before'.

Accordingly, in April 1926, the BBC set up an Advisory Committee on Spoken English under Professor A. Lloyd James. Tricky individual words were solemnly discussed and the 'correct' pronunciation laid down. The first list of pronunciations for announcers, published in July 1926, included:

gala	gáhla
Northants	Nórth-ámptonshire
char-a-banc	shárrabang

Announcers also had to learn to pronounce difficult foreign names and to cope with the 'minor inconsisten-

GIVE US A "WIRELESS" VOICE!

A page from the book *Daily Mirror Reflections* of 1934.

cies' of language between England and the United States, like the sounding of the 't' in valet and the pronunciation of Sioux as 'soo'. The idealistic Lloyd James even believed that radio, by standardising pronunciation, had a part to play in 'bringing closer understanding . . . between the British and American people' and in establishing a league of English-speaking nations 'speaking one clear, intelligible, living English through all communities in the dual Commonwealths'.

The first purpose of the Committee, however, was to keep announcers in line with 'current practice in pronunciation' and with each other. The right education helped. In his biography of Reith Garry Allighan told the sad story of one announcer 'who had managed to squeeze on to the staff without the preliminary qualification of a University education. . . . He was heard one night announcing that a certain politician had 'indickted' another. . . . The hierarchy met in solemn conclave and called for the erring Announcer's history. To their horror it was discovered he had never been properly educated.' The end of the story was not related.

'Announcers' English' always provoked correspondence in *The Radio Times*, as in this letter from a lady in May 1929.

I quite agree with your correspondent, 'A. F. Hole', when he states that the pronunciation of some of your announcers is very 'exasperating'. Is it really necessary to pronounce 'suit', soot? What has poor 'u' done that it should be pronounced as 'oo'? Modern is invariably 'mod'n', Education 'educat'n' and why not say 'gentlemen' and not 'gentlem'n'? It is really quite easy to use the *tongue* and give the *nose* a rest. It is a real treat to listen to Sir Walford Davies, with his charming voice and perfect enunciation.

Members of the BBC staff were, then, required to be pure in word (literally) and deed. In other respects,

also, broadcasting possessed moral implications. Several writers made the philosophical point that broadcasting was *intrinsically* moral since there was an infinite supply of ether and air-waves. No listener, therefore, could benefit selfishly at the expense of another. 'It makes no difference to the individual listener whether only one or one million people erect aerials and listen to the programmes radiated from the central source,' wrote the author of a pamphlet 'The Art and Technique of Broadcasting' published by the Marconi company in 1924, and went on:

There are only a few things in this world which can be enjoyed by the multitude without impoverishing the source of supply and thereby making it more difficult and more costly for others to participate in the same enjoyment, and broadcasting is one of these things. . . . Just as the rain from the clouds provides nourishment to any and every plant which has established its roots in the earth, so does a broadcast programme carry pleasure to any and every person who takes the trouble to install a receiving apparatus in his home.

The same point, with the 'nature' analogy, was developed by Reith himself in *Broadcast over Britain*.

For parallels [to broadcasting] we must turn to Nature . . . when the sun shines and the sky is blue, it is for all to enjoy . . . the broadcast is as universal as the air. There is no limit to the amount which may be drawn off. It does not matter how many thousands there may be listening; there is always enough for others, when they too wish to join in. . . . It is a reversal of the natural law that the more one takes, the less there is left for others.

The same argument was stated in a political rather than philosophical sense by Sir Michael Sadler, Master of University College, Oxford, in *The Radio Times* in December 1933: 'Broadcasting has increased enormously our power of sharing,' he wrote. 'Millions are admitted to a share in what, till quite lately, was the privilege of a few. . . . It may truly be called the communalising of opportunity.' He hastened to add that 'communalising' was not Communism.

Another supporter of the 'great moral virtue' of wireless was G. K. Chesterton. 'Wireless does not throw people out of work,' he wrote in an article called 'The Mystery of Broadcasting' in *The Radio Times* in 1932.

In its chief form of broadcasting it rather gives them work. There are not a thousand Lancashire lovers already getting a living by talking across six counties to Kent, until the BBC beggars them all by its one big machine. It really does find in the air a new field for employment, without taking away land or labour. . . .

'Quaecunque' could obviously be made to cover not only ethics, aesthetics and linguistics, but economics as well.

'The largest parish of all'

(description of 'the ether' by a radio preacher in 1928)

For early listeners the mystery of wireless carried with it vaguely religious associations. One evening in 1924 Reith described 'taking up our headphones . . . without having looked at the programme. It was the eve of Good Friday. In the pressure of business we had forgotten the Calendar. We heard a voice, not a pulpit voice, giving a quiet message about the meaning of Easter, which came like one of the voices that the Maid of Domrémy used to hear while she tended her sheep.' There were voices, also, in an early wireless advertisement, complete with church-style gothic arches (*bottom*).

The new religious broadcasting studio in Broadcasting House (*top*) gave the 'voices' a neutral setting. The designer was briefed to 'create a temple where Catholic and Calvinist, Jew and Moslem, should feel equally at home'. In order to 'command the assent' of most listeners, however, the line was drawn at Fundamentalists and Free-Thinkers, Christian Scientists, Spiritualists and Mormons. Maurice Gorham, *Radio Times* Editor, called the studio 'a monstrous piece of make-believe'.

The BBC's religious day started at 10.15 a.m. with the Morning Service, 'that lovely little service from Daventry' (first broadcast on 2 January, 1928) and ended with the Epilogue. 'With its quiet suggestions through hymn and reading' it 'brought the day's programmes to a close . . . a brief interval of simple beauty for millions who would be the first to claim that they are not religious.'

The BBC itself made wide claims for its religious broadcasting which brought 'religion to the hearthside as a source of comfort to the sick, the isolated, the timid among religious people, and vast numbers of irreligious or semi-religious outsiders'. It hoped that broadcasting would 'act as a stimulus and a means of recruitment to the Churches', but many churchmen had their doubts, like the vicar who sent this story to *The Radio Times* in 1934:

BBC (blithely brazen customer): Can you give me a Bible, Hymn Book, and Prayer Book?
VICAR: What for?
BBC: The wireless services.
VICAR: Do you come to church?
BBC: No, but I was christened there.
VICAR: When?
BBC: Forty years ago.
VICAR: What have you been doing since?
BBC: Waiting for the wireless!

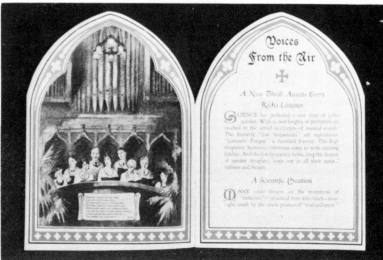

WHAT THE
OTHER LISTENER
THINKS

'What the other listener thinks';
A page where listeners air their kinks;
Where colonels grouse and rip and roar,
And maiden aunts lay down the law.

Now if I were the BBC,
And had such letters sent to me,
I shouldn't worry what to do –
Please the many or anger the few . . .

But for each and every item
That people wrote, who didn't like 'em,
From the programme I would strike 'em.
Oh! I'm sure that I'd delight 'em.

I'd drop light and classic music
Talks and concerts I'd delete,
And on the ether golden silence
Then would reign as king complete.

'W.H.H., WOODINGDEAN',
The Radio Times, 19 June 1931.

'WHAT is the listener like and what does he like? There is a veil that separates the two ends of the wireless chain.' So wrote the anonymous contributor of a facetious article in the *BBC Hand Book* for 1929.

From its earliest days the BBC made efforts to peer through the veil, although no one wished to tear the veil aside. Reith and his colleagues were well aware that in broadcasting 'the listener's like or dislike of the programme as a whole' was 'the programme maker's only guide to its effect'. There was 'no applause, no box-office receipts' by which to measure the listeners' reactions. Nor was there any advertising revenue to be derived, as in the United States, from ratings.

In these circumstances the roughest guide to listener satisfaction was simply the number of wireless licence-holders, and these grew from 2,300,000 in 1927 to 4,800,000 in 1932, almost doubling again by 1939. The nine-million mark was reached just before the war broke out. 'A steady increase in this number' was 'taken to indicate general approval and support of existing policy', said the *BBC Year Book* for 1932. 'But,' the writer wisely warned, 'this is not enough, the contemplation of these figures will not tell the BBC which part of its programme policy has won this approval, and in what respect a change would be welcomed.'

Listeners' letters were treated as the main source of intelligence, and from 1928 onwards a weekly page of *The Radio Times* was devoted to 'What the Other Listener Thinks'. By 1932 2,000 letters a week were pouring into Broadcasting House of which, a BBC spokesman hastened to point out, 'the really unfavourable letters do not amount to one per cent of the whole'. In 1936 the BBC received 160,000 letters excluding those received by *The Radio Times*, and it was claimed,

a little smugly, that 'all suggestions, criticisms and appreciations were recorded and most of the requests for information were met'.

Significantly, what was *not* claimed was that the BBC always acted on those suggestions, criticisms and appreciations. As early as 1932 the BBC admitted the importance of 'Studying Listeners' Tastes', the title of an article in the Hand Book for that year, but cautiously pointed out the drawbacks of building on the individual's preferences, as they were 'too slender a foundation'. Nor, thought the writer, could many listeners 'criticise helpfully the actual handling of a programme . . . a technical question of craftsmanship, to be thrashed out between experts'.

Another danger to be guarded against, Reith and his colleagues believed, was the practice of simply counting 'votes', the opinions expressed in letters, to determine programme planning, especially for minorities. There were two problems – first, 'most honest and sincere opinions can and do conflict with one another so radically', and second, 'the information gained in this way is too often purely negative. "I didn't like that programme. I don't know why, but I didn't," is not a very helpful foundation for building up a system.'

A very different reason for not placing too much confidence in letters as a means of determining listeners' views was expressed by Kenneth Baily in an interesting article, 'Mysterious "Mr Listener"', in *Radio Pictorial* in April 1937:

Letters can never be a comprehensive guide to the BBC of its audience's likes and dislikes. A large section of the audience never writes letters at all. Another large section is under the impression that it is useless to write. The section of the population which is not really a letter-writing one is at the same time the one which values broadcasting probably more than any other, because it cannot afford any other kind of entertainment or knowledge.

Nonetheless there were listeners and listeners, even within the group who did write letters to the BBC. Here are a few extracts from the Post Bag of 1937, printed in the *Hand Book* for 1938:

'It is becoming more and more palpable that you take sides against anything that tends towards the Left.'
'For some time past (together with many other listeners) I have been alarmed and annoyed by the attitude, almost amounting to Communist propaganda, of the BBC.'
'Just a few lines to let you know that I think the BBC is alright if only they would let the dance bands play every night at 6.0 instead of at 5.0.'
'I have now been a regular listener for ten years, that is from the age of twelve, and I should like to take this opportunity of thanking the BBC for the part it has played in my education, pleasures, and formation of my tastes and opinions.'

'I was glad of the Test accounts and had great difficulty in prolonging my illness so as to have breakfast in bed and listen in the height of comfort.'

When it came to matters of programme planning, the BBC, when it deemed it wise to look outside, always turned to special advisers. The opinions of 'Mr Listener' would be noted but not necessarily acted upon. Instead, the BBC invited representative 'experts' in different fields of broadcasting and public life to join a series of special Advisory Committees. Religious broadcasting significantly came first, in 1923, followed by Music in 1925. 'Such committees are awfully difficult to handle,' wrote Reith after its first meeting. 'Spoken English', with Bridges, Shaw and Kipling numbered among its distinguished and out-spoken members, must also have presented problems of co-operation. Whatever the committee the purpose was the same: 'to pass on to the BBC their [members'] great experience in their various spheres, together with suggestions of how this experience can be used to the best advantage in the new medium of broadcasting.'

The tone and composition of these expert committees hardly reflected the 'Other Listener' of *The Radio Times* correspondence column. Experts could be used to back up the philosophy of 'giving the public something slightly better than it thinks it likes', a fair contemporary summing-up of BBC attitudes to pro-gramme planning during the twenties. The ordinary listener was to be kept in his place: he could express his opinions (and it always *was* 'his' in the BBC's own writings) but like a child must not necessarily expect to get his own way. The *BBC Hand Book* for 1929 quoted an improving story to illustrate this point.

'Exercise is what you want,' said Mr Carter's friend in the *Dolly Dialogues*. 'Exercise is what I need,' he corrected. So in the case of the broadcaster who, in spite of the valued co-operation of listeners, is necessarily the actual chooser of the programmes. A false step would be taken if, carried away by his sense of what the public needs, he supposes it to be the same as what the public wants.

As the thirties went on, the down-trodden 'ordinary listener' acquired his (or her) own vociferous cham-pions outside the BBC. One of them was *Radio Pictor-ial*, whose characteristic article championing the non-letter-writing classes is quoted above. The editor reminded his readers that 'the average working man' was the piper who ought to call the tune and 'every person on the staff of the BBC, from the Governors down to the page boys, are on the wage-roll of the listening public,' although, he complained, ' . . . at the BBC they appear to think . . . that their masters are either the Government, the Church, or the combined educationalists of the country'.

In September 1937 the same editor, Garry Allighan, reported an imaginary court trial, 'BBC versus the Listener', in which the BBC as defendants were prose-cuted by 'Mr Lissner, KC'. The eloquent Mr Lissner, alias Allighan, is worth quoting at length.

I submit, m'lord, that the BBC have an entirely wrong frame of mind. Their mental approach to their job is in an absolutely false direction. The hierarchy of the BBC is com-posed of men who have been carefully hand-picked and, equally carefully, moulded into one definite pattern. I suggest they are men who, by birth, breeding and training, are citi-zens of a world that is entirely alien to the world of which most of my clients are citizens. They believe they are, and act as if they were, Our Betters.

I contend that as the listening public is four-fifths of the whole British public it must be an exact reflection of that whole. Now, m'lord, it is an established statistical fact that the British public consists of 85 per cent workers. That elementary fact is known to every entertainment-monger except the BBC who act as if the proportions were in exactly the reverse ratio.

They deliberately ignore the lowest common denominator and cater for the highest abnormal equation. They not only believe that London is Britain but that the West End is London. They have a Mayfair complex and their stilted Uni-versity accents are as artificial as their general concept of national life. . .

All the evidence points, relentlessly and inescapably, to the fact that the BBC ills grow out of the BBC concept that their function is to elevate, not entertain, the public. They have gathered around their brow an aura of superiority, supercili-ousness and saintliness which suggests a 'Not-as-Other-Men-Are' attitude. There is no snob so snobbish as a moral snob, m'lord, and I contend that the BBC believe themselves to be many cuts above the listeners and that their duty is to bring the listeners up to their lofty altitude of moral and intellectual grandeur.

Not surprisingly 'Mr Justice Fairplay', after hearing telling evidence from key witnesses 'Lux M. Bourg' and 'Norman Dee', found the BBC guilty of 'failing to perform their full duty to the listening public'.

The popular press did not always range itself against the BBC, however. Newspaper editors, too, were interested in finding out 'What the Other Listener Thinks'. After all, the 'Other Listener' *was* at times the 'Other Reader' of newspapers. Their interests were shared and sometimes identical. Several popular news-papers ran radio ballots on programme preferences, with the *Daily Mail* leading the way in 1927. There was no entrance fee, and the first prize was a modest £500. It applied only to programmes between 7 and 10.30 p.m., did not include Sunday, excluded religious broadcasts, and lasted ten days. The results were as follows:

1. Variety and concert parties.
2. Light orchestral music.
3. Military bands.
4. Dance music.
5. Talks, topical sport and news.
6. Symphony concerts.
7. Solos, vocal and instrumental.
8. Opera and oratorio.
9. Outside broadcasts.
10. Short plays and sketches.
11. Talk, scientific and informative.
12. Glees, choruses, sea chanties.
13. Chamber music.
14. Revues.

The *Daily Mail* was justified in saying that 'listeners want to be amused, not to be educated'.

Biggest and best of the ballots was that organised by the *Daily Herald* in 1931. *The Radio Times* gave full coverage to the event: celebrities like Gracie Fields cast their votes publicly to encourage the rest ('Miss Fields, not unnaturally, puts Vaudeville first', whilst 'a number of distinguished MPs have put Military Bands first'). The ballot ran nearly three months, every vote cost sixpence, and the first prize was a possible £15,000. The results were as follows:

1. Vaudeville (variety).
2. Dance Music.
3. News.
4. Light orchestral music.
5. Military bands.
6. Opera.
7. Symphony concerts.
8. Gramophone records.
9. Concert parties.
10. Talks.
11. Sports commentaries.
12. Plays.
13. Chamber music.
14. After-dinner speeches.

Sir Robert Donald, in a long article on radio ballots in *The Radio Times* in May 1931, commented severely: 'I cannot follow the claim that the winners of the tempting prizes which were offered "showed skill in judging public taste". No "skill" was called for, and the desire to help hospitals was subsidiary to the hope of getting a big prize for sixpence. As the paper was able to hand the hospitals £20,000 it is to be congratulated, but the result of the voting as an index to public taste and a guide to the BBC is subject to qualifications.' (An interesting sidelight on the ballot was that the BBC was criticised by another newspaper for alleged 'political partiality' in cooperating with the Labour *Daily Herald* in organising the ballot and thereby helping the newspaper to sell more copies.)

When Lord Knutsford, the newspaper chief, pressed Reith to classify the replies submitted in a listeners' competition on the grounds that he would 'never have a better chance of gauging popular opinion', Reith characteristically replied that his main interest in ballots and competitions was that they would stimulate interest and discussion of programmes. He did not want them to guide programme policy. A writer to *The Radio Times*, 'Jigsaw' of Crook, complained of this attitude in June 1932:

There appears to be one source of opinion completely ignored by the BBC – the popular ballots organised by sections of the Press. They have been unanimous in giving first place to vaudeville. Now I would submit that the competitive spirit does not invalidate the general verdict of the ballot. For any competitor will naturally give his forecast of the order of poularity according to his own estimate of the total vote of the competitors, and as the vast number of people like to believe themselves of 'average' opinions, they will naturally give the first places to those features in the ballot paper that appeal to themselves. This average opinion must therefore be largely reflected in these ballot results.

Whatever the BBC's attitude to ballots, it nevertheless knew that it needed *some* guidance from its invisible public. As Reith wrote in a letter to the *Daily Herald* in 1931, congratulating the editor on his new weekly feature of radio criticism: 'Any extension of intelligent and honest interest in broadcasting is warmly welcomed at Savoy Hill.'

'Nonsense! I don't agree'

The 'warm welcome' to listeners' opinions continued after the move to Broadcasting House in 1932, but a merely passive 'welcome' to letters in the Programme Correspondence Department was soon seen to be an inadequate method of determining listeners' views. Furthermore, the BBC wanted to be loved as well as respected. Reith's insistence on elevated middle-class standards in the conduct of broadcasts and broadcasters had, according to Kenneth Baily, writing in *Radio Pictorial* in 1937, 'made the simple people who don't write to the BBC consider broadcasting a lofty fortress, caring nought for an ordinary person's views. . . . For years the BBC was considered highbrow, supercilious

Actually, madam, only the last eight bars were faded out, and you will understand...

Gertrude Adcock

and autocratic.' Clearly the newly appointed (1936) BBC Listener Research Officer, Robert Silvey, whose sole duty was 'to get to know the BBC's audience', had prejudices as well as statistics to break down.

A year earlier Sir Stephen Tallents, who had made his reputation with the Post Office and the Empire Marketing Board, had become the BBC's first Controller of Public Relations, a job done earlier and in different style (not always to Reith's liking) by the Canadian Gladstone Murray. 'You want a consumers' council to guide the policy of the BBC programmes,' the *New Statesman* remarked, welcoming the appointment. Tallents more cautiously continued to emphasise exploration: 'As to people's habits there is a lot of information to be got indirectly . . . the Water Engineer at Portsmouth has just sent us a graph showing how everyone ceased to use water for cooking, washing etc. while the broadcast of the King's Funeral was on.' This was in line with tradition: 'The surrender of programme policy to a "plebiscite",' Tallents insisted, 'would undermine the responsibilities imposed on the BBC by its Charter.'

The same year, 1936, the BBC Annual for the first time contained a chapter called 'Public Relations'. It was a new chapter for the BBC in a broader sense: not only was it finding out what listeners liked in a more professional way, but it also realised it must be seen to be doing so. 'Public undertakings grow increasingly complicated nowadays,' wrote the contributor of this chapter, 'and at the same time a healthy public curiosity as to how things work is growing. . . . Public interest is not confined to the programmes alone. It extends to the BBC itself.'

First, there were sections on the BBC's journals, the *Radio Times*, with its 'freely illustrated Television Supplement included with the London edition'; *World-Radio* which gave the programmes of foreign stations all over the world; and *The Listener*, started in 1929, at 3d, a penny a week dearer than the other two, and 'designed to preserve the best of the talks broadcast during the previous week'. Next, supplementary publications to Empire and Schools listeners, announcements to the Press, visits by radio correspondents and groups of VIPs such as Members of Parliament to Broadcasting House, radio exhibitions and press conferences, all contributed to what the BBC described as 'the outgoing traffic of the public relations system'. In addition to these attempts to appeal to special groups the BBC had commissioned in 1935 'Voice of Britain', a prize-winning documentary film about 'the daily round of broadcasting' encouraging those who saw it 'to look behind the scenes'.

By then the BBC had its viewers as well as its listeners, although there was some doubt as to what the 'viewers' were to be called. Were they just 'lookers-in'? They were all in the London area and it was in London too that Tallents arranged a conference of 400 women to discuss the morning radio talks for housewives.

The listeners were still in the overwhelming majority, and in 1938 the BBC provided them with a new service, the Telephone Enquiry Bureau, to deal with individual queries. Typical questions, during the first year, included, 'Did the announcer pronounce "Winterreise" correctly yesterday?' 'How is Mr Hibberd's cold?' and 'Will Herr Hitler's speech from the Reichstag be translated and broadcast in full?' On the eve of the war the Oxford University Institute of Experimental Psychology was called in to develop projects to increase listener participation – an even more remarkable step than the appointment of Tallents.

Meanwhile, Gale Pedrick devised in 1939 a poignantly titled (with hindsight) summer mystery serial 'To be continued', with the listeners themselves contributing weekly instalments. The mystery was finally solved just before war broke out.

'We want more talks and debates on
economics and industrial history.'

'Oh, do turn Daventry into a dance station so
that we can dance from 8 till 2 every night.'

'Music and Drama—nonsense. We want hourly reports of
Stock Exchange quotations and latest prices.'

In my opinion three-fourths of programme time
should be given to brass bands.'

'The Scot dominates England, therefore the bagpipes
should broadcast more than any other instrument.'

'Please spread the Children's Hour over the whole
evening, and give us some helpful talks on knitting.'

'Give us plenty of good ballads and sea shanties
—they are the backbone of any good programme.'

'That 7 o'clock Announcer is such a dear,
I long for television.'

'Talks on applied science will add interest—let us have
courses on chemistry, electricity and metallurgy.'

'The Hellish Department'
(Lionel Fielden on the BBC's Research Department)

The man in control will be able to tell at a glance what proportion of the public is listening, and where.

"I don't care if you *do* disagree with the referee's decisions, you're not going to throw bottles at the radio!"

'Remember the cab-driver's wife from Wigan' was a condescending BBC adage (without Orwellian overtones) before regular statistics were collected to provide a true 'barometer of public opinion'. Meanwhile, advertisers made fun of listener correspondence (*above*, Grape Nuts advertisement, March 1933), while BBC satirists foresaw an Orwellian shape of things to come (*top left*, *Radio Times* cartoon by Eric Fraser, 1930).

PRECOCIOUS.

ALTHOUGH I am only twelve, I am writing to tell you that about one out of every ten wireless listeners like the programmes that you give. It is nearly all weak, dry music. The people don't want that, they want a good laugh. What is needed is more vaudeville and only a little music. The talks of abroad are no good to ordinary working people ; they also ought to be cut out. The Children's Hour ought to last about one and a half hours instead of three-quarters of an hour. I expect if the public read this letter they will agree with me.—*G. Bailey, High Street, Barnes.*

[We print our juvenile correspondent's letter as received and without comment.—*Ed., The Radio Times.*]

'ERNEST THE POLICEMAN.'

WITH reference to the Children's Hour on February 2, 'Ernest the Policeman,' my son, aged nine, asked me why the policeman was so common. My daughter, aged fourteen, has also passed this comment on several occasions when supposed policemen have been taking part in sketches, etc., and has even remarked : 'It makes me almost feel ashamed that you are a policeman, daddy.' Surely in this advanced age when children are more than ever taught to rely on the police, and to look on them as their friends, which they are, it is wrong to give them the impression that they are a common, ungrammatical body of men. I fully appreciate that policemen are supposed to be so thick-skinned that they are immune from any finer feelings, but, after all, they are human beings and a remark such as my daughter's above is a nasty stab that hurts.—'*Sergeant, Met. Police.*'

'Sobs and Sentimentality'

I WOULD like to reply to K. P. MacLeod's letter which appeared in *The Radio Times* of March 3. As one of the 'lads' referred to, I think I am entitled to say that dance music is in no way responsible for the 'growing spinelessness' (if any) among boys of school age. Those of us who have had a little education do not take jazz seriously ; nevertheless, we can derive some enjoyment from it. We realise that the words in some numbers are rather ridiculous, and regard them as humorous. Dance music is essentially a relaxing music, and it has a peculiarly soothing effect on one's mind. It has no effect on our spines, is not immoral, nor has it anything to do with religion.—'*Seventeen-Year-Old*'

Forgotten Places

I HAVE many friends in outposts of the Empire, and I thank you on their behalf for all the pleasure you have given them through broadcasting those everyday events, which though so ordinary to us, give them glimpses of the dear land they love so well—though Duty calls them far away to the forgotten places of the earth.—*D. A. Kendrick, Birmingham.*

Strong Drink

WITH reference to the otherwise admirable talk on sport during 1934 by Mr. Howard Marshall, on December 29 many who heard it like myself deplore and regret his reference in it to intoxicating drink. There are a very large and happily increasing number of people in this country intensely interested in all manly games who are connected with Sunday School Cricket and Football Clubs, to whom the reference would be very objectionable, and as one who followed his commentaries on the Test Matches between the English and Australian cricketers in the summer of 1934, I hope he will never again when broadcasting mix up imbibing strong drink with manly sport.—*J. W. Ibbotson, Sheffield.*

Buz-z-z

I LISTENED this evening to the Spelling Bee, and my pleasure was tempered by a feeling of disgust at the low standard attained by the players.

May I suggest a team of working men against a team of the 'educated' class ? My qualification for the former side is the fact that I am a fitter, aged 48, with an elementary school education only.

I could quite easily beat, unaided, any team that the BBC has ever broadcast. My score this evening, taking both sides, was 100 per cent.—*G. E. Salmon, Feltham.*

Reciprocities

WE like that nice Announcer
Who sends the cheery call
After the Daily Service—
'Good morning to you all'.
We wait to hear him say it,
And then, as is our due,
Politely we reply with—
'Good morning, sir, to you'.
—'*Us Twa*', *Helensburgh.*

Joke !

WHAT! the other listener thinks ?—*J. M. Saunders, Nuneaton, Warwickshire.*

THE MICROPHONE AT LARGE

'We are now going down to Brighton to hear a concert from the . . .'

How often have we heard that sort of announcement, and on our wireless set we have been taken here and there and everywhere? Now it is a statesman at a dinner, now we hear them clapping an encore at a dance hall, and in a few seconds it is someone in Edinburgh, or the beat of waves on the red rocks of a West Country beach.

How many stop to think how it is done? Who knows of that little band of 'OB' Engineers, as they are called, who have such an anxious time, on whom so much depends, and who work so often under very difficult circumstances?

from an article 'Outside Broadcasts,
by One Who Does Them', *The Radio Times*, January 1926

'OUTSIDE Broadcasts' 'OBs' – and the term was particularly English – were among the most appealing of all broadcasts, whether they covered what are now called dramatic 'media events', like the Coronation of George VI, or the regular round of football matches and concerts. The commentators and the 'little band' of 'OB' engineers were also felt to have the most appealing positions in the BBC. 'Who would not have a job that takes one to Twickenham one day, Epsom or Aintree the next, and Aldershot the day after?' asked the announcer Alan Howland, who was familiar with all the routines, in *Radio Magazine*, in May 1934. 'The work is forever full of variety, even though it has its elements of danger and periods of tiring work.' He admitted that there were humdrum periods too, like '. . . going over to the Savoy Hotel for Dance Music until midnight', but he did not dwell on these for long: his article was called 'Thrills – according to the BBC'.

Much was made in the first years of the contrast 'inside – outside'. Much as he enjoyed 'the sound of a good band in the open air with its suggestion of festivity and of gala', Filson Young wrote in 1933, 'broadcasting is essentially a thing for close quarters and indoors'. This was obvious enough: the microphone was not a megaphone. Nor were most outside broadcasts broadcast from outdoors, even if much was always made of 'the beat of waves on the red rocks' and the first outside broadcast to become an almost universally-known annual feature was the sound of the nightingale in the Surrey woods in 1924.

C. A. Lewis, the BBC's first Director of Programmes, added to the repertoire of outside broadcasts 'the ripple of woodland streams, the sighing of the wind in the treetops, the crash of the surf on shingle and, indeed, any of the manifold noises of Nature'. Meanwhile, Reith himself pictured 'men and women confined in the narrow streets of the great cities' listening to 'the voices of nature' brought by radio, though characteristically he warned that it would be a 'dire fate'

if people should 'prefer the song of the nightingale in the loudspeakers instead of in the lanes'.

Equally characteristically, football managers thought that it would be a dire fate if people preferred the football match in the home to the football match in the field, and because of press restrictions Outside Broadcasts of results were forbidden until January 1927, when the so-called 'seven o'clock rule' was relaxed. It was not only Nature, therefore, which came into the reckoning. Nor was it only the sounds of nature which listeners wished to hear. 'Those of us in the quiet parts of the provinces,' wrote a listener in 1932, 'longed for an occasional glimpse of dear old London, with its ceaseless roar and rumble, shrill hooters, and everything else that makes up its characteristic atmosphere.' The BBC Regional Programme Director in Glasgow wrote of the enthusiasm of Scottish listeners for whom London was 'the hub of their heavens'. This 'very elixir of life', as he called it, was duly administered in *In Town Tonight* which began with 'the mighty roar of London's traffic'.

There was also a quieter London, however. Every November from 1928 the Armistice Service was broadcast from the Cenotaph, in due course to the whole Empire. In that first year the Home Secretary grudgingly informed the BBC that they would be allowed to broadcast the service on the condition that no visible apparatus was employed on the ground except one microphone in the form of a lectern. 'The climax of the Ceremony is, of course, The Silence,' wrote H. H. Thompson, the Chief Engineer of BBC Outside Broadcasting, looking back in 1935 on seven years of experience in relaying the Service.

Its impressiveness is intensified by the fact that the Silence is not true silence, for Big Ben strikes the hour, and then the hubbub of sparrows, the crisp rustle of falling leaves, the creaking of their wings as they take to flight uneasy of the strange hush, contrasts with the traffic din of London some minutes before.

Naturally, viligant control of the microphone is essential: the muffled sobs of distressed onlookers, for instance. Audible groans near a microphone would be amplified, would give a false impression to listeners, would create a picture out of perspective as to the crowd's solemn impassivity and control of pent-up feelings.

The editor of *The Radio Times* commented gravely: 'Here is one of the great paradoxes of radio; that no broadcast is more impressive than the Silence following the last vibrating strokes of Big Ben.'

Many listeners to outside broadcasts craved neither urban ceremony nor pastoral idyll: they wanted 'intimate relays of popular events and everyday happenings'. In an article in *The Radio Times* in October 1934,

Laurence Gilliam, soon to be considered the outstanding initiator of radio features, envisaged broadcasting as 'truly holding a mirror up to life'. Britain was best at 'real-life' programmes, he thought (the article was a reply to earlier contributions on 'actuality' by German and American broadcasters). There were, for example, the 'village broadcasts' from Midland Regional, which presented 'the voices of the villagers, telling in simple, unadorned language the stories of their lives', creating for listeners 'a mental image of the place more truthful, more authentic, and infinitely more real than the most cunning descriptive writing could give'. The territory to be covered in such broadcasts was in no sense parochial: it was 'nothing less than the panorama of life itself. The life of city streets in all their roaring complexity . . . thousands of individuals with a story to tell . . . great crowds with a purpose and a personality of their own . . . forgotten villages full of buried treasure . . . tiny workshops where craftsmanship is still a practised ideal, and vast factories whose thunder is the means of existence to thousands . . . .'

Turning from the rhetoric to the facts, the *BBC Year Book* for 1929 described outside broadcasting as falling into two main categories:

There are, on the one hand, the concerts arranged by the BBC and presented in outside halls, where unrestricted space and the presence of an audience make possible the performance of more important musical works than could be undertaken even in the largest studio; and, on the other hand, events of public interest which broadcasting is able to bring into the homes of many who are unable to attend in person.

The *Year Book* gave examples of both categories: 'of the former,' it said, 'it is only necessary to mention the series of concerts from the Queen's Hall and the People's Palace, and the Chamber Concerts from the Arts Theatre Club. The second category requires rather more careful analysis, as it includes broadcasts of such contrasting types as Grand Opera, Searchlight Tattoos and boxing. Roughly speaking, there are three sub-divisions: sporting commentaries, musical events, and ceremonies.'

The first 'outside' concerts arranged by the BBC were transmitted during the season of 1924–5 from the Royal Opera House, Covent Garden, whose management had already proved friendly to the BBC in allowing direct broadcasts of opera from their stage at a time when most theatre managements were hostile to broadcasting. From the start the BBC had no difficulty in engaging the most distinguished conductors of the day to direct the BBC Wireless Orchestra, usually augmented to eighty on special occasions. Pierre

8.15 *on Wednesday, as Arthur Watts imagines it—*
'WE ARE NOW GOING OVER TO THE QUEEN'S HALL.'

Monteux, Ernest Ansermet and Bruno Walter conducted the first three concerts. Sir Hamilton Harty, Richard Strauss (conducting his own music), Honegger and Sir Edward Elgar followed in subsequent years, and the *BBC Hand Book* for 1928 reported that in addition to a performance of Schoenberg's *Gurrelieder* conducted by the composer, the 1927 concert series 'had a brilliant finish, in a programme of Wagner works, conducted by the Master's son, Siegfried Wagner'. 'Listeners all over Britain, as well as overseas, heard these concerts by wireless with a clarity and distinctness which are all too often lacking in the hall,' added the writer.

Since Savoy Hill had no studio capable of holding a symphony orchestra, all concerts arranged, or merely transmitted, by the BBC were of necessity outside broadcasts, but when, in 1932, the BBC moved to Broadcasting House the intention was to broadcast most concerts – at least in London – from the studio, the great new Concert Hall in Broadcasting House. However, the six-hundred-seat Hall could not be used for this purpose: the designers had provided insufficient accommodation for the orchestra and, as Garry Allighan related in his biography of Reith: 'In despair at last Sir John Reith agreed to the BBC renting the Queen's Hall and the new BBC Symphony Orchestra [it had been formed in 1930] giving all their broadcasts from there.' Thus the outside broadcasting of large-scale concerts perforce continued until the BBC acquired its studios in Maida Vale – an old skating rink – in 1934.

Little backstage glamour was associated with orchestral concerts, and on the whole little attention was paid to the problems of the OB engineers who transmitted them. It was very different with relays from stage shows. In 1929 *The Radio Times* ran a series called 'Moments in Broadcasting'. Number one was 'Backstage at the Coliseum' which showed what happened behind the scenes and how fascinating it could be for the listener:

The time is 9.54 p.m.; at ten o'clock an 'act' is to be relayed. . . . In a gallery high up on the 'OP side' of the stage two BBC engineers stand with their amplifiers and other gear. On the 'prompt side', his eyes fixed on a watch, sits the Assistant OB Director, timing the 'act' in progress. In a minute he will give the warning to be passed on to the Studio. . . . Behind the gaunt canvas scenery the great vault of the stage is in half-darkness and as quiet as a cathedral. The only splash of light comes from a dressing-table in the wings, where two dancers in tinsel skirts are putting the final touches to a 'quick change' make-up. On the revolving stage, which will swing into place at the touch of a lever, the next 'set' stands ready. 'Two-minute warning' speaks the voice into the telephone. The dancers on the stage have begun their final number. A dozen silently-moving stage-hands are ready to pounce. 'Is that Control Room? One minute, please.' In the Studio Jack Payne is already playing, ready to be 'faded out' as the Coliseum is faded in. A crashing chord by the orchestra and down comes the curtain. The stage-hands jump, the stage revolves, the next artist waits anxiously in the wings. The number of the turn goes up. Applause and music. 'Control Room? Fade over!'

By the middle thirties, the BBC was presenting its own revues and variety shows every August from Radiolympia, the great wireless manufacturers' trade fair, and itself a 'media event' par excellence. There were exciting live appearances of the stars who, in many cases, had made their names in the radio studios. In 1934 the bill included the sixteen Radiolympia girls, 'most of them blonde and all of them beautiful'; Tommy Handley, who was described as 'still in the front rank of comedians', (although ITMA was not to start for another five years); and, of course, Henry Hall and the BBC Dance Orchestra, fresh from their triumph at the Royal Command Variety Performance. A mock-up of a broadcasting studio was built so that visitors could see how a broadcast programme was

performed – 'and were able to see the different technique that is required when playing to the microphone, as compared with an ordinary theatre performance'.

Interestingly, in these Radiolympia shows, outside and studio broadcasting almost merged. As the *BBC Hand Book* for 1934 put it: 'Personalities of the air are to be personalities of the stage at Radiolympia.'

Paradoxically, the greatest broadcasting personality of all, certainly the most famous Outside Broadcaster, was not in the normal sense a radio star. Nevertheless an article about King George V in 1935 was called 'The Chief Broadcaster'. 'It gives me the greatest pleasure and satisfaction to come here today with the Queen for the purpose of opening the British Empire Exhibition' were the first words he ever broadcast – at the beginning of a speech delivered in Wembley Stadium on St George's Day, 1924. Writing in 1936, on the King's death, *The Radio Times* commented:

It is difficult now to recapture the full thrill and wonder of that historic moment, when for the first time in history millions of British people, of every rank and station, were able to hear the voice of their King. . . . There was general agreement that he possessed an ideal voice for broadcasting . . . beautifully modulated, deliberate, admirably clear and resonant, in every way consonant with the dignity of his phrases. One of the most satisfying discoveries of the broadcasting age was the fact that no one spoke the King's English better than the King himself.

Four of the twenty-two occasions on which the King broadcast were at Christmas when, to use his own phrase, he addressed his people as 'the head of this great family'. These were outside broadcasts which made listeners feel like insiders. Something of the majesty and mystery of the King's Christmas broadcasts is conveyed by this description in *The Radio Times* in January 1933 of the first and most historic of them:

Two microphones were in use for His Majesty the King's Christmas broadcast. These, and the red-light signal, were mounted in solid stands of Australian walnut. Framed, too, in walnut, was the printed 'reminder' regarding broadcasting procedure. His Majesty spoke from the Master of the Household's office. Next door, in the office of the clerk to the Keeper of the Privy Purse, the BBC engineers had established their control point. Once the red light had ceased its warning flicker, the King was in touch not only with five million homes in these islands, but with short-wave listeners throughout the Empire.

One woman who felt that the King was in touch with *her* lived in the Isle of Man. In a letter to *The Radio Times* in 1933, she described listening to the King opening the World Economic Conference.

I invited a woman to listen with me whose wireless is out of order. I knew she was interested, because she had been working in the canteen every morning providing coffee, etc., for the T.T. riders. Now, while we were listening to the opening of the Conference, and when the King started to speak foreign, I thought my hearing was playing me tricks. Quite pat came her reply, 'He is saying it in French.' Now the only French she knows is what she has heard on the wireless, as she has never even been to England. Isn't it wonderful?

It *was* wonderful that the woman could participate in such a remote occasion at such a distance, but as the thirties went on and such link-ups became almost routine from an engineering viewpoint, the BBC began to adopt an almost blasé tone. In 1937 the *BBC Annual*, summing up OB in the previous year, commented: 'A review of the year's work must not be taken up with an account of such recurrent broadcasts as the Trooping of the Colour, "The Derby" or the Cenotaph Service. . . . After fourteen years of broadcasting these must now be taken for granted, and attention must rather be directed towards new broadcasts and new developments in technique.' Perhaps it was natural that the BBC should adopt such an attitude to the routine in a year which had, as it observed, 'yielded its own crop of special events', which included 'the sombre pageantry of a Royal Funeral', the Accession Proclamations of King Edward VIII in London and Edinburgh, and the Abdication address. It is interesting that the writer went on to suggest that the Abdication was not a true outside broadcast since it took place in 'what were essentially studio conditions'. At such a time, he observed, 'the listener's natural desire for a wealth of detail from the "observer" – on such occasions more properly so called than "commentator" – must yield to the dignity of the occasion'.

One occasion famous for its lack of dignity was 'the Fleet's lit up' episode during the Coronation Naval Review in 1937. *Punch* described it joyfully as 'like the man in the top-hat slipping on the banana skin', adding, 'The BBC should do it again!' A full account of the episode was given by *The Daily Telegraph* in 1977, in its obituary of Commander Tommy Woodrooffe, the unfortunate protagonist.

As the Fleet was illuminated at dusk, listeners heard the BBC commentator, Commander Tommy Woodrooffe, say, from his old ship, *The Nelson*, anchored in the line of battleships: 'The Fleet is all lit up . . . by lights. It is like fairyland; the ships are covered with fairy lights.'

He repeated from time to time 'The Fleet's lit up'. Then, after a muffled conversation, he told listeners: 'The lights have been switched off. It has all gone and there is nothing between us and heaven. The Fleet has disappeared.'

The broadcast, scheduled to last fifteen minutes, was faded out after only four. The BBC played dance music and explained that the commentary was unsatisfactory and had been curtailed. After a high-level investigation the BBC accepted that Mr Woodrooffe had been overworked at the time and took him off the air for four months.

Far from deciding to follow *Punch's* advice and 'do it again', the BBC, as a direct result of the incident, introduced a new and more flexible de-centralised continuity system which would allow more immediate 'fading out'.

The BBC had always known that OB was a precarious art and in 1932 *The Radio Times* even invited their star commentators to relate their worst moments. Holt Marvell's worst was when he had to 'talk, talk and talk' when awaiting Amy Johnson's delayed arrival at Croydon aerodrome:

I described the air-port, the crowds, the sunset, the room I was in, how I had spent the day – anything and everything; I even gave a discourse upon aeronautics, probably the most inaccurate discourse ever broadcast. At length as I was on the point of 'passing out', the heroine of the evening arrived. I was never more pleased to see anyone in my life.

Captain Wakelam recalled setting fire to his trousers with a cigarette during an engrossing 'gents' double' at Wimbledon.

Unable to summon the engineer on duty outside the box without informing all my audience of my rather ridiculous predicament, I had to stamp and press the flames out whilst still keeping up my talk, and as some rubber insulating mats were also just beginning to catch as well, the atmosphere of the tiny hut was almost stifling. However, after what appeared to be several really frenzied minutes, I won through all right, though I welcomed even more than usual Borotra's final smash which allowed me to close down and really sort things out properly again.

The new art of the commentator called for such special skills and temperament that the BBC admitted that 'The perfect commentator, like the economic man so convenient to the hypotheses of nineteenth-century philosophers, does not exist. There are, indeed, commentators who can please all the people some of the time and some of the people all the time, but there never has been found, and there never will be, the man who will please all the people all the time.'

The very word 'commentator' was controversial: the same article continued:

The Oxford Dictionary defines a commentator as a 'writer of a commentary', a definition, of course, laid down before the days of Broadcasting. A commentary, according to this excellent and useful work, is an 'expository treatise, or a comment'. Were the BBC to announce in their programmes that 'an expository treatise' on the Derby or on the Boat Race would be broadcast, there would be trouble. 'Comment', too, is hardly satisfactory, and the use of the word resulted in a good deal of quite unmerited criticism after the first Broadcast of a Rugby football match because the nimble-tongued gentleman in the observation box gave his hearers a thrilling picture of the game but did not, while play was in progress, give his own views of what ought, or ought not, to have been done. It was, in fact, a narrative and not a commentary. He and all his species are, strictly speaking, narrators and not commentators. Still, the English language gives one every excuse for using a word in a sense somewhat different from its classical definition.

Whatever else the 'perfect commentator' could or could not do, he had to be a keen and knowledgeable sportsman. Month in, month out, he had to broadcast commentary on football, rugby, tennis, racing, the Boat Race and boxing. One striking result of the intensive radio coverage of sport was that the most unlikely people became interested in it, although not always intelligently so. In addition, the range of sports popular with listeners greatly increased. By 1939, in a Bristol University survey of listening habits, ice hockey, tennis, golf, boxing, the Derby, and the Boat Race were instanced as 'always listened to' by people who never had witnessed or ever expected to witness an actual contest. The survey gave the following examples from listeners:

'I always listen to the tennis commentaries, but confront me with the actual game, and I should be all at sea.' 'I always listen to golf,' said an old lady, 'but of course I've never seen a game and I don't understand really what they are talking about.'

Football has for long been an absorbing interest to men and boys, but women enthusiasts are for the most part new recruits. 'I don't believe there's a woman took any interest in football,' said one of them, 'before we had the wireless, not without she was proper sporty. Now most women listen – though I wouldn't go to a match myself.' 'I always listened to the Cup Final,' said another, '*always*. Of course I didn't understand anything about the game, but it was very interesting to listen to.' Most of the women listeners had no desire to watch the game.

The sport which, more than any other, has leapt into popular favour with men, women, and children is boxing. Here again, there is little desire among women to see a contest. In fact many emphatically stated that nothing would induce them to do so. . . .

It was not possible, so far as women listeners were concerned, to get any definite statistics. Some were ashamed of their interest. But in a group of ten middle-aged and elderly women, six said that they habitually listened to boxing, while a group of fourteen young mothers all listened, and some even took the wireless up to bed with them, when there was a relay from America.

The Boat Race figured prominently in most listeners' minds: it was one of the most successful of all outside broadcasts. In 1929 the *BBC Hand Book* had observed that it 'formed an admirable subject for a running commentary: it lasted long enough, but not too long, and, thanks to a fine technical achievement on the part of the engineers, the commentators were able to follow just behind the crews with a perfect view of the race'.

John Snagge, writing in *The Radio Times* in 1932, told readers of the advice he had been given by an eminent rowing Blue before his first Boat Race commentary in 1931 to 'keep commentating on the race, no matter if Hammersmith Bridge was on fire'. He was to follow that advice for nearly fifty years.

Just as millions of listeners who had never been to Oxford or Cambridge thrilled to the Boat Race, so thousands of women who had never been to a football match, 'the new recruits to the game', thrilled to the sound of Cup-Ties. The writer Winifred Holtby described how 'excited' she was when she listened to her first Cup-Tie commentary: 'I had not, I have not to this day, the remotest notion of what they were all doing. But I know that I was excited. No one could listen with cold blood and sluggish pulses to the quickening crescendo of that roar preceding the final shout of "Goal!" I wanted more goals. I didn't care who shot them.'

To the football commentaries of the late twenties and the thirties the English language owes the expression 'Back to Square One'. It began on 28 January 1927, the week of the English Cup-Tie Fourth Round, when, to help listeners, *The Radio Times* printed a plan of the ground split into eight numbered squares. The commentator often had a 'Number 2' whose main job was to interpolate discreetly 'Square One', etc. into the main commentary. The system was used for rugby also, and Captain Wakelam, the famous rugby commentator, wrote in *The Radio Times* in March 1932, in an article called 'This "Square 2" Business':

A clever No. 2 . . . can, by watching the game and listening to his companion closely, almost foretell exactly when his voice will momentarily pause, and so can come in with his 'Square 5' without in any way interfering with or muddling up the stream of talk; and he knows almost by instinct when his remark would prove superfluous and merely repetition. . . . He has instantly to realise the difference between an actual and a rhetorical question. 'That was a line kick, wasn't it?' obviously requires no answer but 'Someone's down on the ground. Can you see who it is?' must be replied to at once and sometimes in the excitement of the moment it is not always easy to understand exactly what the 'voice' is driving at.

Describing the positions at cricket was just as difficult, but by 1939 there must have been many listeners who had never been to a cricket match and yet who had become familiar with such terms as 'square leg' and 'silly mid on'. Cricket came to mean as much or more to many listeners as football. In the 1939 survey one listener claimed that it was more popular. 'You see, a poor man hasn't a chance to watch cricket, that costs money and if you want to see the thing through, it's two or three days . . . but now everyone can follow.' The most distant of all OBs came from Australia at the oddest possible times.

The BBC was always more cautious about racing, refusing persistently on moral grounds to broadcast the odds. The commentators had to work out a completely different technique from the cricket commentators or from John Snagge at the riverside. As the *BBC Hand Book* of 1928 put it:

The solitary commentator has by no means a clear view even in a short race like the Derby, and all his skill has to be concentrated into three short minutes; whilst in the Grand National only a tiny circle of experts is able to pick out the colours at the far end of the course, with the result that their

faculties, for a time at least, are concentrated on seeing rather than on speaking.

Of course, the whole question of seeing was fundamental to outside broadcasting. The perfect running commentary was the one which could make the listener 'see' the event. And, not surprisingly, the *BBC Annual* for 1936, one year before the Coronation, described outside broadcasting as 'in many ways the forerunner of television – for it must transport the listener from his fireside and make him feel that he not only hears but sees what is going on in the world outside'. Long before television's *Panorama* and radio's *Kaleidoscope* there was the sense both of panorama and kaleidoscope in outside sound broadcasts, and it scarcely needed pictures at all to convey the message when Neville Chamberlain arrived back at Heston waving an unseen scrap of paper in 1938.

'Peace for our time': Neville Chamberlain confronted by a barrage of microphones at Heston Aerodrome on his return from Munich in 1938.

This sporting life

'Well, no, I don't exactly do the commentary; I give the numbers of the squares.'

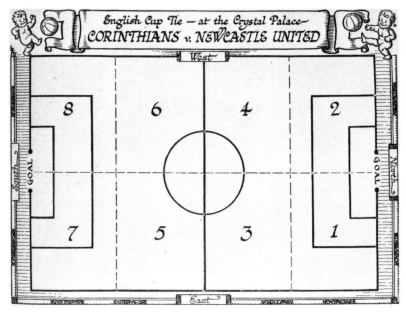

Sport was a national preoccupation, yet the outside broadcasting of sport – perhaps for this reason – had a stormy history. The Press prevented the pre-Corporation BBC from broadcasting football results before the first evening editions, while from time to time the Football Association was unwilling to cooperate with the BBC because of the alleged adverse effect of broadcasting on gates.

George Allison, Arsenal Manager, was a shining exception to the rule – and an able and enthusiastic commentator (*top right*, on the occasion of the first broadcast football match – Corinthians *v.* Newcastle United, 4th-Round F.A. Cup, January 1927).

Early broadcasters of football found it difficult to keep their eyes on the ball. *The BBC Yearbook* for 1930 vividly described their problems: they had to behave 'rather in the manner of the ride from Ghent to Aix'. They were expected to view the whole game, assess the performance of the individual players, 'detach themselves from their wedged-in positions in the crowd and sprint from the Stadium exit a quarter of a mile to the microphone'.

Listeners had their problems too. To help them visualise the game, *The Radio Times* advised them to follow the 'square' plans in *The Radio Times* (*bottom right*). The young man in the *Punch* cartoon (*above*, 1937) was one of the 'no. 2s' who called out the numbers.

*The Grand National, first broadcast in 1927, required less explanation
for listeners but a mass of activity behind the scenes.*

Great occasions

BROADCASTING THE TEST!

A glimpse into the future, by the light-hearted cartoonist of the "Daily Express."

Each sport required its own brand of commentator, though the BBC's Director of Outside Broadcasts wrote in 1937 that they all needed 'a pleasant voice, a quick wit, an eye for the significant detail and a vocabulary to describe it'.

Howard Marshall was the star cricket commentator, bearing 'the most important news of the day' to his eager listeners. Test matches had been staple broadcasting fare from the start and as early as 1926 a *Daily Express* cartoon (*above*) had offered 'a light-hearted glimpse into the future'.

For many the Derby was the greatest of all the great occasions (*right, Radio Times* Epsom course plan, 1927). Its broadcasting offered new settings for old jokes:

'JACKSON: May I take the day off tomorrow, Sir? My-er-grandmother-er.
THE BOSS: Don't worry about that Jackson. Just come here at 2.30 and ... hear all about it on the portable set' (*The Radio Times*, 1927).

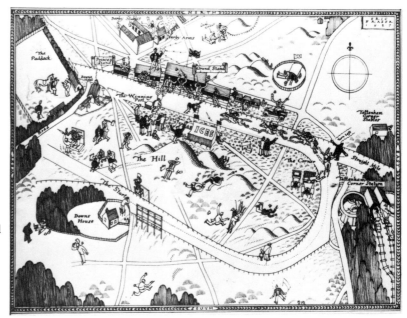

Armchair sportsmen

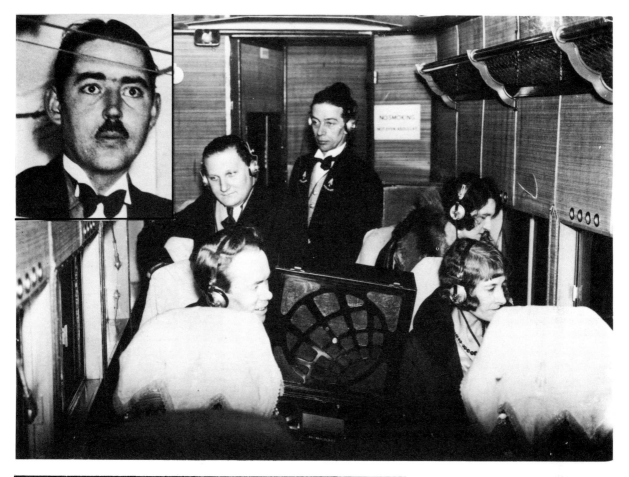

THE OLD BLUE.

In March 1931 fortunate passengers in a radio-equipped airliner could watch and listen to the Boat Race from above the Thames (*above*). Radio commentaries encouraged other types of armchair sportsmen also, as *Punch* pointed out in 1936 (*left*).

John Snagge, most famous of all Boat Race commentators, sometimes covered boxing events also. (*Top left*, formally attired for the Peterson-Neusel fight at Wembley in January 1935.) Boxing was the most popular radio sport of all: the London Electricity Authorities stated that during the Farr-Louis fight, relayed from Yankee Stadium in August 1937, the extra light and power used threw an additional load of 106,000 kw on the generators. Such statistics often provided useful information on the size of BBC audiences in the absence of 'proper' listener research.

'The travelling microphone'

(phrase used by Hilda Matheson, 1933)

'Entertainment by radio telephony may be shared by poor and rich alike,' *The Illustrated London News* proclaimed portentously in 1923. Its illustration, however, of what happened behind the scenes during an outside broadcast, 'the newest wonder of our times', was far more interesting than its text (*right*).

The first outside broadcast – a performance of *The Magic Flute* from Covent Garden – was scarcely designed for the poor, but very soon there was a wide range of outside broadcasts from 'an open-air tattoo of marching troops' to 'a run on a fast express' and 'a religious service down a coalmine'. The BBC's 'tentacles' were said to be everywhere.

Pantomime figured prominently at the right time of year (*below*, the BBC broadcasting *Jack and the Beanstalk* from Drury Lane, 1935). So, too, did the revived Royal Command Variety Performance which secured a *Radio Times* front cover (*opposite*) in May 1931. Popular access to serious music remained a source of pride and a cultural preoccupation of the BBC. 'Music-making has been taken into the heart of the East End itself . . . in a series of Symphony concerts organised at the People's Palace and conducted by Sir Henry Wood.'

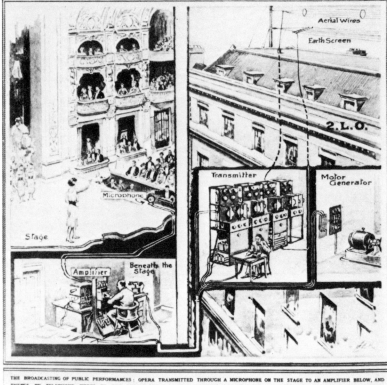

THE BROADCASTING OF PUBLIC PERFORMANCES : OPERA TRANSMITTED THROUGH A MICROPHONE ON THE STAGE TO AN AMPLIFIER BELOW, AND THENCE BY TELEPHONE WIRES TO THE BROADCASTING STATION (POSSIBLY REMOTE) FOR DISTRIBUTION TO THOUSANDS OF LISTENERS.

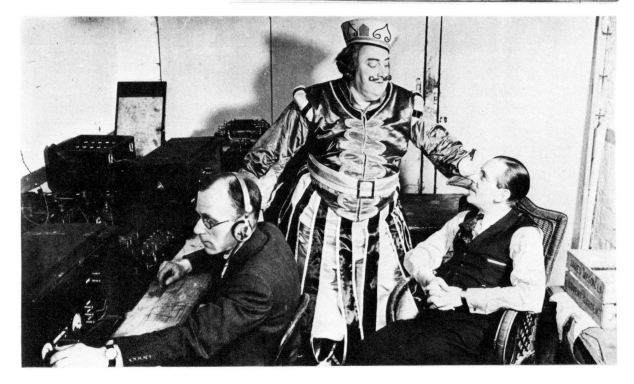

Radio Times, May 8, 1931.

Articles by W. Rooke-Ley: Ivor Brown: Percy A. Scholes: Ashley Sterne: Filson Young

THE RADIO TIMES

THE JOURNAL OF THE BRITISH BROADCASTING CORPORATION

NATION SHALL SPEAK PEACE UNTO NATION

Vol. 31. No. 397. [Registered at the G.P.O. as a Newspaper.]   MAY 8, 1931.   Every Friday. TWO PENCE.

MONDAY: ROYAL COMMAND VARIETY PERFORMANCE

'A nightingale sang...'

BROADCASTING THE NIGHTINGALE.
It is hoped that the song of the nightingale will be made accessible to listeners-in this Spring.

I.

II.

The Nightingale (*proudly*). "I WAS BROADCASTED LAST NIGHT— GREAT FUN!"
The Owl (*not to be outdone*). "AH! I'VE BEEN APPROACHED BY A RADIO COMPANY TO SUPPLY THE HOOTS FOR A SCOTTISH CONCERT."

One genuine out-of-doors 'O.B.' was the annual relay from the Surrey woods of the nightingale, accompanied and encouraged by the cellist, Beatrice Harrison (*top right*). Before the first broadcast in June 1924 a letter to *The Radio Times* praised the BBC for 'bringing to the ears of listeners, some of the voices of the multitudinous soloists in the great orchestra of the world ... a great work in support of those of us who have helped to bring about a new renaissance in the lore and love of Nature.'

Punch tried to see the nightingale's point of view (*above*, April 1924). He even wrote verses *To Philomel*:

...'*Linked henceforth with life's busy hum*
By valves and waves and "magna vox",
The nightingale will soon become
Familar as our hens and cocks.'

(*Punch*, May 1924)

Twelve years later the nightingale was still broadcasting and *Punch* was still commenting (*right* June 1936).

" NOW IS THAT THE NIGHTINGALE, OR MORE INTERFERENCE?"

'In Town Tonight'

'IN TOWN TONIGHT'

GRANDPA: *''Old 'ard Maggie. Another minute, and you'll hear the BBC chap shout 'Stop!' and we can cross in peace.'*

IN TOWN TONIGHT

A SCHOOLMASTER was examining a mixed class in an Elementary School. Ages about nine. The schoolmaster asked: 'Is London a town or a city?'
1ST SCHOLAR: 'Please sir, London is a city.'
2ND SCHOLAR: 'Please sir, London is a town.'
SCHOOLMASTER TO SCHOLAR: 'Why do you think London is a town?'
SCHOLAR: 'Please sir, if you listen to the wireless on Saturday night at 7.30 you'll hear – "In Town Tonight".'

(October 1937, from a letter to *The Radio Times*.)

The Radio Times columnist, announcing the new 'last-minute' feature show, *In Town Tonight* (first broadcast on 18 November 1933) hoped that 'what with it and the News listeners in the country will know far more about doing in the Big City than we ourselves, who, when we *are* in Town on a Saturday night, usually go to a quiet movie and then straight home to bed'.

The programme was a skilful blend of outside and studio broadcasting.

Not only Eric Coates's *Knightsbridge Suite*, but also the familiar 'mighty roar of London's traffic' and the Cockney flower-girl crying 'Lovely sweet vi'lets', were safely recorded and transmitted from the studio. Credulous listeners, imagined by *The Radio Times* in December 1936 (*left*), thought otherwise, and Michael Standing, at least, really *was* 'Standing on the Corner' on location (*above*, at Paddington Station, December 1935).

For C. F. Meehan, producer of *In Town Tonight*, every show was a first night; the programme was complicated '... a cue light to the wrong studio, an over-run at a street corner by Michael Standing, a missed cue ... in the gramophone room, would immediately throw the programme out of balance and ruin a hard day's work'.

A typical mixture of guests, a woman onion-peeler, an explorer, a fishmonger and actor Robert Donat – all previous 'visitors' – made brief comebacks for the 200th performance in May 1939.

'The Queen Mary: a floating BBC'

(title of article in *Radio Pictorial*)

'There is so much to be said about the broadcasts from the *Queen Mary* that we hardly know where to begin,' commented *The Radio Times* in May 1936. For her maiden voyage to New York this 'floating BBC' was equipped with a special broadcasting studio and 22 microphone points strategically placed all over the ship 'from the boiler rooms to the crow's nest'. The BBC was proud that the radio cables had been laid before the ship went into the hands of the decorators and 'are now permanently installed behind the artistic panels about which such controversy was raised'.

There was little controversy, however, about the BBC's achievement in presenting 'the greatest "actuallity" event ever' – 56 broadcasts in five days, including a grand radio tour of the ship from 'ballrooms and turbines . . . to chain locker and garden lounge'.

Henry Hall and the BBC Dance Orchestra were in attendance to play for the real passengers as well as for 'armchair' travellers like E. N. F. of Sanderstead, who wrote afterwards to thank the BBC for a 'delightful trip to New York via the BBC'.

NATION SHALL SPEAK PEACE UNTO NATION

Everyone knows that it was in November of 1972 that the foundation stone of the International Broadcasting Corporation was laid in Geneva.

So began a prophetic article, 'Broadcasting in 1979', by the novelist C. R. Burns, in *The Radio Times* of 20 September 1929. Burns deliberately chose November 1972 as it would be the fiftieth anniversary of the old British Broadcasting Company. He went on to describe the imagined ceremony in which the 'President of the United States of Europe' referred 'most felicitously' to the 'coping stone of the magnificent cathedral of world-peace erected by the League of Nations'.

Idealistic views on broadcasting as an instrument of peace were put forward from the earliest days of radio, long before the newly-incorporated BBC chose as its motto 'Nation Shall Speak Peace unto Nation' early in 1927. 'Fraternal', 'brotherly', 'fellowship', were words which appeared often in the early literature of wireless.

The Marconi company was one of the first to use such stirring language. In 1923 it brought out a leaflet, *Broadcasting*, encouraging potential customers to buy wireless sets, which ended grandiloquently:

Broadcasting brings the world into one listening family. Alexander wept for a new world; we today live in a new world, a world that is happier, more enlightened, and will be some day more brotherly, through the coming of the 'new thing under the sun', the Broadcasting of music, news, knowledge, and all that man is interested in, by wireless.

The same elevated note was taken up by the *BBC Radio Supplement* (later to become *World Radio*). In its first leading article in July 1925, it described radio as 'this instrument of international comity', a means of 'international intercourse'. Later the same year, in wishing its readers at home and abroad a Happy Christmas, it expressed the hope that,

More and more, as this season of friendliness and good will comes round, may the growth of international broadcasting promote throughout the world that spirit of understanding and of mutual endeavour which radio more than any secular agency – if, indeed, it should be called secular – is potent to achieve.

Reith must have approved of the Editor's tactful skirting around the appropriateness of the word 'secular' in relation to radio. He was also delighted when in 1929 the aged Poet Laureate, Robert Bridges, sang the praises of broadcasting in his Testament of Beauty:

Now music's prison'd rapture and the drown'd voice of truth
mantled in light's velocity, over land and sea
are omnipresent, speaking aloud to every ear,
into every heart and home their unhinder'd message,
the body and soul of Universal Brotherhood.

Reith himself believed passionately that 'wireless ignores the puny and often artificial barriers which have estranged men from their fellows', as he wrote in 1924 in a chapter called 'In Touch with the Infinite' in *Broadcast over Britain*. But Reith was in touch with the world too, and in 1925 took a lead in setting up the International Broadcasting Union in Geneva. This 'voluntary association of broadcasting authorities for mutual benefit' tried to create the practical conditions necessary for establishing international brotherhood by allocating wavelengths to countries in an orderly manner. Arthur Burrows, Reith's first Director of Programmes, became the first Secretary-General of the IBU. Although he stayed in Geneva for many years, he was not destined, however, to supervise the laying of the great foundation stone of which Burns dreamed. Instead, within a decade the League of Nations itself lay in ruins.

Even before Hitler's advent to power, just ten years after the Marconi leaflet was issued, the language

First Lady: *'I wonder what they're laughing at?'* Second Lady: *'Better not inquire. I expect it's too LO!'*

of internationalism, taken up eagerly by listeners themselves in letters to *The Radio Times*, could provoke some controversy. Compton Mackenzie, in hardhitting form, denounced the BBC in a commissioned article as 'the apostle of a watery internationalism which does more to promote war than all the armament manufacturers'.

Marconi himself, much as he liked to talk of internationalism, was also willing on the right occasion to talk to Mussolini. When he appeared in 1936 in Leslie Baily's 'Scrapbook for 1901', he recalled how he had felt, in those distant days, 'absolutely certain that the day would come when mankind would be able to send messages without wires . . . between the furthermost ends of the earth'.

In 1932 *The Radio Times* summoned the aid of no less a prophet than Professor Arnold Toynbee to 'settle the issue' of whether or not broadcasting favoured international understanding. 'The new social forces which we have evolved can be used with equal effect for good or evil,' he began his reply, and went on to say that while 'the new technique of flying has hitherto lent itself mainly to the service of War, the technique of broadcasting, which came to birth at almost the same moment, is helping to redress the balance by bringing people together – and this in spirit and not merely by ear'.

'There seems to be something about this art', he concluded, 'which makes "Nation shall speak Peace unto Nation" a singularly appropriate motto for any national broadcasting corporation.'

Mottoes were in fashion at that time; in the same year *The Listener* ran a competition for the best motto based on the initials 'BBC'. True to the international spirit, two of the winners were 'Bring Brotherhood Closer' and 'Bond Between Countries'.

The bond which the BBC favoured most of all was that of the Empire. As early as 1923 the Company began technical experiments which eventually led to the founding of the Empire Service. Reith believed the BBC had a duty to promote a greater sense of inter-Imperial unity and understanding. He dreamed of sharing with the Dominions and the Colonies the most evocative sounds and the most solemn ceremonies of the Mother Country – the time signal from Big Ben, the service from the Cenotaph – to be 'heard alike by the favoured few who are present . . . and . . . in due time by our countrymen in the very outposts of the Empire'. So Reith wrote in the summer of 1924. (The broadcast chimes of Big Ben had already welcomed in the New Year a few months earlier, though it was to be another three years before Reith broke down establishment prejudice against broadcasting the Cenotaph service.)

Such hopes were also part of a greater and more general dream, for Reith believed that 'Whatever is practicable within the Empire is practicable also between all the countries of the World'. The Empire provided lessons and examples for the rest of the world with the help of broadcasting.

Tom Shaw, Ramsay MacDonald's Minister of Labour in the first Labour Government, took up the theme more enthusiastically than the Treasury did: 'Think of the Prime Ministers, Viceroys, and Governors, all being able to attend an Empire Conference without leaving their posts!' he wrote in *The Radio Times* in August 1924. 'What is to prevent it? He would be a bold man who would maintain, with the present extraordinary development before his eyes, that the idea is impossible of realisation.'

King George V himself used broadcasting to address and thereby, he hoped, to unify the Empire as no other monarch had ever done before. His first broadcast, in April 1924, was an Imperial event – the opening of the British Empire Exhibition at Wembley. 'The Exhibition at Wembley strongly enforces the magnitude of the British Empire,' wrote the Dean of Durham wordily in *The Radio Times* soon afterwards, ' . . . and the broadcasting of the King's Speech . . . cannot but serve to accentuate beyond all preceding records the effect of the speech . . . as inculcating and illustrating the lessons which the Exhibition itself teaches.' That lesson, the Dean went on, was that 'The British Empire is the abiding guarantee of truth, justice and freedom all the world over'.

The first broadcast to be heard 'all the world over' was the King's speech at the opening of the Naval Conference in 1930. 'As always, the King's fine resonant voice came over perfectly,' reported *The Radio Times*. 'Listeners in the fog of London by-streets, in Australian sunshine, amidst the roar of New York, in the cherry-gardens of Japan – this first world-broadcast was a romantic occasion. The Broadcast was introduced from Savoy Hill by the Director-General.'

The next great landmark in Empire broadcasting, the inauguration of the Empire Service itself, did not come from Savoy Hill. Neither was it introduced by the Director-General, although by coincidence it took place almost exactly ten years from the day Reith joined the pay-roll of the BBC. Ten years later, in December 1942, the wartime *Radio Times* looked back on the historic night:

What years they have been! On 19 December 1932, when Mr C. G. Graves, the first Empire Service Director (now Sir Cecil Graves, joint Director-General of the BBC), hopefully sent out his first experimental programmes to the ears of British listeners in every part of the globe, the world was at

THE BIRTH OF EMPIRE BROADCASTING.
DECEMBER, 1932.

the *New York Times* enthusiastically. 'His message, spoken at the end of a chain of greetings that miraculously girdled the earth, fired the imagination not only of Britain's twenty million listeners, but of countless hosts beyond the seas,' wrote Leslie Baily in 1935 in 'A Christmas Scrapbook' in *The Radio Times*.

Something of the romance and wonder that listeners felt in the early days of the Empire Service comes across in this *Radio Times* announcement of the broadcasting of the Armistice Day ceremony to the whole Empire in November 1933:

It is an impressive thought that it will be possible to keep the Silence, wherever Empire broadcasting reaches, at the same moment of time. This will not be practicable, probably, in such places as Vancouver, where 11.0 a.m. Greenwich Mean Time is 3.0 a.m. But for the greater part of the Empire it will fall within the waking hours. In Nigeria it will be midday; the Sudan and South Africa, 1.0 p.m.; in India and Ceylon, 4.30; North Borneo and Western Australia, 7.0; South Australia, 8.30; Melbourne, Sydney and Adelaide, 9.0, and in New Zealand and the Pacific Islands somewhere about 10.30. Empire broadcasting is making us realise the meaning of that saying about 'the Empire on which the sun never sets'.

The 'bond of unity' was soon to be put to the test: when those words were written, Hitler had already swept to power and Goebbels had taken over German broadcasting and was broadcasting propaganda in foreign languages by short-waves to many countries. At home there was a tacit agreement in the BBC that the motto, 'Nation Shall Speak Peace unto Nation', was becoming inappropriate and should be quietly and gradually dropped. As early as 1931 (see p. 229), the Cambridge undergraduate magazine *Granta* had headed its spoof edition of *The Radio Times* with the words 'Nation Shall Shoot Peas unto Nation'. (This, of course, may have been normal undergraduate irreverence rather than an early manifestation of anti-pacifism.)

The motto still had some support among readers of *The Radio Times* in 1933. One Londoner wrote in December: 'You have a great motto on the front page of *The Radio Times*: "Nation Shall Speak Peace unto Nation." These words should be spoken just before your announcer gives out any international announcement. I should like to hear more from the heads of the big Government Departments.'

With the final sentence of that letter Reith would have been in complete agreement. 'No response for three years,' he wrote many years later, in his autobiography *Into the Wind*, when describing his efforts to persuade an apathetic Cabinet to begin short-wave broadcasting in foreign languages to foreign countries. Reith believed that in this respect Britain should play

the top of the long slippery slope that has led to war. Hitler was about to seize power in Germany. On that very night the British Prime Minister, Mr Ramsay MacDonald, was broadcasting to listeners at home on the problem of unemployment. But the same years that saw a gradual deterioration and disintegration of the political situation also witnessed the rapid strengthening by means of radio of those ties of kinship which unite the world-wide British Commonwealth. The BBC short-wave service developed almost unbelievably, and by the time war broke out was ready to develop still further. Now that the BBC broadcasts regularly in 47 languages over 24 hours of every day, now that the short-wave service has become not only a bond of unity but a war-weapon of power incalculable, it is good to look back and realise what a great step was taken by those pioneers of a brief decade ago.

On that day in 1932, however, and, even more, a week later, when the King gave his first and most famous Christmas broadcast, 'through one of the marvels of modern science', no one was thinking of Empire broadcasting as a 'war-weapon of power incalculable'. 'Distant Lands Thrill to "God Bless You",' reported

Goebbels's game, except, of course, that the BBC would always tell the truth.

It was November 1937, when, as Reith put it, 'almost every month brought news of extensions of activity in totalitarian lands', before the Government agreed to make a start in foreign broadcasting. The BBC insisted that it should run the new services since 'the BBC would be trusted where the Government might not be'. At last Britain would have this 'war-weapon of power incalculable'. But at the BBC truth must always prevail. 'The aim of the new service is not to meet propaganda with counter-propaganda,' said the *BBC Hand Book* for 1938, 'but to secure a wider audience for a broadcast news service which has, in English, won a high reputation in all parts of the world for fairness and impartiality.'

The Arabic service of the BBC was ceremonially opened on 3 January 1938; the Spanish and Portuguese services for South and Central America in March; by September 1938, at the height of the Munich crisis, daily news bulletins in French, German and Italian were broadcast to Europe. No wonder *Punch*, looking back on 1938, could write in his *Almanack* for 1939:

> This is the year that made us tireless
> At listening-in to the evening wireless

By then war was only months away, and the prophecies contained in a remarkable article by Stephen King-Hall, 'The Uses of Broadcasting in War', were about to come true. King-Hall's article was written for *The Radio Times* in August 1929, within a month of Burns's unfulfilled fantasy of the 'Broadcasting Cathedral of Peace':

I wish to say at the outset of this brief attempt to suggest the position of broadcasting in any great war of the future which humanity may inflict upon itself, that in my judgement the invention of broadcasting is one of the most powerful preventatives of war now functioning in the world. When its possibilities in this direction are better appreciated than perhaps they now are, I anticipate that international action will be taken to co-ordinate what I will describe as the peace-maintenance forces of broadcasting. . . . In the meantime, however, the possibility of future war cannot be ignored, and it is interesting to speculate what would be the effect of war on broadcasting.

The last war . . . proved conclusively that the weapon of propaganda has become a most subtle, deadly and far-reaching instrument of national policy, and with the net of popular education spreading . . . a belligerent Ministry of Propaganda, suitably camouflaged under some respectable title such as Bureau of Information, will be a key Ministry.

In that Ministry the national broadcasting organisation will occupy many floors. Expert broadcasters, men of persuasive voices, artful talk-writers, will not be allowed to risk their bodies in the fighting lines, the nation will need their voices at the microphone.

The air forces of the belligerents will naturally make every attempt to seek out and bomb the enemy broadcasting centres, and these will probably be protected by having their power station underground. A government at war would use broadcasting chiefly for three purposes. Firstly, to hearten and inform its own people; secondly, to influence neutrals; thirdly, to discourage the enemy. . . . Government loud-speakers will probably be established outside every village post office and in public places. . . . In the late war, if broadcasting had existed, it is certain that Dutch loud-speakers would have transmitted many talks spoken in Dutch into British and German microphones. In order to gain the neutral ear, it will be necessary to sugar the pill, and a first-class orchestral concert may be the framework which will enshrine a passionate statement of war propaganda, artfully interpolated into the intervals between items on the programme. . . . A peculiarly unpleasant consequence of broadcasting in war will be the possibility of listening to great religious services appealing for victory being simultaneously conducted from several national cathedrals. . . . One may be thankful there are no loud-speakers in Heaven, for hell is the spiritual home of war.

The Cathedral of Peace would be built only on the ruins of war.

PANDORA'S BOX. 'Be a bit less gloomy – or I'll —' (from *Punch*, 22 February 1939.)

'A girdle round the earth'

(Shakespeare, *The Tempest*, often quoted in the early days of broadcasting)

The freedom to twiddle the knob of the wireless set and pick up foreign stations did not necessarily add to international understanding. There were difficulties of reception (*right*, *Radio Times* cartoon, December 1925) and there were enthusiastic bores who were more interested in totting up the number of stations they received than in anything the stations had to say. Bateman (*bottom right*) made fun of the listener whose wireless set was always better – if not bigger.

As late as 1936 the cartoonist Arthur Ferrier invented the 'Twiddleknob Family' for *Radio Pictorial*. The Family's not-very-sparkling dialogue consisted solely of comments about wireless reception. ('Listen to those bass notes. It's so clear it might be in the room' and 'What's the matter with the beastly thing? It won't get China!!')

Reith's sense that wireless was a force uniting nations and men, 'taking continents in its stride' and 'outstripping the winds', was too idealistic for the radio advertisers, whose copy was more down-to-earth. The couple in a 1929 Marconiphone advertisement (*below*) are praising their new set:

'I say, Jim, this is great!'

'Yes, we must have sampled pretty nearly every programme on the Continent in the last few minutes.'

"I know. And didn't you say it was only three valves?"

"Rather. Good enough for five, eh?"

"Those logging dials are such an excellent scheme, too. It won't take a second to find a station now – and, hallo! here's another!.... How wonderfully clear those guitars are. It must be Madrid. Let's jot it down."

Where Willie Scored.

With his little radio set Willie listens to his bed-time story from the local station without interruption—

Whereas, Mr. Millions has a set powerful enough to listen to the programmes of the entire radio world—and finds it almost impossible to get one clearly!

MARCONIPHONE MODEL 35

"THE MAN WHO BOASTS HE CAN GET TIMBUCTOO ON ONE-VALVE"

"I believe I've got America. I hear a persistent chewing sound"

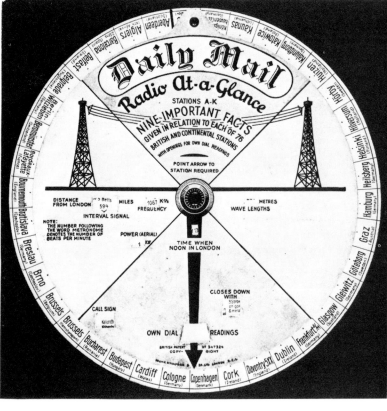

The new technology of foreign radio link-ups appealed to many – from the Prince of Wales to *Punch*. In March 1924 *The Illustrated London News* featured 'Mill Hill's First Royal Visitor' (*left*). In his speech to the schoolboys the Prince praised the school's wireless installation: 'I was interested the other day to hear that Mill Hill had got America. I think this school is among the first of the schools to wireless the Atlantic, and I congratulate you. This work is done by a boy (Mr C. W. Goyder) in his spare time; and I consider the proper and profitable use of spare time plays a very big part in education.'

The *Daily Mail* agreed, producing for its readers in 1932 a 'Radio-at-a-Glance' chart (*bottom left*), a 'girdle' in paper: 'By pointing the arrow at any one of the seventy-six British and Continental stations named on the disc, the listener could read off the station's distance from London, its frequency, wavelength, aerial power, call sign, closing-down signal, and interval signal, as well as providing space for his own dial readings.'

A cartoon in *London Opinion* as early as 1924 spanned the Atlantic (*above*), but an anonymous letter, quoted in *The New Statesman*'s 'This England' column, summed up a perennial problem of foreign listening. 'My knowledge of foreign languages is rather shaky and they always seem to be harder to understand on the air except when an Englishman is speaking.' (c. 1932)

The magic carpet

In October 1922 *The Broadcaster* called its editorial 'Exploring': 'Throughout all the ages of Mankind men have been possessed of "Wanderlust",' it declared, 'but many [now] explore thus: By the turning of a switch, the adjustment of a tuning coil, or condenser, many "Nations" journey – in the passing of a second of time – to lands afar. Many hear, and fancifully almost see, New York or "The land of the Rising Sun"; or travel to the West where the Amazon rolls in flood to the sea; to the Gateway of the East, Singapore; or to Iceland's one Radio Station.... All by the turning of a switch and the lighting of a Radio Valve.'

A 1928 advertisement for the *Lands and Peoples* Encyclopaedia borrowed the 'magic carpet' theme (*right*). It used the still undeveloped but eagerly anticipated new medium of television as a bait: both books and television would enable readers/viewers to 'see the world'.

Meanwhile they had to be content with radio. In 1935 *World Radio* carried an advertisement for the 'Transatlantic All-Wave Superhet model', 'the set that brings the World to your finger tips' (*above*).

In a *Punch* cartoon of 1936 a butler standing at the wireless asks the Duke, 'Do you wish me to summon Berlin or Rome, your Grace?'

See the World as by Television

Before your children have grown up, Television may enable them and you to "see by Wireless" any part of the world. This will be unending delight for those who live to enjoy it, but they must wait for wireless vision to be perfected.

You need not wait more than a few hours for a work that gives you in six lavishly illustrated volumes a vision of the interesting lands and peoples of all the world in full colour, and vivid, exciting descriptions of them written in the most engaging manner by eye-witnesses of every scene.

Here you see the religions, superstitions, witchcraft and magic of tropics and arctic circle. Here the eyes of the great cats haunt the jungle, to stalk the unconscious hunter. There the gorgeous colours of strange birds shift and shine in the sun, volcanoes burst into fire and great waterfalls rush down in foam. Some savage king is heavy with stifling clothes for his naked people to admire, and whole races wear little or nothing. All this and more, in full colour, with thrilling descriptive chapters you will find.

6 VOLUMES SENT TO YOUR HOME FOR 5/-

Here is a FREE Book that shows you, by samples, the nearest thing yet to television, and tells you what these volumes are like.

Lands & Peoples SIX SUMPTUOUS VOLUMES Edited by J.A. Hammerton

'Crossing continents in your armchair'

(title of *Radio Times* article, October 1924)

CHILDREN'S HOUR Annual

Edited by
"UNCLE MAC"

(Derek McCulloch
of the BBC)

Hullo Children!

—and grown-ups, too, are invited to listen—This is Uncle Mac speaking. I want to announce the third edition of our "Children's Hour Annual". This Annual is really the response to many, many requests that some of our most popular broadcast stories should appear in book form. Here, then, is a collection of our best authors in their most entertaining vein; in addition to the regular London broadcasters are included some from other Regions. Please keep this book, adding it to your own special library.

Parents, uncles and aunts are also strongly advised to bear this book in mind as a gift suitable for all occasions, particularly at Christmas.

Punch celebrated the global powers of broadcasting early (1924) and in verse:

WIRELESS AT NIGHT

TALL as a village spire
A slender fir-tree set upon the hill
Carries the news – or CHOPIN – at your will
    Along the fine-drawn wire.
    Aerial and telephone,
Batteries, valves (so little for so much),
And half of Europe answers to your touch,
    Whispers to you alone.

    The dogs of Paris bark
For us; . . . within a voice comes through:
'Bon soir, Mesdames, Messieurs, I hear it say,
'L'audition de ce soir est terminée.'
Monsieur, good-night to you—.

Children too could explore the world by wireless (*top left*, advertisement for the 1937 *Children's Hour Annual*). Realists, however, like the cartoonist Bert Thomas (*bottom left*, *Punch*, February 1931), recognised that they could add to the family chaos which listening to at least one foreign station is said to have caused.

In one cartoon (*below, Punch*, July 1938) Fougasse imagined what the other listener thought – the foreigner puzzling over an English cricket broadcast. The caption read:

'A radio expert declares that foreigners listen to our programmes just as keenly as we listen to theirs. In this way no programme is entirely wasted.'

Grannie. "THE HOUSE HAS NEVER BEEN THE SAME SINCE WE GOT MOSCOW ON THE WIRELESS."

". . . I got him caught in the gully off a wrong 'un . . ."

Home and colonial

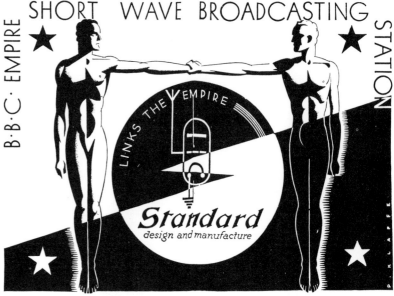

The BBC could be considered (letter to *The Radio Times*, July 1928) as an 'apostle of human brotherhood', although it acquired, and prided itself on, specific imperial responsibilities. Following the 1932 Christmas programme to the Empire, Hilda Matheson wrote eloquently that 'the listener could feel himself travelling in person to each place of call in the World's circumference, could almost feel the earth roll as he chased the hours from night to day, from winter to summer'. No aeroplane could do better.

For the advertisers, too, (*top right*, Standard Telephones and Cables Ltd. advertisement, 1933) short wave broadcasting linked the Empire, and in one of its advertisements the Co-operative Wholesale Society (*bottom right*, 1934) even took over the BBC's motto (soon to be quietly dropped), 'Nation Shall Speak Peace unto Nation', adding the words 'and mutual trading establish good will throughout the world'.

The BBC's coat of arms was elaborately described in the 1930 *Year Book* (*top* – it then still included the motto): 'Heraldic language almost justifies the plea that "there is nothing new under the sun". Ancient symbols have been found for the electrical nature of broadcasting (the thunderbolt and lightning flash), the speed of it (eagles), its work of public proclamation (bugles), its scope and breadth (the world and universe), and its ultimate ideal (the motto "Nation shall speak peace unto Nation").'

Extract from a Tanganyika listener's letter Christmas 1934.
'God bless you gentlemen! The programmes were so alive, so expressive, so Christmassy that one lived in a haze of England. There were a few moist eyes during your Empire Exchange and the King's Speech, and I had to swallow a lump too.'

'A link with the old country'

(Cape Town listener's tribute to the BBC Empire Service, April 1933)

GSA	A for Aerial
GSB	B for Broadcasting
GSC	C for Corporation
GSD	D for Daventry
GSE	E for Empire
GSF	F for Fortune
GSG	G for Greeting
GSH	H for Home
GSI	I for Island
GSJ	J for Justice
GSL	L for Liberty
GSN	N for Nation
GSO	O for Ocean
GSP	P for Progress

'For simple beauty and dignity in the new realm of radio there has never been anything like the Empire Broadcast on Christmas Day 1935,' wrote a Dominion newspaper. The climax was George v's Silver Jubilee year message (*above*, photo-montage, with imperial-sounding radio call-signs from *BBC Year Book* 1938). It proved to be a royal farewell to the Empire: a month later the King was dead.

'No better medium than the radio exists to strengthen the bonds and ties of Empire,' wrote an 'ordinary' Canadian listener in 1934. He had left England at the age of nine and tuned in to London programmes with 'affectionate and patriotic enthusiasm'. The bonds were not all political, however, as is made clear in two *Radio Times* cartoons, (*bottom left*, 1932, *right*, 1934).

Outposts of Empire
THE SYMPHONY CONCERT

Outposts of Empire
COOKERY TALK

THE TELEVISIONARY.

"I DON'T CARE HOW LONG IT TAKES ME, I'M GOING TO TURN AND **TURN TILL**
I GET A SIGHT OF PEACE."

(*Punch*, 2 September 1936.)

HERE'S LOOKING AT YOU

In the olden days the belle of every ball
Used to be the toast of fellows one and all.
Now that television's at our beck and call,
I'll play host.
Here's my toast:

Here's looking at you
From out of the blue.
Don't make a fuss
But settle down and look at us.
Here's looking at you –
It seems hardly true
That radio
Can let you sit and watch a show.
This wonderful age
Goes to show that all the world is a stage.
And you wonder what the next thing on the list will be!
What a hullabaloo!
We are just peeping through
To say 'How do!'
Here's looking at you!

Song lyric written for Radiolympia in August 1936 by Ronnie Hill.

'Now television's at our beck and call,' boasted the Radiolympia song in August 1936, the month when the first television programme from Broadcasting House was transmitted. Yet at that time, and down to 1939, it was only at the beck and call of a few thousand people in London.

The words 'settle down and look at us' had too complacent a ring – a world away from the language of a speculative editorial in *Popular Wireless* only fourteen years earlier, in June 1922, a few months before the BBC was born. It predicted 'Wireless Wonders to Come': 'Shall we ever see by Radio?' was one of the questions it raised ' . . . what will the general public think when they install apparatus which will enable them to *see* as well as hear by wireless? To the novice in wireless work this suggestion must savour of black magic or the ravings of Munchausen and De Rougemont rolled into one. Jules Verne himself would have paused before suggesting such a possibility.'

The Editor of *Popular Wireless* did not pause, however. He believed that, 'amazing as it may seem . . . this great ambition is within the bounds of practical possibility.' In the same year, *The Broadcaster* even predicted what programmes would be seen: women, it thought, would be particularly well catered for 'should this innovation be perfected':

In their homes they could view 'wirelesed' pictures of mannequins in the latest fashions created by European dress kings. No longer would the privilege of viewing the march of fashion be restricted to those who had facilities for visiting the mannequin parades in the stores of big towns. Women living in isolated villages or in inaccessible parts of the country could watch the newest fashions as easily as their sisters in the cities.

There had been predictions of 'seeing by wireless' since the nineteenth century. *Punch*'s Almanack for 1879 contained a Du Maurier cartoon entitled a 'Radio Prophecy' the caption of which ran, 'Every evening before going to bed, Pater- and Mater-familias set up an electric camera-obscura over their bedroom mantelpiece, and gladden their eyes with the sight of their children at the Antipodes, and converse gaily with them through the wire.' (See p. 208.)

The sub-title, 'Edison's Telephonoscope', suggested correctly, however, that *Punch* was thinking not of broadcasting, but of person-to-person communication. Nor was Marconi broadcasting when, almost twenty years later, he sent his first faint wireless telegraph signal through the ether: his message, too, was an individual one with a specific destination.

Almost as soon as sound broadcasting actually began in the early 1920s, television, 'the transmission of living and moving scenes to a distance by wire or wireless', was thought of as the natural complement of sound. Within a year of the birth of the BBC, in October 1923, a writer in *The Radio Times* prophesied that 'within ten years "television" will be as far advanced as telephony today', and in a short article two months later on 'Wireless Vision' in the London *Evening News*, a scientist, Dr Fournier d'Albe, predicted: 'When once our sense of hearing extends all over the world, our sense of sight will follow.'

In 1925 J. L. Baird, more of a shoe-string inventor than Marconi had been at the start of his career, gave his first public demonstration of television in London. 'Mr Baird . . . has demonstrated a cheap and practical solution to the problem of television,' wrote *The Radio Times*, 'a new department of wireless activity.' Yet the beginning of a regular television service was still more than ten years in the future, and in December 1935 a *Radio Times* editorial explained the reasons for this long interval between the first dreams of television and all but the most experimental reality:

The early history of television will necessarily differ from that of sound broadcasting for two critical reasons. There is no apparatus for receiving television comparable in simplicity and cheapness with the crystal set, and the range of stations is limited by certain physical factors over which engineering can exercise no control.

For these reasons, television cannot hope to grow with the incredible rapidity with which broadcasting covered the country in 1922 and 1923. When television programmes from the new station at the Alexandra Palace start next year, they will be capable of reception only by people in the London area.

To these 'official' BBC explanations of the delay in setting up and, having done so, developing a television

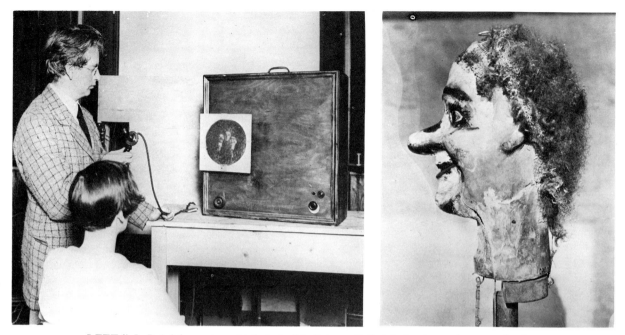

LEFT *J. L. Baird demonstrates his 'televisor' in July 1926. Baird gives instructions over the phone to his assistant, who can be seen on the screen with two puppets.*
RIGHT *One of the puppets, the first object ever to be televised.*

service – true as far as they went – were added more critical ones. R. S. Lambert, editor of *The Listener* from 1929–39, wrote, after he left the BBC:

In its infancy the new Service was sadly hampered by lack of money . . . it was extremely costly, and the BBC had already spent, upon luxuries such as Broadcasting House, the funds they might otherwise have had to spare for it. Television found itself caught in a vicious circle – not enough money for programmes; not good enough programmes to make the public buy viewing apparatus; manufacturers unwilling to take risks by cheapening apparatus till sales improved.

Garry Allighan in his biography of Reith, suggested that another reason for the delay in developing television was Reith's own lack of enthusiasm:

From the beginning of television's struggle for BBC recognition, Reith's advisers were anything but helpful, and the story told by Sydney A. Moseley [Programme Director to the Baird Television Company] of his fight to get television inside the BBC refers more than once to the BBC engineers, 'aloof, suspicious and supercilious'. It was not until 1929 that Sir John Reith consented to witness a test of television at the Savoy Hill studios, despite many previous invitations to go to the television studios in Long Acre and see for himself the progress made. 'I had failed to get the Director-General to come over to see television so we took the mountain to Mahomet,' is Sydney Moseley's caustic comment.

Reith's *Into the Wind* certainly contains little reference to television: a factual paragraph on the BBC's negotiations with the Government on financing the Television Service; a few sentences on the problems of televising the Coronation (but none on the achievements). Reith seems to have felt none of the excitement which he felt at the birth of sound broadcasting.

Whatever the causes for the delay in developing a television service – and they were more complex than the BBC or its critics suggested – the BBC nonetheless provided the London area with the first regular television service in the world. Moreover, the ten-year waiting period yielded many interesting predictions about the new medium: sociological and technical; excited and sober; serious and facetious.

George Fyfe, writing in *The Radio Times* in June 1924, foresaw a new lease of life for the BBC 'when it becomes, as we must suppose it will, the British Broadcasting and Television Company'. Writing before Baird's demonstration in April 1925, he predicted that television would

enter completely into the life of the community and be used for many other purposes than mere entertainment. The housewife will naturally order all her goods by the aid of the new method. When she telephones the butcher, she will be

MARCH 1928   TELEVISION

SOME NEW USES FOR TELEVISION

FOR THE TOILET—ENABLING THE TELEVISIONER TO SEE THE BACK OF HIS HEAD WHEN BRUSHING HIS HAIR

FOR THE CONVENIENCE OF THE ANGLER, PERMITTING HIM TO KEEP HIS EYE ON THE BAIT WITHOUT UNDUE EXERTION

A HANDY SET FOR SCHOOL MASTERS ENABLING THEM, WHILE ENJOYING THEIR MID-DAY SOLACE IN QUIET, TO KEEP AN EYE ON THEIR PUPILS

A GENTLEMAN 'LOCATING A LOST STUD WITH THE AID OF A NEAT DRESSING ROOM TELEVISION SET.

W. HEATH ROBINSON

Drawn by W. HEATH ROBINSON

able to see what sort of chops he has to offer that morning. It will be the same with the fishmonger, or the florist, or the draper. 'Shop by television' will be the new motto at the big stores.

At the cinema theatres, big events will be shown as they are happening all over the world, with additional thrills in between. You will be taken up with a pilot in an aeroplane and, as you listen to the roar of the engine, the world below will be seen with his eyes in order to let you participate in his experience without leaving the ground.

The idea of doing business without moving from the house was attractive in the early days of broadcasting. 'We are gradually accustoming ourselves to do our business without transferring our body from place to place, and it is becoming necessary that we should be able to see documents and to be able to see our friends at a distance,' wrote Professor A. M. Low in an article 'Wireless Television' in *Wireless Review* in June 1923. Dr d'Albe predicted that once television had become a practical reality, 'our bodily and material limitations are reduced almost to vanishing point'. He imagined a busy doctor in his consulting room; 'he rings up his

patients one after the other. He talks to them, examines their tongues and their general appearance, interviews the nurses, and inspects the sickroom – all without leaving his house.'

Even before there was a television service, some writers were already afraid that, convenient although it might be, television would become a substitute for life. In a heavily ironic article, 'The Armchair Millennium', in *The Radio Times* in January 1927, Rose Macaulay wrote:

As to the drama, the arrangements for its transmission to an arm-chair audience are not yet completed; at present they can only hear it, which is unsatisfactory, if economical and comfortable; but one understands that before long television will give us quite a good view of the stage and performers. That, for many of us, will be the millennium. To see and hear a play every night, without the further trouble and expense that one's own wireless set entails, without the tedium of going out and coming back and the discomfort of being surrounded by other people as noisy and tiresome as ourselves (for those in our homes we should be able, with a little firmness, to keep in order) – here indeed is bliss, only a little marred by the fact that we cannot choose what play we see, but must accept what is given us. . . . And as to our recreations, why should we not have dinner parties by wireless of an evening, instead of sallying out from our homes to the homes of others? Turn us on to any dinner party where there is jollity, wit, the feast of reason and the flow of soul, transmit to us the taste of savoury viands (this should be a simple business) and let us sit and enjoy the evening without trouble.

In later years, when television had arrived, there were writers who believed that to view a play at home was inferior in *principle* to going to the theatre to see it, quite apart from the technical problems of television, which they predicted would be solved. 'Do we not, when we go to the theatre, set out to enjoy ourselves?' wrote C. Whitaker Wilson in *The Radio Times* in March 1939. 'At home we might have seen the same play televised – yet, fully allowing for the restrictions of television, we may not have felt in the least like seeing it and moreover were deprived of the stimulus of the surroundings of the theatre to *make* us feel like seeing it.'

In March 1939 *Punch* predicted a not-so-distant time when television would be perfected and when 'we shall complete our pleasant slavery, I suppose, to that series of strange boxes to which we are already, like monkeys to barrel-organs, very largely bound: Men and women, words and music, deeds and drama, and the whole wide world will come like food from cans. There will be no need to see any real person, nor look at any real thing, nor move nor think nor read at all.'

More serious radio critics had feared the effect of television on the imaginations of 'lookers', as early televiewers were often called. 'Uncle Mac', for example, was afraid that the television version of *Toy Town* would destroy the original radio version, making young viewers too lazy to 'visualise'. W. E. Williams, writing in *The Listener* in August 1935 regretted that 'television is unhappily soon going to reverse the good tendency of radio to make people listen blindfolded. Give us our ears back again!' he pleaded. '. . . When the wireless play succumbs to television, we shall have another example of the irresponsibility with which scientific precocity can destroy an aesthetic definition of purpose . . . the listener to a wireless play is compelled to use his imagination in the way of an Elizabethan audience.'

The players, some felt, might suffer as much as the play from the change from sound to vision. One woman listener in the Isle of Man had written to Filson Young in 1930, wondering if 'when television comes, we shall weave as much romance around our favourite broadcasters as we do now. Listening is different from looking.'

There was more than one way of looking, too. Sharp contrasts were drawn between the techniques of television and cinema and the kind of enjoyment each provided. The BBC, accustomed from its earliest days to the hostility of theatre and cinema interests, always tried to play them up, in order to show how little the other entertainment interests had to fear from the competition of broadcasting. In 1939 S. John Woods wrote in *The Radio Times* that the mighty cinema industry had nothing to fear from the infant television:

Film magnates don't have to worry; television will have little effect on films, for between television and films there is a vast No Man's Land. At first sight this may seem odd, because both are viewed on a screen in black and white, and accompanied by sound. There, however, the similarity ends. The ordinary commercial film is not suitable for transmission by television. The reason? Because in television the most important part of any film is lacking: the audience. A film appeals to several hundred people at the same time; a comedian cracks a joke and there are several hundred laughs; the heroine sheds a tear and several hundred eyes are moist; at the shot of a gun several hundred hearts stop beating. Mass emotion. It is far, far easier to make a crowd of people laugh or cry than to produce the same effect on a solitary person.

In 1930 the *BBC Year Book* had suggested that 'even perfected television would never overcome human reluctance to admit mechanical impediment between man and man.'

The 'mechanical impediment', however, was the very instrument of what was beginning to be called 'actuality'. Early viewers, far from objecting to the presence of the television set, felt grateful for, and sometimes excited at, the sense of being present at and even participating in distant events which they could never have visited in the flesh. 'To see an event actually happening thousands of miles away is one of those alluring dreams that few wireless experimenters have not enjoyed.' So wrote one radio critic in *The Radio Times* as early as 1925, conscious, as Reith never was, of the magic of television. 'No familiarity with even the simplest crystal receiving set ever causes the owner to cease wondering,' he went on, 'and it is not difficult to believe that a looking set will soon provide an indispensable addition to the enjoyment at present derived from the head-phones.'

In the same year 'A Listener's Diary of Forty Years Hence', an imaginary glimpse into the distant future of 1965, described the writer's reactions to seeing 'The Ride of the Valkyrie' being performed live in Paris 'about as clearly as if I'd been there myself'. His set had 'all the up-to-date improvements . . . fitted with the stereoscopic attachment'.

TELEVISION

LYRIC BY JAMES DYRENFORTH
MUSIC BY KENNETH LESLIE-SMITH

A mighty maze of mystic, magic rays
Is all about us in the blue,
And in sight and sound they trace
Living pictures out of space,
To bring a new wonder to you.
The busy world before you is unfurled –
Its songs, its tears and laughter, too.
One by one they play their parts
In this latest of the Arts,
To bring new enchantment to you.
As by your fireside you sit,
The news will flit,
As on the silver screen.
And just for entertaining you
With something new,
The stars will then be seen.
So there's joy in store!
The world is at your door –
It's here to pass you in review,
Conjured up in sound and sight
By the magic rays of light
That bring Television to you.

1936

The excitement of 'actuality' in sound broadcasting was communicated by Peter Eckersley in an article he wrote for *Wireless* in September 1925, but he also looked ahead to the days of television outside broadcasts: 'I suppose in a hundred years we actually shall be auditors and spectators of the world's happenings.' He imagined a typical extract from a television news bulletin of 2025:

SEEING THE NEWS

1st General News. – 'New British Ambassador lands at New York,' says a voice in our room. We are aware immediately of the hum of propellers and on the wall of our living room a great shape, the world's largest Transatlantic Airship, glides into view. We can see the crowd waving handkerchiefs. A cheer breaks out. 'Clank! She is moored.' Down comes the caisson from the mooring mast, the Ambassador steps out, we hear him, 'I am glad to have arrived. We did a record trip in 24 hours 3 mins. 19 secs. . . . My policy . . . etc., etc.' We are glad he has arrived, too, and he's looking very well, better than when he was in South Africa that time he spoke on the inauguration of the half-day service to London.

'We see no barrier to the linking of the world by broadcasting theoretically today,' Eckersley commented. 'Where broadcasting can percolate, so, assuming a practical system, will television. We dream, and the dreams of today are the facts of tomorrow, but let no one expect tomorrow to dawn before the earth's necessary revolutions. Science and Technology have accomplished many wonders. Do not let us in imagination try to force a pace that is logically determined by our advances not in this section or that, but, as they said in the war, "on a wide front". When we send movies by wireless, much water will have passed under the bridges. In the meanwhile, let us face present problems, which are plentiful enough, and not be too (tele)visionary.'

Writers foresaw drawbacks, some of them comic, in the imaginary world of television 'actuality'. A novelist, Noman Davey, wrote a story called 'A Radio Dream' for *The Radio Times* in October 1928 in which the host, who has the most advanced radio installation in England, demonstrates 'TB' (Television Broadcast) from Paris:

'You can see for yourself,' boasted the proud owner, 'I'll show you TB from Paris; let me see, it's five-thirty now; Raminoff's *thé dansant* should be on. I'll put you through. Look at the screen at the end of the room there.'

The little man fiddled with some discs and plugs and the next instant the room was filled with the noise of the jazz band and the wall at the end had vanished and I found myself gazing upon a crowded dance floor, as if I had been a spectator on the edge of the *piste*.'

But trouble was on the way – the result of seeing too much: I was about to express my wonderment, when my host suddenly uttered a strange, half-inarticulate cry.

'What's the matter?' I asked.

'My wife!' he cried, in a kind of frantic stammer. 'M-m-y wife – dancing at Raminoff's – with that half-caste – and she told me she was going to stay with her mother at Buxton. My ——!'

And suddenly before I could interfere, he had seized a large porcelain jar from the mantelshelf and hurled it at the screen.

One aspect of the excitement of 'actuality' in television, compared with the cinema, was summed up by S. John Woods in *The Radio Times* in 1938:

In films the scene is rehearsed time and time again until the action has the precision of a machine, everything just so, every moment accounted for, every movement calculated. In television there is the delicious knowledge that at any moment something may go wrong. The leading lady may get hiccups, the hero may trip up, the lights may go out. These things don't happen. But they easily might, and this feeling of actuality is an absolutely fundamental part of television.

This kind of excitement, a kind of *Schadenfreude* in anticipation, compensated viewers for the presence of the 'mechanical impediment' and the absence of an audience. Gerald Cock, the BBC's first Director of Television, writing in *The Radio Times* in October 1936 a month before the opening of the Television Service, suggested that 'viewers would rather see an actual scene of a rush hour at Oxford Circus directly transmitted to them than the latest in film musicals costing £100,000 – though I do not expect to escape unscathed with such an opinion.'

Viewers, however, were not fobbed off with such unexciting fare, and by 1939 the *BBC Hand Book*, reviewing television in the previous year, could boast:

The most spectacular achievements of 1938 were outside broadcasts. . . . viewers in their homes twice saw the Prime Minister as he stepped from the plane at Heston: first after the visit to Berchtesgaden and again on his return from Munich. Viewers were among the first to see him holding aloft that fluttering piece of paper (the writing was visible) bearing his own signature and that of Herr Hitler. Eager viewers scrambled round television sets on Derby Day, after seeing the race from the start, to get an amazing glimpse of Bois Roussel beating the field on the post at Epsom; private sitting rooms became part of an immense theatre auditorium when scenes were televised direct from the stage at the St Martin's and Palace Theatres. Arm-chair critics came into their own when Test Matches were televised direct from Lord's and the Oval, and when Emitron cameras peered through the tobacco smoke at Harringay to see Foord v. Phillips and McAvoy v. Harvey. These were the highlights in a year of highlights.

Cock, who had previously served for ten years as BBC Director of Outside Broadcasts, believed that 'actuality', useful in sound broadcasting, was all-important in television. By 1939 an advertisement for

Selfridges' television studio and showrooms summed it up. Over the last three years since the television service had begun, it claimed:

Viewers have seen history being made. They have seen as well thousands of studio productions – variety, plays and ballet. Leaders of thought come to address them at their own firesides. Mannequins show them the latest fashions in the comfort of their own homes. And everything they see is taking place at the moment they see it. That is the thrill of television – its immediacy. It combines the best of the cinema with the urgency of a radio broadcast, taking the best from both of them and building for itself a new technique.

Every member of a television audience hears every word, every voice inflection, and sees every detail of the performance often more clearly than if he were actually present.

The developments and applications of television are innumerable. To what extent the new art will affect social life it is difficult to foresee. Whatever the social effects it will have, we can be sure that it will raise the general standards of knowledge and culture, even more than sound broadcasting has done.

"I didn't realise you had Television, dear."

The sense of intimacy was as important as the sense of immediacy. Cock went on, 'Perhaps the most important part of television is the feeling that the action that is taking place is actually happening at the moment you are watching it in your home.' Where television was viewed was as important as what was viewed. The 'hearth' theme, so familiar in early writing on sound radio, was even more stressed in television. Lord Birkenhead predicted in 'The World in 2030', quoted by *The Radio Times* in 1930, that by 2030 'the development of broadcasting and television will enable a family gathered round its own atomically radiant hearth (no

more coal and gas thanks be!) to watch and listen to a variety of spectacles. . . . It will be possible to create in a private house the exact illusion of physical presence at a stage performance hundreds of miles away.'

So important for the right television experience was the home setting, that one writer in *The Radio Times* in 1938, Ian Hunter, attacked the practice of potential customers viewing television sets 'with even a small crowd in a demonstration room'. 'I believe,' he went on, 'you must make the dealer bring television into your home and leave it with you for a few days. After that, I cannot imagine you will allow it to leave you again.' What was the use of crowding into a non-domestic environment like an inferior cinema, he asked, when 'it is the synthesis of intimacy and immediacy gives television its really unique appeal – an appeal that can be appreciated only in the home.'

Hunter even believed that every fortunate owner of a television set should

. . . consider it his duty, as a pioneer, to convert friends by inviting them round to enjoy it under domestic conditions. Only by a great expansion of the viewing habit can the present service develop – or perhaps go on at all.

When you arrange your television parties, take care to choose an evening when there is something extra good on – such as a short play, a cabaret, or an outstanding personality. And don't ask too many at a time – five is about my ideal number.

Sooner or later one of your guests will exclaim: 'Yes, it's very wonderful – much clearer than I imagined possible – but I suppose it is still in its infancy, isn't it?'

That remark is based on a widespread misconception you might do something to remove.

Many kinds of people were prepared to risk backing the 'infant' and buy a television set; by 1939 when the Television Service closed down there were an estimated 20,000 viewers. Most of them lived within the recommended 25-mile radius of Alexandra Palace, but some took a very big chance and bought a set although they were far from London.

In February 1939 *The Radio Times* gave a whole page to an article on a farm labourer, Mr George Boar of Long Melford, Suffolk, who, 'without even troubling to see a demonstration,' had 'invested his whole fortune (and £126 is certainly a fortune to a farm-hand) in his set.' The worthy man gave shows to his neighbours. 'He has demonstrated a courage, a spirit of sacrifice, and a desire for self-improvement which are unique,' commented *The Radio Times* approvingly. 'For here we have the remarkable picture of a simple farm-hand thoroughly enjoying, and actually entering into, a television programme composed of quotations from literary classics, and saying at the end of it, "Those are the

SAUCE! YOU KNOW YOU SHOULDN'T LOOK

items we folks like".' Mr Boar was described as fondling the television set 'with all the love which a stockman gives to a new-born calf or a leggy foal'. 'Television's far more entertaining and much less trouble than a wife would be,' was his verdict.

At the other end of the social scale the television critic of *The Radio Times*, 'Scanner', wrote in April 1939, that while 'the possession of a television set will not automatically give you access to Ascot's Royal Enclosure, it will at least ensure that you are in the swim with the best people. The fact that you are a viewer might help you to qualify for an appearance in one of the fashionable illustrated periodicals.' Owners of sets on 'Scanner's' list included cartoonist David Low; the Egyptian Ambassador; Basil Dean, theatre manager and producer; Prince Bira, Siamese motor-racing 'ace'; dance-band leader Henry Hall; newspaper magnates Harmsworth, Kemsley and Rothermere; comedian and amateur astronomer Will Hay; Cyril Mills of the

Olympia Circus; Harry Curtis, manager of Brentford Football Club; and, of course, Leslie Mitchell, 'whose wife puts the coffee in the percolator for him on Thursdays directly she sees the last item finish in "Picture Page".'

Members of Parliament, too, were among the earliest viewers. The *BBC Annual* for 1937 reported that daily reception of the television programmes was arranged in the Grand Committee Room, Westminster Hall, from 30 November to 11 December 1936, soon after the opening of the Television Service.

Whoever they were, early viewers often took their viewing very seriously indeed, and the BBC encouraged them to do so. The *BBC Annual* for 1936, published a few months before the Television Service was inaugurated, laid down some quasi-moral precepts for viewers: 'He who wishes to obtain reasonably full value from his set will be called upon to make and keep appointments with it; in other words to study the published programmes selectively, and to give an undivided attention to those items which he chooses for his entertainment or instruction. The habit of switching-on vaguely on the chance of finding a pleasant musical background to other activities would have to be modified.' 'Background' viewing was, indeed, thought to be impossible, 'For some reason the prospect of television background programmes seems more appalling than the bad-enough actuality of background sound radio,' wrote Kenneth Baily in October 1938. 'What else but downright waste will it be if the television screens are illumined with stirring drama or Variety high jinks while most householders have their backs turned to them as they do their domestic duties?'

Another contributor to *The Radio Times* in 1938 was Irene Stiles. 'Television puts an end to haphazard, half-hearted listening,' she wrote. 'You may be a "background listener" but you can't be a "background viewer".' She quoted disapprovingly a woman, reported in the Press, who 'gave as her case against television the fact that it would *demand her whole attention* and that she would have to put down her knitting'. That, said Mrs Stiles, was exactly what she liked about television. She would like to 'take some of these men and women with butterfly minds away from the several things that distract or disturb them and set them down in front of our screen when a programme is in progress. I believe that a course of television would soon effect a cure.

'Many people fail to realise that the attitude of mind governing one's leisure may affect the attitude of mind governing one's work. Those who are desultory and dissatisfied in their leisure moments are quite likely to be so when they are working.'

Mrs Stiles described viewing in her own home: it was a very serious affair.

Preparations for watching the television programmes are, in our case, invested with a certain amount of ceremony. Just before nine o'clock chairs are drawn into a circle. Lights are switched off, a screen shuts out any interfering reflections from the fire, and once the tuning signal is radiated silence prevails by common consent. All this may be due to the fact that television has its time limit and that, unlike ordinary radio, it is not 'on tap' at all hours. Whatever the reason, it gets our full attention.

One woman, very different from the high-minded Mrs Stiles, was interviewed in a television demonstration studio in March 1937. A *Radio Times* 'special representative' described her as 'a perfect model for one of Bert Thomas's Cockney studies'. Turning to her friend this woman exclaimed: ' "Blimey, Lil, this is too good! If ever we get one of those things at home, we shan't have an excuse to go out to the pictures." Her friend's reply was even more mournful. She said, "No, we shan't, and we shan't be able to get rid of the men on Saturday afternoons either. They'll want to sit in front of the fire to watch the football match." They evidently believed that television as a home entertainment was going to make a difference to them!'

At this time – and for the first eighteen months of the service – television programmes, far from being 'on tap', as Mrs Stiles approvingly noted, were limited to two hours daily, at 3 p.m. and 9 p.m. In April 1938 about an hour of 'live' programme was added regularly on Sunday evenings and on occasional Sunday afternoons – from January 1939.

A typical weekday's viewing in March 1937 consisted of (between 3 p.m. and 4 p.m.) a demonstration of archery; 'Cook's night out: the preparation of crêpes flambées by the Chef Marcel Boulestin'; the current Gaumont British newsreel and 'The Policeman's Serenade', a 'Grand little Opera' by A. P. Herbert and Alfred Reynolds. Between 9 p.m. and 10 p.m. viewers could enjoy ten minutes of light piano music; a (live) repeat of the crêpes flambées demonstration; the Movietone newsreel, and a 25-minute cabaret. There was no separate television news programme but a recorded version of the nine o'clock sound radio news was introduced as a service at the end of the evening service.

Scarcity of resources partly accounted for the limited transmission time, but it was thought, in any case, that the degree of concentration required for viewing precluded long hours. Short as they were, the programmes were to be deliberately interrupted at frequent intervals. 'To avoid eye strain, there should be interval signals between individual programme items, lasting not more than half a minute,' wrote Cock in 1936. 'These intervals should be marked by means of a modern clock, the dimension of whose face should be roughly the same as the dimensions of the received picture.' Cock did not foresee a time when programmes would be continuous. In 'A personal forecast of the future of television' for *The Radio Times* in 1936, he wrote: 'We are entitled to imagine that programme hours would be few – perhaps four a day – and that they would be confined to events of outside interest and entertainment, for television will, I think, mean the end of "background" listening.'

Three years later it was television itself which was to end, closed down 'for the duration' on the outbreak of war. The *BBC Hand Book* for 1940 told the sad story of the shut-down: 'During the afternoon [of 1 September 1939] an engineer in a grey overall had stepped in front of the camera at an Alexandra Palace rehearsal and turned down his thumbs – thus bluntly signifying that a great pioneering achievement, in which Britain was leading the world, had to put up its shutters. The BBC was on a war footing.' Television was no longer 'looking at you'.

'Ah tahnk ah kees you now.' – the last image broadcast on television before it closed down 'for the duration' in 1939.

Personalities of the Palace

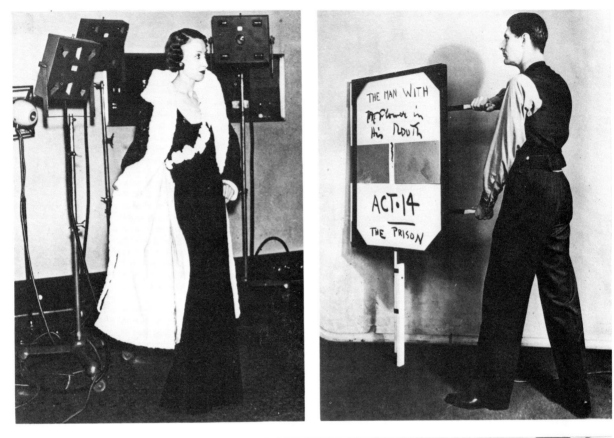

In August 1932 the BBC introduced an experimental (Baird) television service of four programmes a week, very limited in scope. 'Dancers, acrobats and jugglers have been successfully televised,' reported the *BBC Handbook* of 1933, (*bottom right*, the Paramount Astoria Girls, televised in 1933).

Fashion shows were televised, too (*above*, a mannequin in a Broadcasting House studio in October 1932), and a fashion expert commented: 'Soon it will only be necessary for Madame or Mademoiselle to ring through to the establishment she fancies, ask for the televiser, say she is wanting a new hat or dress, and within a few minutes she will see displayed before her in her own home the very latest models ... What visionaries, these dressmakers, what dreamers!'

A 'visionary' in television drama, Lance Sieveking, was the producer of the first television play in the world, Pirandello's 'The Man with the Flower in his Mouth' (July 1930) (*top right*, Sieveking with a 'caption' during rehearsal).

'A pleasant and informal manner'

(the BBC's requirement for television announcers, 1936)

'Television cavalcade'

(title of advertisement for Selfridge's TV studio and showroom, 1939)

'The film has found a voice, while radio is as yet only blinking its eyes,' *Radio Magazine* asserted in September 1934. Yet within three years *The Radio Times* could boast that the 'journey from crystal set to television has been made at so breathtaking a speed that we are apt to forget how far it is'.

By then the experimental stage of television had ended, the great individualist pioneer, Baird, 'Mr. Television', had lost, and EMI teamwork (led by Isaac Schoenberg) had triumphed. With the triumph, 405-line pictures entered Londoners' homes (the provinces were still outside the range of the camera).

Performers now stole the limelight from the technicians, although in Freddy Grisewood's words, '... their faces were ... so deathly white that their noses vanished, and had to be outlined by means of thick black lines ... What with this and their vicious, purple lips ... they seemed a cross between a ghost and a clown.'

Henry Hall, neither white nor purple, 'looked back' in 1937 (*right*), five years after his first television broadcast in 1932.

HENRY HALL
LOOKS BACK

'You will be able to count her teeth!'

(television producer's claim, December 1932)

Cecil Madden, Television Programmes Organiser, presented the television 'magazine', *Picture Page*, first relayed from Alexandra Palace to Radiolympia in August 1936 and described by *The Morning Post* as 'real television'. Madden made unique and invaluable photographic montages of the many celebrities he produced between 1936 and 1939 (*above*, Madden's own photograph is below his name in the montage – near the Coronation coach, another television 'celebrity' of 1937).

Joan Miller, the 'hello girl' of *Picture Page*, broke new ground by operating a switchboard to plug the celebrities through to the programme 'after a few preliminary words of description'. 'In every way the technique is novel,' claimed *The Radio Times* (*left*, photograph for the opening of the scheduled Television Service, 30 October 1936).

'Ally Pally'

Some early television outside broadcasts were simply out-of-doors 'studio' broadcasts. In Alexandra Park, the latest Emitron camera was linked to the interior of the Palace (*above*, August 1936). The *BBC Hand Book* for 1938 claimed, 'The park studio has made it possible to show model yacht-racing on the lake, sheepdog trials, car parades, horse-riding, archery and golf and the Television Garden tended by Mr C. H. Middleton' (*centre right*).

In the wide world beyond 'Ally Pally' there was more for television 'lookers' to see. In November 1938 J. B. Priestley's play *When We Are Married* was televised direct from the St Martin's Theatre (*bottom*), a genuine 'O.B.'. 'Viewers took the trouble to telegraph congratulations from places far beyond the official service area,' claimed the BBC, 'from the Isle of Wight ... and even Gloucestershire.'

'Headlines as they happen'

(title of 1939 article on television 'OBs')

Great public events made great television, according to one optimistic television advertising leaflet of summer 1939. It listed enthusiastically the viewing joys in store.

'You sit in the drawing-room and see the Derby at Epsom. From pounding start to flying finish with Blue Peter, the favourite, out well ahead. . . . *You know who won, before hundreds on the course.* You see the crash of a knock-out blow, the referee counting, a new world champion acclaimed. You see the Test Matches, the Cup Final, wrestling, fencing, jumping. You lean forward in your chair, feint and strive with the sport of it. Your pulse, your breath accelerate. Television has got you! . . . You see Mr Chamberlain step out of his aeroplane back from Munich. He takes a sheet of paper from his pocket. Peace, it means Peace!

These things are unique. We shall tell our grand-children of such days.'

Television covered ceremony also (*top left*, The Trooping of the Colour, 1937) sometimes with news thrown in, like the incident at the Cenotaph in November 1937:

'The Silence, November 11, two years ago. The streets are still. In Whitehall, tens of thousands stand reverently bareheaded. In eight million homes the radio is on, but held by a solemn stillness. Those with television gaze silently at the Cenotaph's sad and sombre ranks. Suddenly a figure thrusts through. A Voice . . . "All this is hypocrisy," he shouts. There is a scuffle, then silence again. What happened? What was it? Television sees it all. Television viewers know; others learn later.'

Royalty had produced the most exciting of all television 'O.B.'s'. In May 1937 'mobile television was gloriously inaugurated on Coronation Day'. Three years later, on what was described as 'The 872nd Day of Television', viewers could watch the scene at Waterloo station. 'Here they are! The Royal Train is coming into the station. Their Majesties are back from Canada! . . . You watch them drive off. Then, by television, you join the expectant crowd lining the Mall, watching the Palace balcony' (*below, left*).

'Clearly the best'

(HMV television advertising slogan)

Advertisers of television sets in the late 1930s tried as many different sales slants as wireless manufacturers. HMV was snobbish and 'scientific', hoping that customers would want to impress their friends by being the first to possess 'the latest achievement of science' (which was, however, 'in a time-honoured tradition') and boasting of their progress 'From the laboratory in 1931 to the Home in 1936'; Pye was snappy: 'Now there's an eye in Pye', and so was Ekco: 'Now *see* what you are missing!' GEC fell back on the familiar 'hearth' image – television would make happy stay-at-home families (*top right*, advertisement for GEC's add-on vision unit): Cossor tried to show – literally – how sight could supplement sound (*bottom right*); and Marconi boasted that its three-in-one Mastergram was 'the most complete home entertainment provider ever known'.

For the final pre-war Radiolympia in August 1939, the Radio Manufacturers' Association – better at puns than at prophecy – came up with its own slogan, 'Television is here: you can't shut your eyes to it' (*opposite*). Soon there was to be a different kind of 'actuality' and, for the duration, television was no longer 'here'.

'A world winner'

(Sir Stephen Tallents on the future of British television, 23 August 1939)

TELEVISION IS HERE

"I little thought we'd ever get a grand view of the boat race from inside our own drawing-room, *while it was actually being rowed!*" This thrilling sense of surprise comes to everyone who first experiences the wonder of Television in his own home. For about three hours a day, every day of the week, you can look in at the rich and varied Television programmes of the B.B.C. Great men, great occasions, famous plays, famous stars, sporting events, news and world affairs appear before your eyes to entertain and inform you and your family. Become an eyewitness of life. Watch the news while it happens — through the modern miracle of Television.

you can't shut your eyes to it

Television is as easy to buy, and to use, as a radio set. Your radio dealer will demonstrate the wide choice of moderately priced receivers. If you live in the Home Counties, write now to the Television Development Committee, 59 [r] Russell Square, w.c.1, for free copy of the new book, *And Now*, telling you all about the Television programmes with pictures of the famous stars and celebrities who appear in them.

Visions of the future

'Before the next century shall expire,' *Lightning*, one of the many popular science magazines of the 1890s, exclaimed, 'the grandsons of the present generation will see one another across the Atlantic, and the great ceremonial events of the world, as they pass before the eye of the camera, will be executed at the same instant before mankind.'

Punch had the same idea even earlier (*above*, from the 1879 *Punch* Almanack, see page 192). Yet there were famous sceptics too. When Bertrand Russell read in 1928 that sets capable of receiving pictures were to be shown at a London exhibition he felt 'a word of warning' was necessary: 'the public would be well advised to discount heavily the flamboyant anticipations that have appeared in the non-technical press on this subject.' Even Marconi was luke warm: 'I do not feel any useful purpose would be served by discussing the subject [of television] at the present time,' he wrote in a letter in 1928. By 1933, however, Marconi's idea of a radio set in 1960 included a television screen (*opposite, above left*, model displayed at Radiolympia). The set acted 'on command of voice'.

A VISION OF THE NEAR FUTURE.
Listening and seeing at the same time.

'Seeing the World from an Armchair'

(title of *Radio Times* article looking forward to television, February 1924)

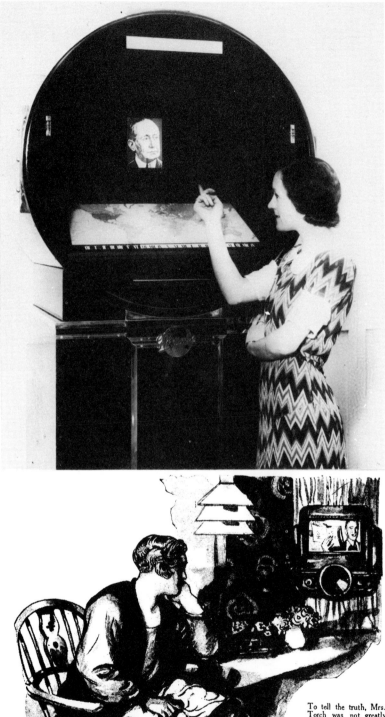

To tell the truth, Mrs. Torch was not greatly interested in antiquities, and it was the pleasure of hearing Tom's voice and seeing his jolly, boyish face on the screen which really held her attention.

WITHIN THE NEXT FEW YEARS.
'Tune in on the New War, Albert. I find these Oriental riots vastly boring.'

Journalists, novelists and cartoonists enjoyed speculating on the future of television. The shape of things to come meant the shape of the sets as well as the shape of the programmes (*opposite, bottom left*, *Radio Times* illustration of a 1924 article, 'Seeing the World from an Armchair'. *Below left*, *Radio Times* illustration by Stephen Spurrier of a science fiction story, 'Old Magic', May 1928, and a *Radio Times* cartoon, May 1931, *above right*).

In Ivor Novello's 'Glamorous Night' the young inventor of a new television process is given £500 by Lord Radio (in a futuristic setting) to keep quiet about it.

J. D. Beresford pictured the householder of 1950 in a *Radio Times* article of August 1931; he was 'seated with his family before an opaque white screen, about six feet by four, fixed on the wall of the principal sitting-room in a simple dark frame. Before him on a movable stand is a small switchboard, and after a study of the daily programme he conducts the evening's entertainment for the amusement and education of himself, his wife, and his children. By manipulating the switchboard he can, for example, bring a moving picture on to the screen of the Prime Minister taking part in a debate in the House of Commons. . . . It is all there before them.'

'Radio has received its sight'

'In the opinion of the leading Wireless and Scientific experts, one of the next great developments of Wireless will be in the fascinating field of Television.' So wrote *Wireless Review* in June 1923, announcing a £500 prize for inventors, to encourage experiments in television. The generosity of the prize testified to the difficulty of the subject.

Unlike the familiar schoolboy wireless constructor, the typical television constructor was shown as a middle-aged man in an elaborate workshop (*top and bottom right*, illustrations from the first number of the magazine, *Television*, March 1928). There were fewer of them, also, since, as the magazine pointed out discouragingly, 'television is a much more complex subject than wireless, and requires a knowledge of science not usually within the grasp of the man in the street.'

'Mr. Baird seems to be on the threshold of great things,' wrote the *Daily Herald* in 1926 of the greatest of all television constructors (*opposite top*, a Baird televisor of 1928). Most would-be television constructors, however, were not on the threshold of even the smallest discovery.

As television developed in complexity during the 1930s, amateur constructors became even rarer. Yet as late as 1937 *Radio Pictorial* could still urge readers to 'Make your own television set', reminding them of the good old days when 'every other man was building his own wireless set'.

'Scene in any suburban living room:
  "Henry, when are you going to clear the table, so that I can lay supper?"
  "Nearly finished, dear...."
Scene in any railway carriage next morning:
  "Yes, I finished my new wireless set. Made it all myself . . . and I got America last night!"'

How much *more* satisfaction there was in making one's own television set, claimed *Radio Pictorial*:

'Something new is exciting the technically-minded man. Very soon those dining-room tables will again be littered with radio parts and gadgets, because television has come to town.

Think of the excitement of holding television parties! You may say "I can't afford to buy a television set, and surely they are much too difficult to build?"

Not a bit of it. You can start today to construct a television set with as much confidence as when years ago you built your first wireless set.'

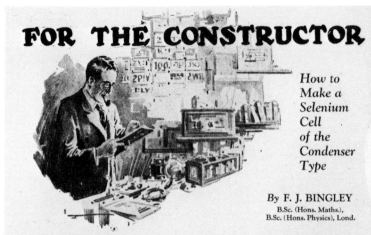

FOR THE CONSTRUCTOR

How to Make a Selenium Cell of the Condenser Type

By F. J. BINGLEY
B.Sc. (Hons. Maths.),
B.Sc. (Hons. Physics), Lond.

THIS type of cell is extremely sensitive and rapid in action, and is eminently suitable for use with the televisor described on page 27. It consists in essence of a copper and mica condenser, one edge of which has been filed down so as to expose the edges of the copper, the filed face being coated with selenium.

Those readers who have taken apart a commercially made cell of this type may be excused for declaring that an amateur would find it impossible even to assemble one, for at first sight it appears to be a very intricate and delicate piece of apparatus. The writer would, therefore, ask them at the outset not to be discouraged, as it is quite possible with a little practice to make very sensitive cells at small cost, and can assure them that he has made several, all of which worked very successfully in the televisor mentioned above.

Commencing with the materials required, the first and most obvious is the selenium. This can be obtained in 100 gm. bottles containing sticks of the element at a cost of about eight shillings from Messrs. Griffin,

The writer used silvered copper foil, obtained in sheets about 12 by 4 inches, from Calipe Dettmer, Poland Street, London, W., though silvered copper is by no means essential. For the insulating material mica about ·008 inch thick, obtainable from any wireless dealer, is used, while the

which will cost about sixpence, and will make four cells. The above, together with a few 8 B.A. steel screws and nuts and brass washers, completes our list of materials.

With regard to tools, very few will be required, and these will generally be already in use in the experi-

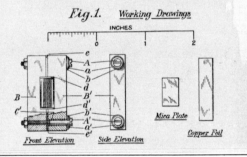

Fig.1.   Working Drawings

Front Elevation   Side Elevation   Mica Plate   Copper Foil

How to make a Simple Televisor

Specially described and tested for "Television" by our Technical Staff.

'The Looking-In Era'

(phrase from pre-television *Daily Herald* article, 1923)

Most 'lookers' preferred to buy a commercially-made set, perhaps after visiting Selfridge's studio to see television 'with the lid off'.

By 1938, television was beginning to be taken for granted, and 'Scanner', the *Radio Times*'s television correspondent, wrote, of Radiolympia, 'Last year television was a sideline of the show – popular, but no more important than the press-button working models in the Science Museum. This year Radiolympia is to treat television not as a scientific curiosity, but as a luxury desirable in every home in the London area.'

A year later, the possession of a new model television set was a status symbol (*bottom left*, *Men Only*'s comment, 1939); and Radiolympia hired glamorous 'hostesses' (*below*) to demonstrate the sets grouped along a corridor called 'Television Avenue'.

Triumfo
30 · VALVE
HIGH FIDELITY
ULTRA · SUPER HET
DE LUXE MODEL
AT 120 gns.
NOT A TOY   THE LAST WORD

C. Salisbury

" When selling this model, sir, we require an assurance
that it is going to a suitable home."

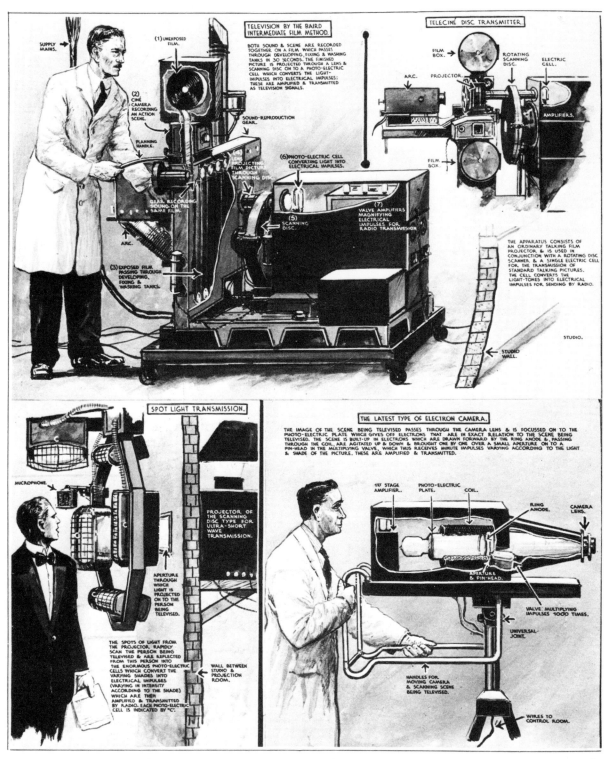

ONE OF THE ALTERNATE TELEVISION SYSTEMS FOR THE LONDON STATION TO BE ESTABLISHED

AREA TO BE SERVED BY THE CRYSTAL PALACE ULTRA-SHORT WAVE STATION.

HATFIELD

LONDON

MAIDENHEAD

SOUTHEND.

CRYSTAL PALACE TRANSMITTING STATION

SEVENOAKS.

THE TELEVISION TRANSMITTING STATION AT THE CRYSTAL PALACE IS CAPABLE OF IMMEDIATELY TRANSMITTING HIGH-DEFINITION PICTURES ACCOMPANIED BY SOUND TO ANYWHERE WITHIN A RADIUS OF 30 MILES.

10-KILOWATT ULTRA-SHORT WAVE RADIO TRANSMITTER.

PROJECTION ROOM.

TELECINE TRANSMITTERS

SPOTLIGHT STUDIO.

STUDIO No. 1.

STUDIO No. 3.

THE BAIRD TELEVISION STUDIOS AT THE CRYSTAL PALACE EQUIPPED TO SERVE AN AREA POPULATED BY 10,000,000 PEOPLE.

ELECTRONIC CAMERA.

CENTRAL CONTROL ROOM.

TERRACE.

OUTDOOR

CAMERA ROOM

THE LATEST TYPE OF TELEVISION HOME RECEIVER. IT HAS NO MOVING PARTS.

THE TRANSMITTING AERIALS ON THE SOUTH TOWER OF THE CRYSTAL PALACE 680 FEET ABOVE SEA LEVEL.

A

B

A.- NEW HIGH-POWER ULTRA-SHORT-WAVE VISION TRANSMITTING AERIAL, WITH RADIUS OF 30-40 MILES.

B. B.- SOUND & VISION SHORT-WAVE TRANSMITTING AERIALS.

STUDIO No. 2.

CATHODE RAY TUBE.

DUAL RADIO RECEIVER FOR SOUND & PICTURES.

SOUND CONTROL.

VISION CONTROL.

FROM AERIAL

POWER COMPONENTS.

LOUD SPEAKER.

A.C. MAINS SUPPLY.

ELECTRODE THAT MODULATES THE STREAM OF ELECTRONS & SO PRODUCES DARK & LIGHT SHADES IN THE PICTURE BEING BUILT UP.

CATHODE OR ELECTRON-GUN WHICH EMITS ELECTRONS.

ANODE DIRECTING ELECTRONS ON TO THE FLUORESCENT SCREEN, WHICH CONVERTS THEM INTO SPOTS OF LIGHT.

THE VERTICAL & HORIZONTAL DEFLECTOR PLATES ARE OPERATED BY ELECTRICAL IMPULSES TO PRODUCE A FIELD IN THE FORM OF HORIZONTAL LINES.

SIMPLE DIAGRAMMATIC VIEW OF THE CATHODE RAY TUBE USED IN THE LATEST BAIRD TELEVISION RECEIVERS.

PICTURE BUILT-UP IN HORIZONTAL LINES ON FLUORESCENT SCREEN.

LATER IN THE PRESENT YEAR: DETAILS OF TRANSMISSION APPARATUS, AND A HOME RECEIVER.

Wireless Wonders to Come

Shall we ever see by Radio? And can Nature's wireless supply us with an unlimited source of power? Both these great ambitions are within the realms of practical possibility.

By THE EDITOR.

THE radio telephone has brought speech and music to our homes on the back of wireless waves. That alone is something to marvel at—the fact that we can hear a man singing to a piano accompaniment fifty or a hundred miles away. But what will the general public think when they instal apparatus which will enable them to *see* as well as hear by wireless? To the novice in wireless work this suggestion must savour very much of black magic or the ravings of a second Munchausen and De Rougemont rolled into one. Jules Verne himself would have paused before suggesting such a possibility.

Photographs have already been successfully transmitted by wireless, but the fascinating problem of transmitting living pictures by wireless is still in its undeveloped stages. Yet it is a possibility—a distinct possibility, amazing as it may seem.

Inventors have already made crude attempts at the accomplishment of this great feat, and there is little doubt in the minds of scientists that a radio telephonic vision will be an actual fact before very many years have passed us by.

The first step in the realisation of this invention has already been reached by the transmission of wireless photographs.

Mr. Edward Belin, a French scientist, recently invented a system of telephonic telegraphy which has thrown light on many dark problems surrounding wireless vision, and Knudsen, a Dane, has made interesting experiments in sending pictures by wireless. Creed has done even better in helping to rend the veil and reach the desired goal of radio vision.

Another interesting wireless experiment lately carried out in the United States was connected with the battleship Iowa.

She was manoeuvred at sea entirely by radio during bombing tests.

The captain, safe on shore, had only to transmit waves in a certain sequence, and the ship would answer to her helm as readily as if a man was actually controlling her from the bridge.

Will naval battles of the future be fought by crewless ships—the respective commanders controlling the vessels from wireless stations ashore? It is quite possible.

And what if we could harness Nature's wireless to do our bidding? Whenever lightning flashes, a terrific radio signal is being sent out. Can we use this energy to drive motors and other machines?

The problem is to find a way to drain the vast atmospheric reservoir of electricity that exists all about us. Undoubtedly the man who invents a means of doing this will die a millionaire many times over.

He will revolutionise civilisation. Imagine the millions of machines we now drive by artificially-generated current being supplied indefinitely by Nature's natural storage battery! Think of the effect it would have on our everyday life!

But however fantastic this may seem, remember the principle is a sound one, and that the harnessing of lightning is a proposition which scientists are seriously studying. If they solve the problem—— But it is a big " if," and, meanwhile, one's imagination is apt to fail when considering the results.

When you have installed your receiver and are getting along with your wireless studies, and the approach of a thunderstorm is heralded in your telephone-receivers by loud, incessant atmospheric " crackers," just pause and think of the titanic energy Nature is letting loose, and try to feel that, however far man has progressed with wireless research, there is still a problem left which will tax his ingenuity to the utmost and will cry shame on his so-called " high-power " wireless transmitters.

Nature's wireless!—people hear it working a lot nowadays—but I wonder if they realise exactly what it means, and what are the possibilities it has in store for us?

THE EDITOR.

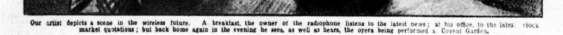
Our artist depicts a scene in the wireless future. A breakfast, the owner of the radiophone listens to the latest news; at his office, to the latest stock market quotations; but back home again in the evening he sees, as well as hears, the opera being performed at Covent Garden.

THE MYSTERY OF THE BEAM

There is one big satisfaction in evolving dreams around wireless. For, unlike fantasies that intrigue the mind in other directions, the visions that one conceives concerning radio possibilities are far more likely to develop into realities than most of 'the stuff that dreams are made of'.

The Broadcaster, August 1922

RADIO always carried with it a sense of fantasy as well as fact. It was not only specialist magazines like *The Broadcaster* which evolved 'dreams around wireless'. To writers of all kinds radio provided an invigorating new topic. In December 1928 'Astyanax' wrote of the 'unfortunate writers of novels and plays':

Theirs is a hard life at the best of times . . . It must be so when you consider the annual output of books and plays – to say nothing of the magazines, whose covers turn railway bookstalls into imitations of a cubist flower-bed – and when you remember that, according to the best authorities, there are only seven (or is it five or nine) plots in the world. Think of the imagination and labour required to ring the changes! Who would be Mr Wallace, after all?

Think, then, of the gasps of joy and relief which must have arisen from garrets all over the country when a brand new incident, in itself peculiarly dramatic and pregnant with limitless possibilities, was launched into the ordinary world. What a change! What a chance! Fleet Street rocked. Bloomsbury and Chelsea trembled. Illustrators everywhere might be seen drawing loudspeakers for practice on the backs of dirty envelopes.

As the illustrators practised drawing loudspeakers, so writers – from the Poet Laureate downwards – practised their radio vocabularies, often with more enthusiasm than knowledge. Both the scientific and the human aspects of the 'miraculous toy' appealed to a wide range of writers. Some tried extrapolation, projecting present patterns into the future, though seldom with any full perception of the options on the way; some took leaps of the imagination, mixing the wildest dreams with a modicum of scientific or social plausibility. Some were light-hearted, some portentous; some were poets, some parodists; only very few were prophets. All alike seized with enthusiasm on 'the brand-new incident'.

Early radio fiction concentrated on wireless telegraphy rather than wireless telephony – broadcasting. Indeed some of the short stories could have been written a decade or more before 1922. A typical anonymous thriller in *The Wireless World* in 1922 showed the exciting uses of wireless at sea. 'Gaudy the bigamist on board SOBRINA under name Sullivan – inform police' was the 'freak' message which Tommy, the Marconi operator in the story, successfully sent across the 'thousand or two miles which separated the SOBRINA from the nearest wireless station'. The hero, who had discovered the villain on board and rescued the girl from his clutches, claims the girl himself. The story ends with a heavy wireless metaphor: Harry embraces

'How wireless put the police on the track of two notorious robbers many miles from the scene of their crime.' (From Popular Wireless, *10 June 1922.)*

'John Clewin leapt up from the table and flung aside the headphones.'

the girl, 'And in this case, although a powerful transmitter was close to a sensitive receiver, it was apparently found necessary to repeat the message an indefinite number of times.' The impetus behind such stories was still the real-life arrest at sea in 1910 of the murderer, Crippen and Ethel le Neve. *The Wireless World* reported that, before Crippen's arrest on board the SS. *Montrose*, he 'would often sit out on deck and look up aloft at the wireless aerial and listen to the cracking electric spark as messages were sent out by the Marconi operator. He said "what a wonderful invention it was".'

At last, with Edgar Wallace's story, *Fluff Wiblington of Berysted, Dorking*, in *The Wireless Magazine* for February 1925, fiction entered the age of broadcasting: the hero, young John Clewin, temporarily estranged from his wife and sulking in the Canadian Rockies, is reunited with her by hearing a daylight transatlantic relay of the English Children's Hour. He learns in a birthday message to his wife's nine-year-old sister that he is a father: 'Hallo Fluff. Many happy returns! I am glad to hear that you are a proud Aunt and have a little baby nephew.' Not surprisingly the previously unexpectant father 'leapt up from the table and flung aside the headphones and yelled for his car'. He was on the CPR steamer bound for England and fatherhood in record time. . . . thanks to a broadcast.

The BBC itself, highly conscious of its own image from the earliest days, was as fond of looking into its future as over its shoulder into its short past, or into a present-day mirror. Future time was divided up by the BBC into satisfyingly neat decades: broadcasting – twenty, fifty, a hundred years ahead – was the subject of many articles and stories in the early *Radio Times*, both by professional broadcasters and distinguished outsiders. Prediction, both warning and witty, was as much a habit at Savoy Hill as nostalgia.

So rapidly did broadcasting develop in the earliest, pre-BBC, days that many wireless fantasies became fact almost as soon as they were written. Indeed, to many early writers about radio – as well as their readers – the astonishing facts of the ether *were* fantasy. There was no need to project into the future since the present was so remarkable. By the later twenties, when radio was taken more for granted, writers had to strive harder for effects to astonish their readers. Radio fantasies, set often in some indefinite future period, began to read more like modern science fiction.

The influence of H. G. Wells's science fiction novels and the Czech Karel Capek's *RUR* (1923, but not widely known in Britain until a few years later) were also beginning to be felt: the monster, Robot, reminded people that the new technology did not always mean human progress. The terror of the machine began to infect the mood of frolic and fun of the first wireless fiction and features.

The article by P. Russell Mallinson quoted at the beginning of the chapter was called 'When Wireless Dreams Come True'. All his dreams were sweet: in 1922 wireless nightmares had not yet begun to disturb such writers. In a series of delightful fantasies Mallinson wrote of the 'premier allurement' of 'radiating music through many hundreds of miles of ether; of enjoying a performance from the opera house in the comfort of your home (a dream that was to come true within a few months with the broadcast of *The Magic Flute* from Covent Garden in January 1923). Mallinson imagined, too, 'doing the foxtrot to the dance tunes that emanate from the simple, loud-speaking trumpet erected in your drawing room,' so that '"radio dances" will assuredly become the vogue in country houses'. Schools would conduct radio lessons 'whereby "Smith Minor" will know the novelty of having the details of a Western ranch and its commercial possibilities explained to him by a real-life cowboy who is speaking into a transmitting apparatus situated somewhere in the heart of the Sierras.' Meanwhile, twentieth-century lovers would enjoy 'radio courtship on the river with the softening influence of music to blend with their sentimental appreciation of life'.

Crime would virtually disappear, Mallinson suggested, since it would be infallibly detected by wireless – like many early writers on the subject, he did not always distinguish between the 'old-fashioned' uses of wireless telegraphy and the new broadcasting – detailed descriptions of wanted criminals would be 'flashed round the world and these particulars would reach not only police stations but would penetrate into entertainment halls, restaurants, and the booking offices at railway stations.' Another contributor to *The Broadcaster* in 1922, K. R. G. Browne, wrote in the very month that the BBC was born that 'no criminal's job will be worth the trouble; he will find it more satisfactory to become a wireless operator'.

One of the safest wireless prophecies of all was simply that there would be much more of it. Browne, whose article was called 'A Hundred Years Hence', predicted that 'in 2022 . . . the man, woman or child not in possession of some species of wireless outfit or apparatus will be considered as having more than qualified for entry into a mental home. In 2022 wireless will be as commonplace and everyday and generally inevitable as Germany's protests about paying up are in the present year of grace. In 2022 the remark that "old Jones is going about without his wireless set" will be as scathing an indictment as "old Jones is going about without a collar on" would be to-day. In other, simpler and plainer words, there will be a lot of wireless about.' Fleet Street in the form we know it, Browne thought, would have disappeared, 'since with the popularising of wireless, newspapers would cease to have any excuse for lingering on . . .' and the site would instead be occupied by a colossal broadcasting station. 'Gone for ever will be the trouble of *reading* the news.' Such predictions were fearsome only to the press interests of the day, lending force to their frequently-expressed fear of the competition of wireless.

The image of that 'colossal broadcasting station' of the future was a potent one, which featured often in radio predictions. The novelist C. R. Burns's story, ironically titled *Nation shall speak peace unto nation: a story of the 'Day after Tomorrow'*, printed in *The Radio Times* in 1928, begins with such a description:

It was close upon midnight. The Central Radio Building towered fantastic, immense, and black against the winter stars. Under their cold, remorseless shining lay the city, its roofs mantled with snow. Above the great doorway, through which one could glimpse the nodding form of the drowsy commissionaire, two storeys flared with the lights of studios completing the evening's programme. Above that rose twenty-six storeys of black darkness. Only at the apex of the central tower gleamed a single golden light, like a beacon.

Descriptive writing like this, with its warnings of the inhumanity of the machine, owed much to writers like Capek and Wells; Burns's story, however, makes humanity, in the shape of a journalist hero, triumph over the wicked manipulators of the machine, the corrupt 'President of the Central Radio Organisation' and a crooked munitions tycoon who plan to trigger off the Second World War by bogus broadcast news reports of a foreign invasion.

By the middle thirties, the early vein of fantasy on radio themes was beginning to be played out: the fun – as well as many of the fears – had been killed by fact. Actual achievements in broadcasting including the establishment in 1936 of a regular television service made much previous speculation irrelevant: predictions of the future course of broadcasting became firm promises rather than wild wondering. Articles in the *BBC Year Books* and *Annuals* described serious work in progress rather than castles in the air. 'The European

" The twentieth-century lovers' radio courtship. On the river with the softening influence of music to blend with their sentimental appreciation of life."

Wavelength Problem' and 'Synchronisation of Transmitters' were typical titles of 1938. By the late thirties, in any case, politics offered a grimmer field for speculation: as Hitler extended his power, once again it was the man rather than the machine who was the devil.

Radio fiction – once the excitement in conquering the ether was gone – was by this time indistinguishable from the traditional type of *Peg's Paper*, boy-wins-girl, romantic mush. In such stories broadcasting provided a useful alternative to films as a glamorous background. Typical stories in *Radio Pictorial* in 1936 and 1937 were 'the thrilling new serial of Love and Radio, *Sponsored Love*' ('Will the revelation that her lover is a famous radio star make any difference to Janet, the waitress with the red-gold curls?') and '*Double Act*' ('Partners – and the magic of Radio brought fame to one'; in this story the unsuccessful ex-music-hall partner never recovers from a chip on his shoulder, summed up by his words: 'You know they aren't our class up at that BBC place. All University men, so I hear').

During the late thirties, science fiction focusing on radio was confined – so far as the BBC was concerned – to *World Radio*, whose far-flung readers included many radio 'hams' with a taste for technology. An anonymous story, *The Mystery of the Beam*, which provides the title for this chapter, unravelled the cause of a series of mystery plane crashes believed to be due to unknown death rays – the time seems to be not far in the future. The professor hero solves the mystery with a brilliant application of science, expounding enough detail to impress even the knowledgeable readers of *World Radio*: '"… The Reading super-power station of 1500 kw on a wave-length of 6½ metres is the latest application of the new possibility of radiating great power on very much smaller waves. … Here is the vital fact, gentlemen," the Professor announced triumphantly to the anxious Air Council. "A wavelength of 6½ metres is practically in exact resonance with the metal framework of the average aeroplane."' Like Erskine Childers's *The Riddle of the Sands*, written before an

earlier war, *The Mystery of the Beam* seems to have had a rearmament message.

Radio fiction had travelled a long way since the 1922 story in *The Broadcaster* with its coy final metaphor about 'powerful transmitter' and 'sensitive receiver'. Throughout the period the fiction and the fantasy of radio concern pictures as well as words. This had always been the case with fantasy and with much of fiction, even in a pre-television age. The picture could be pseudo-realistic or it could be exotic, robot-like or romantic; and the fantasy could relate to everything from the appearance of transmitters and receiving sets to the complete futuristic Radio City – not to mention every possible kind of listener in every possible kind of listening situation.

It is natural to think that the pictorial radio fantasy – if not the fiction – should deal more with television than with sound since television is itself a visual medium. In fact, however, there was as much visual fantasy about sound broadcasting as there was about television.

There was one kind of imaginary writing about both sound and vision which adopted a cool approach to the media – witty rather than prophetic, even at times ironical and satirical: this was parody. Parodists – artists as well as writers – found in wireless a rich and delightful new field in which to apply their talents. Writers from Samuel Pepys to Edward Fitzgerald; from Kipling to Chesterton and artists from Botticelli to Stanley Spencer, all fell victim to the radio parodist's art (see pp 226–9).

The Radio Times itself was given the full-scale treatment in 1931 with both words and the pictures, by *Granta*, the Cambridge University undergraduate magazine. Looking at *The Radio Times* through the exaggerated distorting mirror of *Granta's* parody reminds the reader of its unique style. It had adapted slowly over the years and in any given period it sums up the prevailing style of the day – neither particularly old-fashioned (except in the earliest years before an art editor was appointed) nor avant garde.

Fiction and factual extrapolation, parody and fantasy, were not the only categories of popular writing to be inspired by radio. In some cases, the new medium, like ether itself, touched off a strain of mysticism. Thus Reith called the final chapter of his book, *Broadcast over Britain*, 'In Touch with the Infinite'. In it he speculated about the possibility of thought being made to 'ally with the ether direct' and of broadcasting and communicating thought 'without the intervention of the senses or any mechanical device'. Characteristically, Reith's conclusion was that we should 'turn to the contemplation of the Omnipotence . . . in whom, as in the ether, we live and move and have our being.'

Not all radio mysticism was religious in character, however. 'Is everyone a potential broadcasting station?' asked Arthur Burrows, the BBC's first programme director, in a characteristically semi-facetious article on thought transference. According to a French scientist in sound, he reported, '. . . you received at the moment of birth some days before you were assigned a Christian name or "call letters", a definite wave-length which, operated by the mind in later years, would enable you to establish wireless communication with others tuned in sympathy.' Burrows imagined, with mock horror,

. . . what might happen tomorrow were some misguided professor to discover the wave-length of my thought and to tune in upon it! When he had recovered from the shock there would be nothing, I suppose, to prevent him causing me to fetch and carry and to perform all the labours of life which to him are uncongenial. I, on the other hand, might reverse the process and give the professor a few hectic hours as Director of Programmes to a broadcasting company. (This, by the way, is the trick I really intend to play on all who happen to discover my wave-length!)

But there is nothing new under the sun. Has not the romantic novelist from the earliest days written freely and convincingly about the two minds with but a single thought; the two hearts that oscillate as one?

Filson Young thought that many minds and hearts might think and oscillate as one: the mysterious power of radio could be used for the good of mankind.

What if the thought of the whole human race could be so co-ordinated that at some given signal their minds would function in a common mental effort? . . . Suppose that at some second in an agreed hour of the twenty-four the Greenwich Time Signal of six 'pips' were to be flashed over the world, and that every human being in every country, prepared for it by thought and intention, were to make the six sounds represent 'We . . . will . . . have . . . no . . . more . . . war.' Would it change the attitude of the human race towards war?

By the thirties, Einstein's theory of relativity, involving the notion of curved space, filtered into popular writing about radio, often by non-scientists; Burrows's

notion of 'personal wavelengths' was now joined by the idea of 'eternal wave lengths along which the words of the great poets were travelling for ever'. 'The thought has even haunted many people that it may be possible in some remote future to abolish time in retrospect,' wrote Hilda Matheson in 1933, 'that some super-sensitive microphone may learn to pick up the still-journeying waves set in motion by poets, philosophers, prophets, orators, wits as far back as the dawn of history'. In similar vein the critic and essayist, A. R. Orage, wrote, in an essay in the *New English Weekly* comparing the power of radio with that of the press:

. . . I do not put it beyond the power of Radio to give us, and before long, not only the news of the day, but the news of all the events that have ever occurred. In a universe of curved space in which vibrations are eternal everything that has ever happened is still happening; and if Radio can already pick out, pick up and transmit news from the still vex'd Bermoothes, I see no reason why eventually it may not give us news of, say, the victory of Salamis. No 'better and brighter' Press could compete with that.

In the same year, 1933, the *Cambridge Review* even published a sonnet on the same theme:

TO MY WIRELESS SET

Fount of the fabled music of the spheres!
  By what new godlike magic do you pour
  From out the silent air the mighty roar
Of joyous cymbals, or the plaintive tears,
The lyric love songs, or the horrid fears
  Of those who dwell upon some distant shore?
  Have you the present only in your store,
Or can you give us back the byegone years?

Perhaps some night, when all the world's asleep,
  Orpheus will play to me, Catullus sigh;
Not fashioned echo, but across the deep
  Abyss of years love's very voice may cry:
Perhaps some shepherd, sitting midst his sheep,
  May sing me ancient songs of Arcady.

JOHN J. WITHERS

Communication with one's loved ones – as well as the great figures of the past – was also held out as a possibility. H. de Vere Stacpoole, the novelist, had written in *The Radio Times* in October 1924, of 'the road without barriers . . . ethereal communication. . . . Wireless as we know it,' he went on, 'is the most subtle and perfect method ever devised for the inter-communication of ideas between mind and mind, it uses the only road without barriers, the ether that pervades all things, and if, as many people believe, the mind of man is indestructible, who can say that this new road into which we have broken will not lead us into touch with the minds of those we speak of as "deceased"?'

G. K. Chesterton developed the 'mystic' attitude to wireless in different and characteristically perverse vein. 'I was once asked by a wireless enthusiast to consider what a wonderful and beautiful thing it was that thousands of ordinary people could hear what Lord Curzon was saying,' he wrote in an article, 'Making Listeners Jump', in *The Radio Times* in February 1925. 'I replied,' Chesterton went on,

that it would be much more beautiful if there were an instrument by which Lord Curzon could hear what thousands of ordinary people were saying. But that machine has not yet been invented; and until it is, there will be no true machinery of democratic government. It may be said that some moral qualities are (thank God) beyond the control of any machinery; and that the scientific mechanism that would make Lord Curzon listen to anything which he did not want to hear is beyond the visions of science. But without entering into this question, it may be said that that simple antithesis or reversal, implied in such an anecdote, is the real crux of the question.

Morals always fascinated Chesterton more than technology or, indeed, spiritualism: typically, he used the new medium for an old moral message.

Where Chesterton saw the moral limitation of broadcasting, other writers saw a limitation in the very perfection of radio transmissions. Wireless religious services, for example, with their beautifully sung hymns and nicely-judged sermons, might seem sterile and lacking in reverence to some worshippers, simply because they were too correct to be 'human'. This attitude was perfectly expressed in a Christmas story by J. D. Beresford in *The Radio Times* in December 1933. An old-fashioned couple, Margaret and John, are spending Christmas with their married children who decide to surprise them with the gift of 'a brand-new radio-gramophone . . . got at a big trade discount and absolutely the last word in power and selectivity, with all kinds of special gadgets which Joe would show his father how to use'. The new set was secretly rigged up on Christmas Eve outside the french windows, just as a carol service was about to be transmitted.

It was still very mild, but there was the sound of a rising wind, through which there came all at once with a queer unexpectedness the music of a choir of men's voices, singing 'God rest you merry, gentlemen; let nothing you dismay'.

Everyone got up and went to the open window. It was very dark outside. The moon, at the end of its last quarter, would not rise for hours yet; there was a veil of cloud over the stars; and it should not have been difficult to imagine that a company of singers was actually standing on the lawn, come this Christmas Eve with their comforting message of peace and goodwill.

Indeed, Margaret honestly tried to feel that and wondered why she failed until John, whose arm she was holding, murmured in her ear 'How perfectly they sing!'

Ah, yes! That was it, they sang too well, Margaret reflected. What she had been longing for was the endearing human weaknesses of the old carol singers from the village choir she had known in her youth. They had not sung well, but surely their untrained imperfectly harmonised voices had been warm with a feeling she could not find in the admirable execution of these well-taught, well-drilled musicians. No one went to the village church next morning. The Vicar was an advanced Ritualist, and Margaret admitted that she was so dreadfully old-fashioned as to regret the simple hearty service of her young days. Instead, they listened to the service at the Abbey, which carried through perfectly on the new set, and would have been really impressive if it had not been rather spoilt by the children's blissful unawareness of any need for reverence. Virginia innocently commented on the clearness of the reproduction in the middle of the Absolution and it was evident that she and Peter regarded the performance as some kind of show – with which they became increasingly bored after the first quarter-of-an-hour. Margaret could not blame them. After all, Chester and Joe were both smoking.

Films could do more with plot and atmosphere than short stories. As early as 1923, a silent film, *The Radio*

Roy Stuart, the Radio King himself, the modern Sherlock Holmes.

. . . broadcasted direct from the Apollo Theatre by the Bell Telephone Co. and hundreds of thousands of radio fans 'listened in', not only to the music and 'effects' appertaining to the film, but also to the applause and laughter of the huge audience. The film itself fully lives up to its title, and its big feature is a realistic tempest, when branches of trees hurtle through the air, thunderbolts crash, the wind howls and the rain beats upon the windows. All this, realistically 'rendered' by the orchestra, was plainly heard via radio. This was the first occasion upon which a *première* has been thus broadcasted.

By the thirties, the crime thriller with a well-informed and realistic background in broadcasting had taken the place of such simple 'shockers'. There was *2LO*, a detective story by Walter S. Masterman, while Val Gielgud and Holt Marvell (the pseudonym of Eric Maschwitz) were obviously well placed to produce *Death in Broadcasting House* (1934), in which the actor murderer's alibi breaks down when it is discovered that his voice in a radio play could have been a recording on the newly-invented Blattnerphone. The novel, indeed, was 'produced' in every sense, since it later became a film, with Val Gielgud playing a lightly disguised version of himself.

The Death Pack by Ray Sonin (1937) brought in *The Radio Times* as an essential tool of detection in the plot. The amateur detective hero, glancing through *The Radio Times*, catches sight of the words 'Dance Music from the Weisendorfer Hotel', which enables him to interpret a cryptic message earlier received. 'He realised in a flash that "br . . ." stands for "broadcast".' The villain's secret code is naturally contained in the titles of the various dance numbers in the programme; it is duly cracked by the hero – thanks to *The Radio Times*, which, in real life, was naturally delighted at such recognition, as it had been at the 'compliment' of being the subject of the full-scale – and all-too-accurate-parody in *Granta* (see page 229).

The Radio Times itself was, indeed, the main vehicle for much of the radio fiction and fantasy. With its wide readership from every class, it provided every week not only a convenient set of the following week's programmes, but a running commentary on the present, and, along with nostalgia for the past, intimations, expectations and dreams for the future.

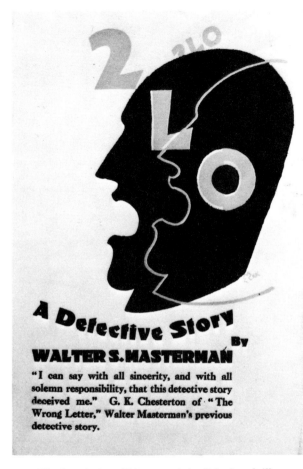

The front jacket of Masterman's 'radio' crime thriller.

King, introduced both radio hero and radio villain. The 'Radio King' himself was 'a deformed and fiendish scientist, using his talents and discoveries not to benefit mankind but to sow villainy broadcast'. He could even electrocute his enemies by radio. Opposed to him was a scientific detective or radio hero, who, in response to a child's cry for help, received by radio, made his way into the villain's secret laboratory.

Another early film, *The Silent Vow*, introduced an instrument for exploding a dynamite charge by radio. The star, William Duncan, was a radio fan and had been responsible for the whole paraphernalia of tuning-coils, spark-breakers, batteries, transformers, condensers, etc. etc., making their appearance in a California studio.

The radio ham, his wife, family and troubles, soon became familiar figures in comic 'two-reelers'; while in New York, *The Broadcaster* reported, a film première, D. W. Griffiths' (silent) *One Exciting Night* was

'A trivial and passing phenomenon'

GEORGE DU MAURIER AS PROPHET.

Musical Mistress of House ("on hospitable thoughts intent").
"Now, recollect, Robert, at a Quarter to Nine turn on 'Voi che Sapete' from Covent Garden; at Ten let in the Stringed Quartette from St. James's Hall; and at Eleven turn the last Quartette from 'Rigoletto' full on. But mind you close one Tap before opening the other."
Buttons. "Yes, Mum!"

By the Telephone Sound is converted into Electricity, and then, by completing the Circuit, back into Sound again. Jones converts all the pretty Music he hears during the Season into Electricity, bottles it, and puts it away into Bins for his Winter Parties. All he has to do, when his Guests arrive, is to select, uncork, and then complete the Circuit. And there you are!

Nineteenth-century anticipations of broadcasting designed for home reading, were, not surprisingly, concerned mainly with the home. George du Maurier in *Punch* (*above*, 1877) forecast canned opera; Albert Robida (*below*, 1883) forecast canned news. The telephone was then the obvious means of transmission, however, not (as yet uninvented) wireless apparatus. Television already beckoned: in a story of 1898 Mark Twain imagined 'calling up' in pictures (not words) one corner of the globe after another. 'Give me Hong Kong, give me Melbourne.'

After radio had become a medium, forecasts were wider ranging. 'Radio College' was one forecast of 1927 – a kind of Open University with all the students in residence, in a new world of educational technology where 'the old days of strikes and lock-outs' had gone for good. Some forecasters were more pessimistic. Wireless could produce 'a "civilisation" of mechanical minds'. But Englishmen would never [agree to] stay awake to listen after midnight!

AN ANTICIPATION OF THE WIRELESS RECEIVER

'In Touch with the Infinite' ...

Broadcasting provided a new frisson for lovers of the supernatural. 'It is a terrifying thing to have left the wireless on, in a house where you are alone, and to come on it, suddenly from another part of the house,' wrote 'EJO' in *The Radio Times* in February 1935. 'For a moment, the mysterious voices cause an interior convulsion. This is natural enough, if one reflects: for the ghosts that traverse Space are as mysterious as those other ghosts that traverse Time.'

In the caption to the illustration (*right*) to Holt Marvell's story for *Radio Magazine*, 'Wavelength Unknown' (1934), the dialogue goes as follows: 'Look the set's out of action – it wasn't even plugged in!' 'But the play – ?' 'There isn't a play tonight.'

New veins of mysticism were waiting to be tapped by radio. In 1928 the *BBC Yearbook* reported that some United States scientists were advancing 'the interesting theory that it should be possible to recall historical events by locating and tapping the wavelengths on which these events are alleged to be permanently recorded.'

In 1930 *The Radio Times* ran a full-page advertisement for the World Radio Research League: 'A large number of listeners wanted the mystery of interplanetary space to be penetrated. Mass listening must succeed where isolated scientists fail.'

Readers were assured that numerous 'technical Authors' and Professors had given the League their blessing.

Sometimes writers of fiction imagined a future dominated by 'the infernal ingenuity of modern science', as H. de Vere Stacpoole called it. Winifred Holtby, writing in July 1931, imagined a time 20 years ahead, in 1951, when a young woman, a student from the Chelsea Poly, invented a receiver by which she could listen to any day after tomorrow. 'The Director of Inventions' at the BBC turned down this invention 'which might have staggered the world'. 'You must destroy the instrument or you will destroy the soul of Britain .... You will destroy Sportsmanship!'

"A pretty fantasy, a brilliantly lighted aeroplane gliding smoothly beneath the stars away from the turmoil of the earth beneath, whilst wireless music is wafted through the aerial ballroom."

... 'The Voice from the Silence'

(titles of chapters from Reith's *Broadcast over Britain*, 1924)

' Silas started as he saw the dim light of the valves gleaming through the transparent form of his uncanny visitor.'

Occasionally ignorance produced a kind of mysticism, as one letter to *The Radio Times* in December 1930 showed:

SAFETY FIRST!

'I can quite understand how the sounds come in from outside when there is a wire to bring them in, but I cannot think how they get indoors and inside a box, too, without a wire for them to catch on to.' So said a middle-aged maiden lady, when for the first time she saw and listened to a portable set with no visible wire. Then, as a man's voice came through on the loudspeaker, 'Most extraordinary!' she exclaimed, watching the set suspiciously as though she half expected some eerie apparition to emerge. 'I call it weird. I would not stop in a room alone with that box for anything.'

The Broadcaster showed an early radio ghost (*top left*, 1923). Fifteen years later *Punch* saw the ghost's point of view (*bottom left*, December 1938).

"How uncanny! I could have sworn that there was a woman singing somewhere quite near us."

THE VOICE.

SHE put on the headphone
 Idly, not knowing what she was to hear,
When of a sudden in her startled ear
That voice, to her once so well known,
Again rang out loud and clear——

That voice whose every tone
And accent once had been so dear :
And now he seemed to speak for all to hear
What then had been for her alone,
And murmured in her ear.

Listening, she caught no word
Of all the learned lore that he broadcast.....
But dreamt that he'd come back to her at last,
As once again love's very voice she heard
Speak out of the dead past.

WILFRID GIBSON.

'With apologies to...'

THE LISTENERS.

"Is there anything good?" said the Listener,
  Turning on the Regional wave,
And his friend in the silence waited, waited
  For the noise that the sound-box gave.
And a song flew up out of the wireless
  Over the Listener's head,
And he turned the little knob again a second time:
  "I don't want *that*," he said.
Nothing was good enough for the Listener,
  For he liked to show his skill;
He kept passing from station on to station
  And he would not hold one still...

So I pulled him away from the sound-box
  And hit him in the face with a stone;
And the weather and the news surged backward
  When the radio fiend was gone.   EVOE.

BBC Fever

(*with apologies to Mr. John Masefield*)
I must part up with ten bob again for licensing
  time is nigh—
And all I ask is a good set, and a knob to
  tune her by,
And a merry song for a man to sing, and a
  lovely girl to sigh for,
And a Middleton talk, and This Week's Sport
  is what I cry for.

—*Ronald A. D. Hanbury, Hounslow*

THE MOVING FINGER

'The moving Finger writes, and having writ moves on.
  Nor all their piety nor wit
Shall lure it back to cancel half a volt; nor
  Tears wash out a decibel of it.'

THE DONKEY

When eagles on my aerial
Fought elephants in pairs,
And I to save my darling poles
Flew up ten flights of stairs;

I heard my proud and precious poles
Break with a senseless crack;
And I was dumb, I could not move,
Step neither fro nor back.

Fools! For this was indeed my hour,
My one fierce hour and sweet,
There was a sheet about my head
And cold air round my feet.

(with apologies to Mr. G.K. Chesterton)

Samuel Pepys, Listener.
By R. M. Freeman.

MAY 5. *My wife and I listening-in this
night, but the heering indifferent; so to
fiddle with the battons, my wife in her busy
way telling me I am like only to make bad worse
by my fiddling. And, as the devil will have it,
in the midst of my fiddling, out goes one of the
valves, through a fused wire. Whereat my wife,
like the fool she is, do lay all to me rather than to
the fused wire, saying, 'There, Samuel, what
did I tell you?' and other taunting things;
so that how I did keep my hands off her, God
knows.*

'IF.'

(*With apologies to Rudyard Kipling.*)

If you can make a choice when all about you
Are praising 'dynes' and 'supers,' 'Reinartz,'
    too;
If you can estimate what it will cost you
To build a set for Rome or Timbuctoo:
If you can listen nor be tired by listening
To friends' romance of what their circuits do,
And in the end settle yourself to making
The set you're keen on (less a valve or two);

              A. J. CAMPBELL.

CIVILIZATION.

Here with a loaf of bread beneath the bough,
A double Scotch, a book of verse and "2 LO"
Beside me, singing in the wilderness,
And wilderness is Paradise enow.

Engineer   Variety   Talks   Drama   The Listening Public   Music   Anti-cyclone   Deep Depression
(*above*) The Spirit
of Radio

HOPE!

A new world in Radio opens before them...

Millais' famous picture —" The Boyhood of Raleigh " — finds its modern counterpart in many homes where world-wide, all-wave radio is every day opening up new horizons.

(With acknowledgment to Tate Gallery)

Model 747
Six-valve All-Wave
Superheterodyne

12½ GNS.
or H.P. terms

and *'New Listening'* holds them spellbound!

PHILIPS
RELIABILITY HAS BUILT PHILIPS REPUTATION

THERE IS A PHILIPS MOTORADIO FOR WHATEVER CAR YOU DRIVE

COUPON
To Philips Lamps Ltd., Dept. B.V.66, 145 Charing Cross Road, London, W.C.2.
Please send me full details of the Philips "New Listening" receivers.

NAME

ADDRESS

Radio parodies

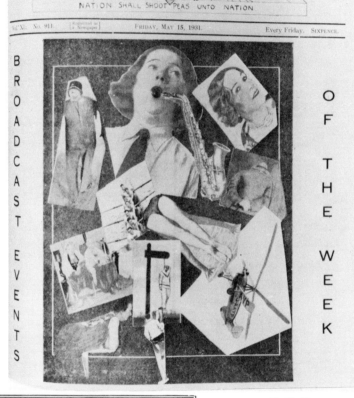

THE GRANTA

RADIO TIMES

JOURNAL OF THE BOTTISHAM BROADCASTING CORPORATION

NATION SHALL SHOOT PEAS UNTO NATION

Vol. XL. No. 914. [Registered as a Newspaper]   FRIDAY, MAY 15, 1931.   Every Friday. SIXPENCE.

B R O A D C A S T E V E N T S   O F T H E W E E K

Granta, Cambridge University's undergraduate magazine, transformed itself into a bogus *Radio Times* on 15 May 1931 (*left*). Its Editor, Alistair Cooke, introduced the 'Journal of the BBC (the Bottisham Broadcasting Corporation)' with its motto 'Nation Shall Shoot Peas unto Nation'. Features included 'A Short History of Art' by Roger Halfbake and a masterly send-up of *The Radio Times* highest-browed music critic analysing 'Grippe Schnupfen's Pastorale'. The familiar correspondence column, 'What the Other Listener Thinks' became 'How the Other Thinker Listens' (with a full quota of typically pretentious and illiterate letters).

A bogus A. J. Alan mystery story – the shortest ever – followed:
'Good evening everybody! Er – the other day an amazing thing happened to me. A friend asked me to meet him at a certain house at 5 o'clock. Well, the time came, and I took a taxi there. I opened the door of his house and my friend – er – shot me through the head. Goodnight!'

There was even a vivid running commentary on dinner in a College Hall:
'...I wish you could see the activity that is going on down below. As soon as the Grace was finished, the waiters rushed forward and at least a third of the men are now well away with the soup. I'll give you the time of the fastest man. From the next stroke. In-Out. IN-OUT, IN-OUT, IN-OUT, IN-OUT. What is it? 29 *I think*.'

And, of course, there were the programme pages ... direct from 'Tella-whopper Trassmission' (*below centre*).

MISS VIRGILIA WOOMF, the New Mistress of Girnham, who will debate this evening with Mr WOOLBERT HUMPH.

7.45   CHAMBER MUSIC
THE BEDMAKERS' QUARTET
Quartet in T ....*Liszt-Starboard*
Les Voleurs de Confiture......*Stravinsky*
On Hearing the First Cuckoo in Spring
Traditional

8.15   OUR ISLAND STORY— II
Professor SCHORTSNOUT : ' The Leanderthal Man '

8.35   GARDENING NOTES
' Chestnuts and their Origin '
Lady SNORTSHOUT

9.0   WEATHER FORECAST (weather permitting), NEWS BULLETIN, S.O.S.'s, AND OTHER LIGHT MUSIC

9.15   **VAUDEVILLE**
JOHNNY DAVENCORP
(the Boy Baritone)
MICHL ROTGRAF
(in Schuplattler Dances, with ELSA PHAR at the Harmonica)
LOUIS LA BRETONNE
(in a Sketch ' Ca, c'est Magdalene ')
DORIS PASTONNE
(in a Comedy Sketch 'Aren't we Mod'n !'

Inspired by radio

A RADIO THRILLER

WILL BE BROADCAST

TONIGHT AT

9.35

The Outstanding Hit of the Production!

ON the RADIO

by
VINCENT LOPEZ
&
OWEN MURPHY

as featured by
VINCENT
LOPEZ
and his
HOTEL PENNSYLVANIA
ORCHESTRA
in the
GREENWICH
VILLAGE FOLLIES

PUBLISHED IN GREAT BRITAIN
FRANCIS DAY & HUNTER
138/140, CHARING CROSS ROAD
LONDON, W.C.2.

Radio inspired serious composers like Hans Eisler whose 'Speed of the Times' (Tempo der Zeit), a Cantata for Broadcasting, was performed by the BBC in May 1930 (*bottom right, Radio Times* announcement of the concert).

Writers of popular songs like *On the Radio* (*top right*, 1924), used the radio theme to give a more personal and romantic message:

> 'Oh Radio, oh lady oh,
> My love I send to you
> From station JOY
> Thru a friendly sky
> I am flashing kisses too.'

By the late 1920s playwrights were writing futuristic radio plays (*above*, *Radio Times* announcement of 'X' by George Crayton, October 1928, than which 'no stranger, more thrilling story was ever written by Jules Verne').

Painters, too, responded to radio. Mouat Loudon, who painted 'the first radio picture', exhibited at the Royal Academy in 1925, described how the model put on his earphones as she sat by the studio fire and 'how becoming the new head-dress looked, like the hair fillets of ancient Greek maidens'.

Music for Broadcasting

A concert of music written specially for broadcasting, including 'Speed of the Times' and 'Lindbergh's Flight,' will be given at 9.40

It is not a strange thing that men has made poems about Broadcasting, for the new magic, which pours the music of the concert room into the stillness of the cottage and brings the song of nightingales into the heart of Town, is of the very stuff of poetry.

(*The Radio Times*, introduction to page of poetry, December 1927)

A TIME TO DANCE

Shepherds on the downs, do it!
Workers in towns, do it!
Highbrows, get down to it!
Tune in!

Every station, every nation,
Every overseas relation—
We're calling you, we're spoiling to begin
Our new year's programme, our featuring-the-future
    programme,
So if you're feeling low ma'am,
If you're ailing sir or failing, tune in!

However sad you were,
Soon you'll be glad you were
Alive to feel our
Appeal and tune in.
Turn your loud-speaker on, sir!—
To-night our chief announcer
Gives that competition's answer,
So tune in!

Revolution, revolution
Is the one correct solution—
We've found it and we know it's bound to win.
Whatever's biting you, here's a something will put life in
    you:
This evening we're inviting you
To share what's on the air and tune in.
                    (C. Day Lewis)

'YOU CAN'T MAKE LOVE BY WIRELESS'

You can't make love by wireless;
    It's like bread without the jam.
There is nothing girls desire less
    Than a cold Marconigram
For it's something you can't speak to
    From a someone you can't see
It's like a village church that's spireless
    Or a little home that's fireless
    Or a motor-car that's tyre-less
    (Or a Selfridge's that's buyer-less)
And it isn't any good to me.

(Song lyrics by George Grossmith
and P.G. Wodehouse, 1923)

BROADCASTING TO THE G.B.P.

"Hushaby baby, on a tree top
when the wind blows, the cradle shall rock,
when the bough breaks——"

    Stop that at once!
You'll give the Great British Public a nervous shock!

"Goosey goosey gander
whither do you wander
upstairs, downstairs
in the lady's——"

    Stop! where's your education?
Don't you know that's obscene?
Remember the British Public!

"Baa-baa black sheep
have you any wool?
yes sir! yes sir!
three bags full!
One for the master, and one for the dame,
and one for the little boy that lives down the——"

    No!
You'd better omit that, too communistic!
Remember the state of mind of the British Public.

"Pussy-cat pussy-cat where have you been?
I've been up to London to see the fine queen!
Pussy-cat pussy-cat what did you there?
I frightened a litte mouse——"

    Thank you! thank you!
There are no mice in our Royal Palaces. Omit it!
            (D.H. Lawrence)

EARPHONES

Sounds came sifting down
As I fastened the phones.
Music crowned the cottage.
The trees outside
Wrung their hands and cried in vain,
Unheard, forgotten. . . .
No latch clicked,
Nor door rattled,
Nor ivy at window tapped,
For I was far away,
Listening to the great orchestra
Bowing and drumming
In Germany.

RICHARD CHURCH

GOOD NIGHT, EVERYBODY

GOOD night, everybody!
   Young and old.
      The play is over,
And the tale is told,
The dance is ended,
   And the song is sped—
Good night, everybody,
   Go to bed!

ELEANOR FARJEON